PLUM BLOSSOM & GREEN WILLOW

JAPANESE *SURIMONO* POETRY PRINTS FROM THE ASHMOLEAN MUSEUM

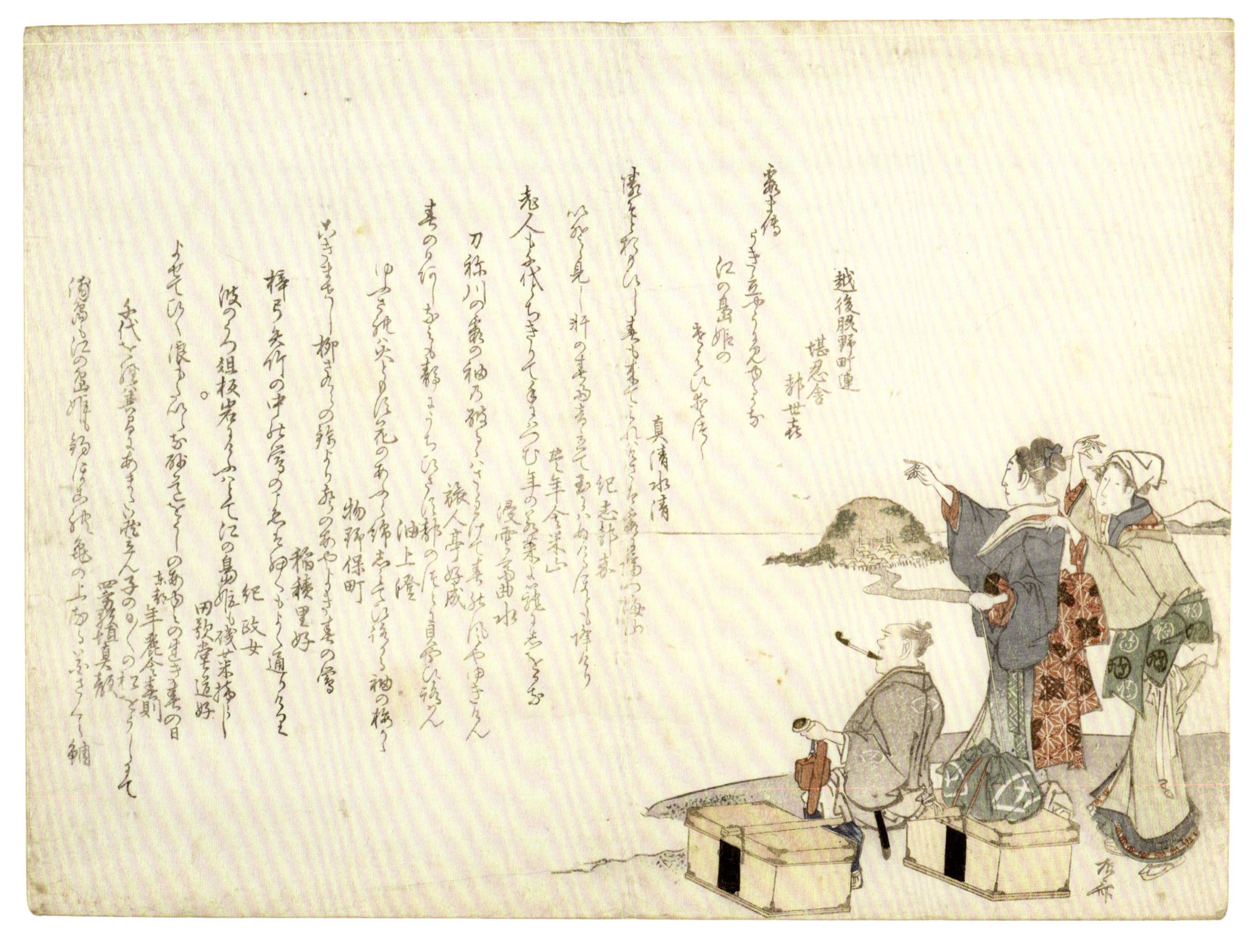

Kiyoko Hanaoka and Clare Pollard

Plum Blossom & Green Willow

Japanese *surimono* poetry prints from the Ashmolean Museum

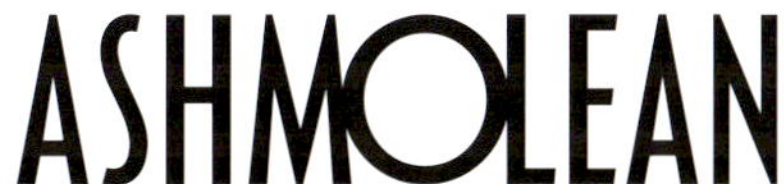

PLUM BLOSSOM & GREEN WILLOW
JAPANESE *SURIMONO* POETRY PRINTS FROM THE ASHMOLEAN MUSEUM
2 October 2018–17 March 2019

Kiyoko Hanaoka and Clare Pollard

British Library Cataloguing in Publications Data
A catalogue record for this book is available from the British Library
ISBN: 978-1-910807-26-2

Catalogue designed by Stephen Hebron

Printed and bound in the UK by Gomer Press

For further details of Ashmolean titles please visit:
www.ashmolean.org/shop

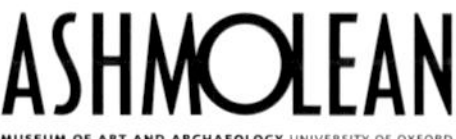

Frontispiece:
Travellers looking towards the island of Enoshima
After Ryūryūkyo Shinsai (active 1799–1823). Nineteenth century. EAX.4667

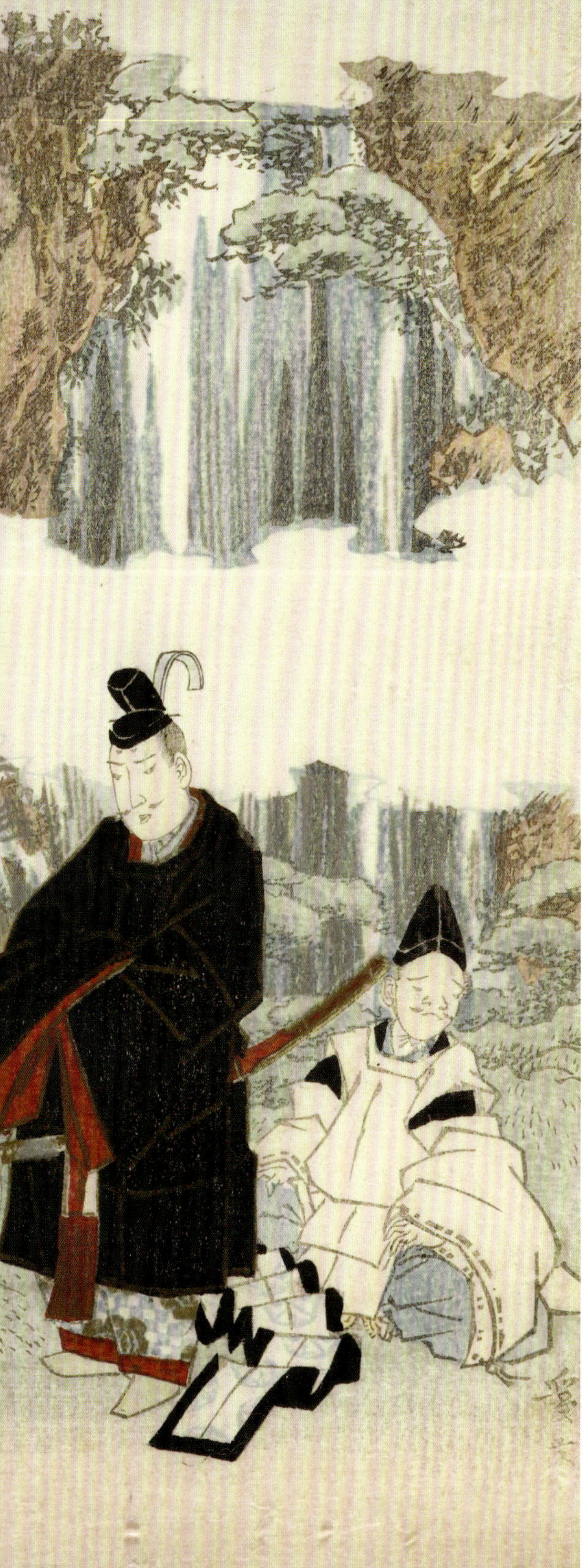

Contents

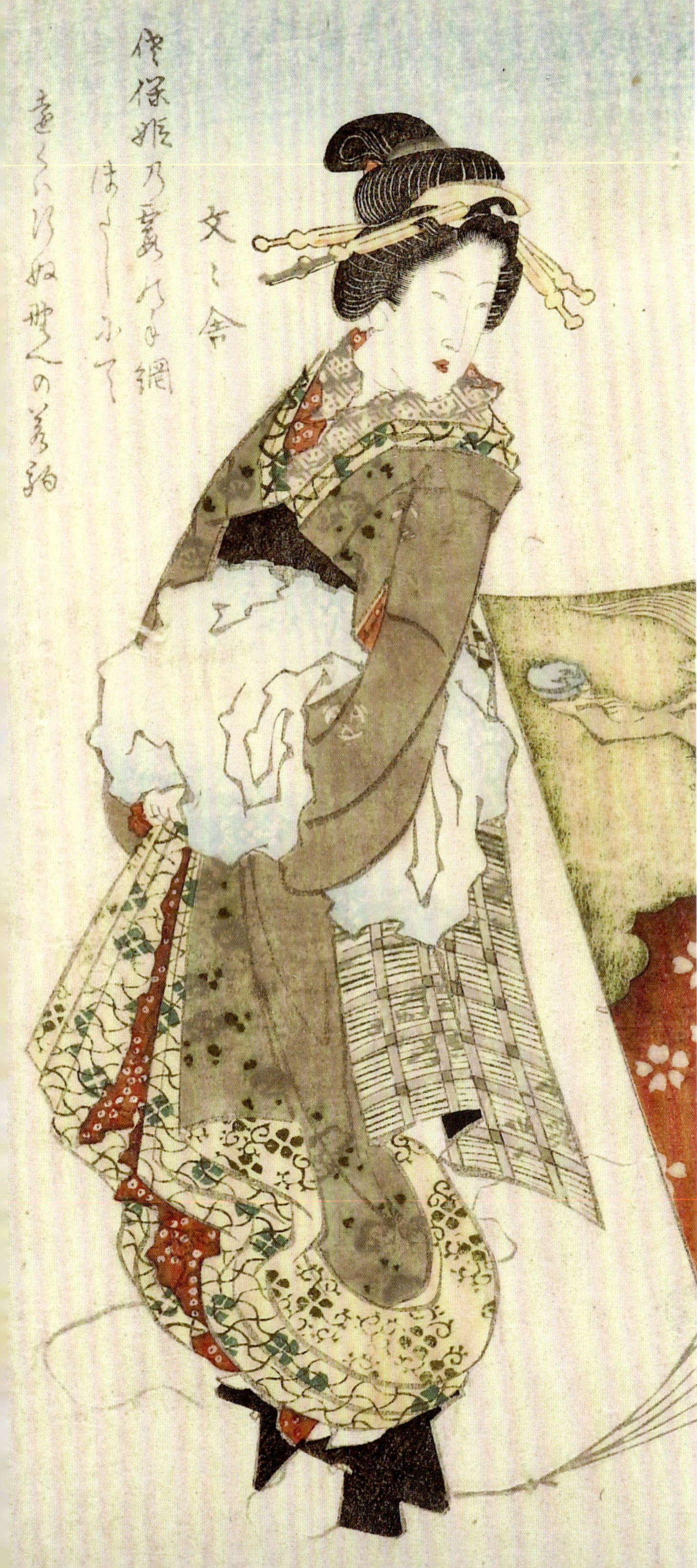

Acknowledgements

We are extremely grateful to the Patrons of the Ashmolean Museum and to the Jeffery Story Fund for generous support of this publication.

We gratefully acknowledge Nora Crook for her help with poetry translations, and Joyce Seaman and Tim Kiggell for their editorial input. We are indebted to Asano Shugo for his scholarly advice and to Israel Goldman for sharing his expertise and for allowing the use of several *surimono* images.

At the Ashmolean Museum we would like to thank Declan McCarthy, Amy Taylor, David Gowers, Annie Hollie, Jo-Hung Tang, Alexandra Greathead, Lara Daniels, and all the staff in the Eastern Art Study Room.

We would like to extend our gratitude to Catherine Bradley for her meticulous copy editing and to Stephen Hebron for his elegant design.

How to 'Read' a *Surimono* Poetry Print

Surimono are viewed from right to left

Poem 2 (left)

水かゝみ
かけをうつして
さほ姫の
すかた海老やも
はるハきにけり

mizukagami
kage o utsushite
sahohime no
sugata ebi yamo
haru wa kinikeri

The reflection of the Goddess Sahohime on the mirror of water looks like a lobster – spring has come.

Poem 1 (right)

羽根つきも
いち度ハ見よと
母親の
けふハゆるしの
いろさとの春

hanetsuki mo
ichido wa miyo to
hahaoya no
kyō wa yurushi no
irozato no haru

Today my mother told me to watch my first ever game of New Year's battledore and shuttlecock, on my free day in the pleasure quarters in springtime.

Poems
Most *surimono* are inscribed with one or more *kyōka* ('playful poems'), a popular, light-hearted version of the classical *waka* verse form with a syllable structure of 5-7-5-7-7. The Japanese poems are written in vertical lines and read from right to left.

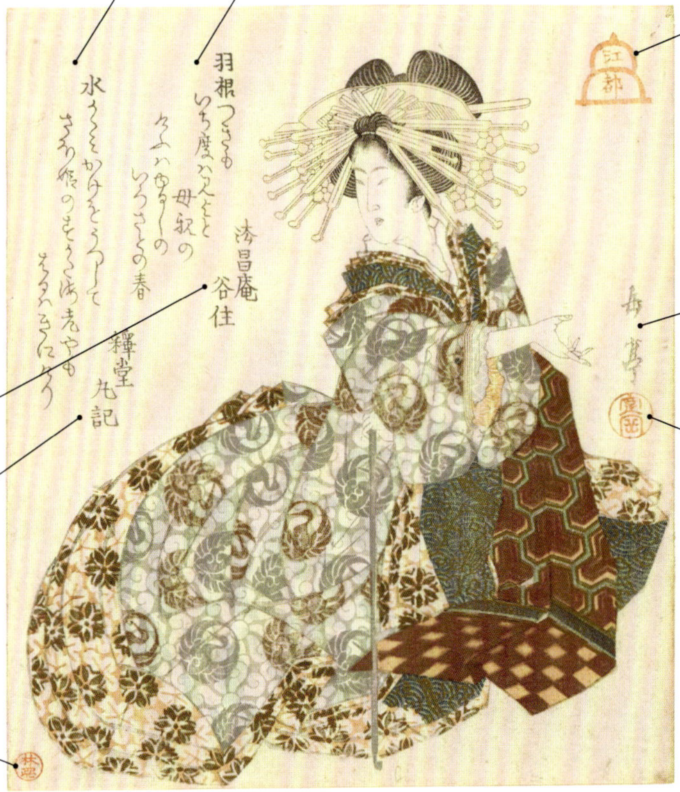

2

1

Print title
江都 (*Kōto*, an elegant term for Edo)
The title cartouche is in the form of a gourd, the emblem of the Hyōtan-ren (Gourd circle). Many poetry clubs had their own emblem which they incorporated into their *surimono*.

Artist's signature
岳亭 (Gakutei), Yashima Gakutei (*c.*1786–*c.*1855)

Artist's seal
定岡 (Sadaoka)

Name of poet 1
法昌庵谷住 Hōshōan Tanizumi

Name of poet 2
釋堂丸記 Shakudō Maruki

Collector's seal
林忠正 Hayashi Tadamasa (1853–1906)

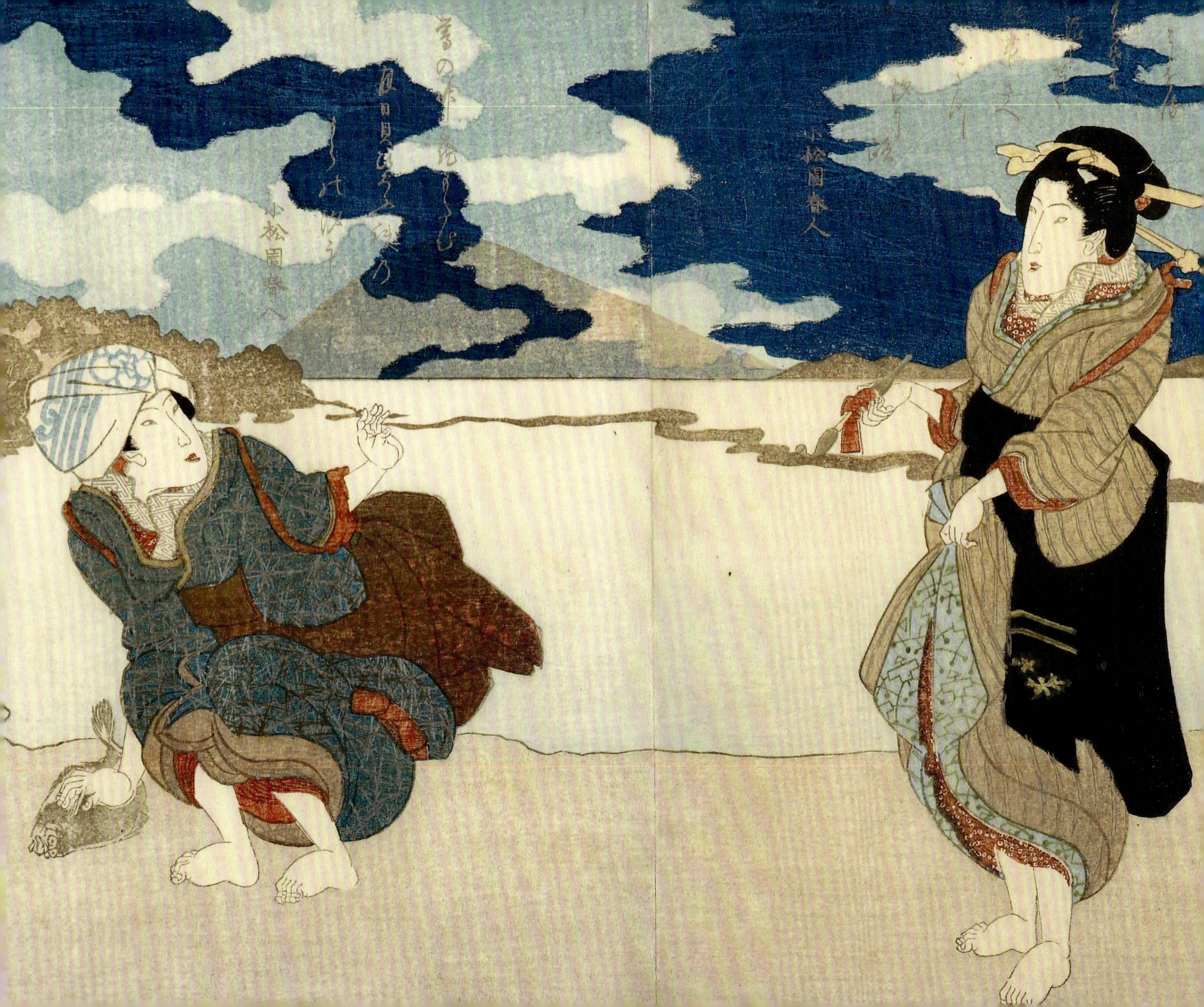
小松園春人
小松園春人

Preface

Within the Japanese collections of the Ashmolean Museum is a small group of sophisticated woodblock prints of the genre known as '*surimono*'. Mostly compact in size and made in the capital city Edo (modern Tokyo) in the early nineteenth century, they combine delicate images with elegant calligraphic poetry. Unlike the *ukiyo-e* prints of actors, courtesans and landscapes that were being commercially published around the same time, *surimono* prints were never intended for sale to the general public. Instead they were privately published in limited editions by wealthy patrons, mostly members of amateur poetry clubs, to present to friends and acquaintances on festive occasions, especially at the New Year.

Most Western collectors, unable to appreciate the subtleties of the poetry, have collected *surimono* for their visual appeal. Often designed by leading print artists, *surimono* were produced using the best materials and the finest printing techniques: intricately carved designs, a wide range of subtle colours and plentiful use of rich metallic pigments and embossing on thick, soft paper. When viewing a *surimono* it is all too easy to pass over the elegant cursive text arranged above and around the images, but it is important to remember that the poems came first. The well-educated intellectuals who issued *surimono* met to compose and share witty, erudite poems called *kyōka* ('playful verse'), demonstrating their knowledge and refinement through clever wordplay and allusions to classical literature and history. Only when they had selected the poems they wanted to commemorate did they commission an artist to illustrate them. The images were designed to complement the poems, but could also add a fresh perspective or surprising new layer of meaning, turning the *surimono* into a pictorial puzzle. The relationship between the poems and the accompanying images formed the essence of *surimono*, and recipients of the prints – usually fellow members of the poetry clubs – took great pleasure in unravelling the complex web of allusions and links embedded within them.

Plum Blossom and Green Willow introduces highlights from the Ashmolean's *surimono* collection, focusing on both text and image. The catalogue presents new translations of the *kyōka* poems that are at the heart of the *surimono* and explains the customs, legends, figures and objects depicted in the images. The *surimono* are grouped by their subjects into seven sections: ingenious picture calendars, in which the date information is hidden within the illustration; animals of the Japanese zodiac; depictions of New Year's customs and activities; figures and events from history, literature and religion; Kabuki actors, both on and offstage; still life, a rare subject within the Japanese print tradition; and the naturalistic subjects typically used in *surimono* that featured *haiku* rather than *kyōka* poetry.

This publication is part of an ongoing series of catalogues designed to introduce the Ashmolean's Japanese print collection. *Plum Blossom and Green Willow* commemorates the Museum's first exhibition of *surimono*, held in the Eastern Art Paintings and Prints Gallery at the Ashmolean Museum from 2 October 2018–17 March 2019. Despite their delicate beauty, very few of the Museum's *surimono* have ever been displayed before, partly because of the difficulty of interpreting them. Through this catalogue we hope to provide readers with an insight into the refined and cultivated Japanese literati culture of the early nineteenth century, and to give some sense of the way in which these rare and beautiful prints were intended to be enjoyed. We have been most fortunate in benefiting from the expertise and dedication of Kiyoko Hanaoka, who transliterated and translated every poem and researched the complex background to each *surimono* in order to write the catalogue entries.

In compiling the catalogue we have drawn heavily on a number of excellent and illuminating books on *surimono*. We are particularly indebted to works by John Carpenter, Matthi Forrer, Roger Keyes, Daniel McKee, Joan Mirviss and Mary Redfern. A selection of relevant book titles is included in the 'Selected Bibliography' section on pp.148–50.

Clare Pollard, Curator of Japanese Art, Ashmolean Museum

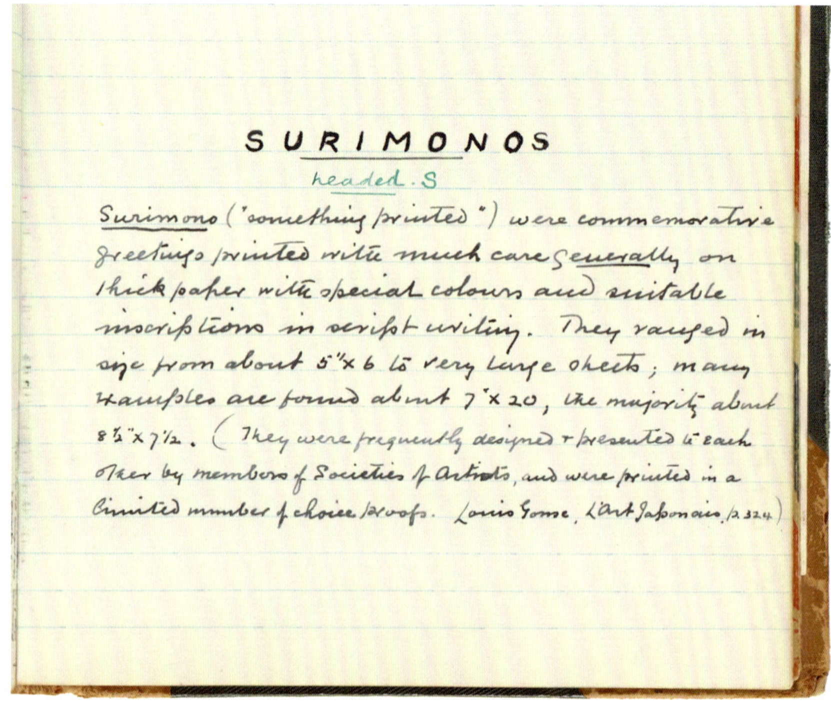

SURIMONOS

headed. S

Surimonos ("something printed") were commemorative greetings printed with much care generally on thick paper with special colours and suitable inscriptions in script writing. They ranged in size from about 5"x 6 to very large sheets; many examples are found about 7"x 20, the majority about 8½"x 7½. (They were frequently designed + presented to each other by members of Societies of Artists, and were printed in a limited number of choice proofs. Louis Gonse, L'Art Japonais, p. 324)

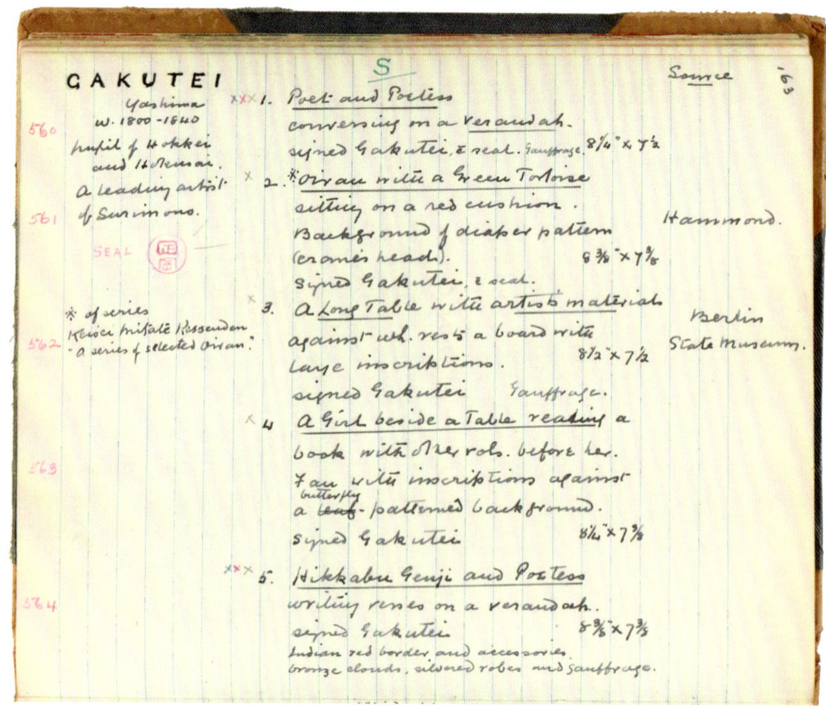

GAKUTEI | S | Source | 63

Yashima
w. 1800–1840
pupil of Hokkei and Hokusai.
A leading artist of Surimono.
SEAL

* of series Keisei mitate Kasen... "A series of selected Oiran".

560 xxx 1. Poet and Poetess conversing on a verandah. signed Gakutei, & seal. Gauffrage. 8¼" x 7½

561 x 2. *Oiran with a Green Tortoise sitting on a red cushion. Background of diaper pattern (cranes head). 8⅜" x 7⅜ signed Gakutei, & seal. — Hammond.

562 x 3. A Long Table with artist's materials against wh. rests a board with large inscriptions. 8½" x 7½ signed Gakutei Gauffrage. — Berlin State Museum.

563 x 4 A Girl beside a Table reading a book with other vols. before her. Fan with inscriptions against a butterfly-patterned background. signed Gakutei 8¼" x 7⅜

564 xxx 5. Hikkaburi Genji and Poetess writing verses on a verandah. signed Gakutei 8⅜" x 7⅜ Indian red border and accessories. bronze clouds, silvered robes and gauffrage.

Figs 1 and 2 Excerpts from Herbert Jennings' hand-written print catalogues.

Surimono Poetry Prints at the Ashmolean Museum

Clare Pollard

The Ashmolean Museum owns 135 *surimono*, of which 110 arrived as part of a large collection of Japanese prints presented to Oxford University's Museum of Eastern Art (later to become the Ashmolean's Eastern Art Department) in 1953. This collection was formed in the early twentieth century by Herbert H. Jennings (1868–1946) and donated by Mr and Mrs H. N. Spalding, founders of the Spalding Trust, a charitable organisation committed to the promotion of intercultural understanding through the study of comparative religion. The Spaldings had acquired the prints at a bargain price from Jennings' daughter, Mrs Evelyn Allan, on behalf of the Ashmolean in 1952. This was a highly significant gift for the Museum, forming the core of the Museum's Japanese print collection.

We know little about the collector Herbert Jennings, but from two detailed handwritten catalogues of his print collection we can learn a good deal about how the collection came together. In his introduction he describes his admiration for Japanese prints, which he regarded as constituting 'one of the greatest forms of artistic expression that the world has known' and which he believed to 'show the genius of the [Japanese] race for design, colour and line, and for the selection of essentials and the exclusion of unnecessary details'. In Jennings' catalogue the prints are meticulously listed by artist and series, along with their sources, acquisition dates and prices, plus notes on the quality of each impression. The collection was formed over about 35 years, for he seems to have started buying Japanese prints in 1910, with the last purchase recorded in 1945, shortly before his death. Jennings bought from dealers and auction sales, mostly in London but sometimes further afield in Paris and New York. *Surimono* were among his earliest purchases; they came mostly from sales of leading European collections of Japanese prints, including those of Major J. J. O'Brien Sexton, Sir Leicester Harmsworth and Paul Blondeau. Jennings begins the *surimono* section of his catalogue with a translation from Louis Gonse's book *L'Art Japonais*, one of the first European books to discuss the subject of Japanese art:

> Surimono ('something printed') were commemorative greetings printed with much care generally on thick paper with special colours and suitable inscriptions in script writing. They ranged in size from about 5″ × 6 to very large sheets; many examples are formed about 7″ × 20, the majority about 8½″ × 7½. (They were frequently designed and presented to each other by members of Societies of Artists and were printed in a limited number of choice proofs.)
>
> *L'Art Japonais*, 1883, p.324

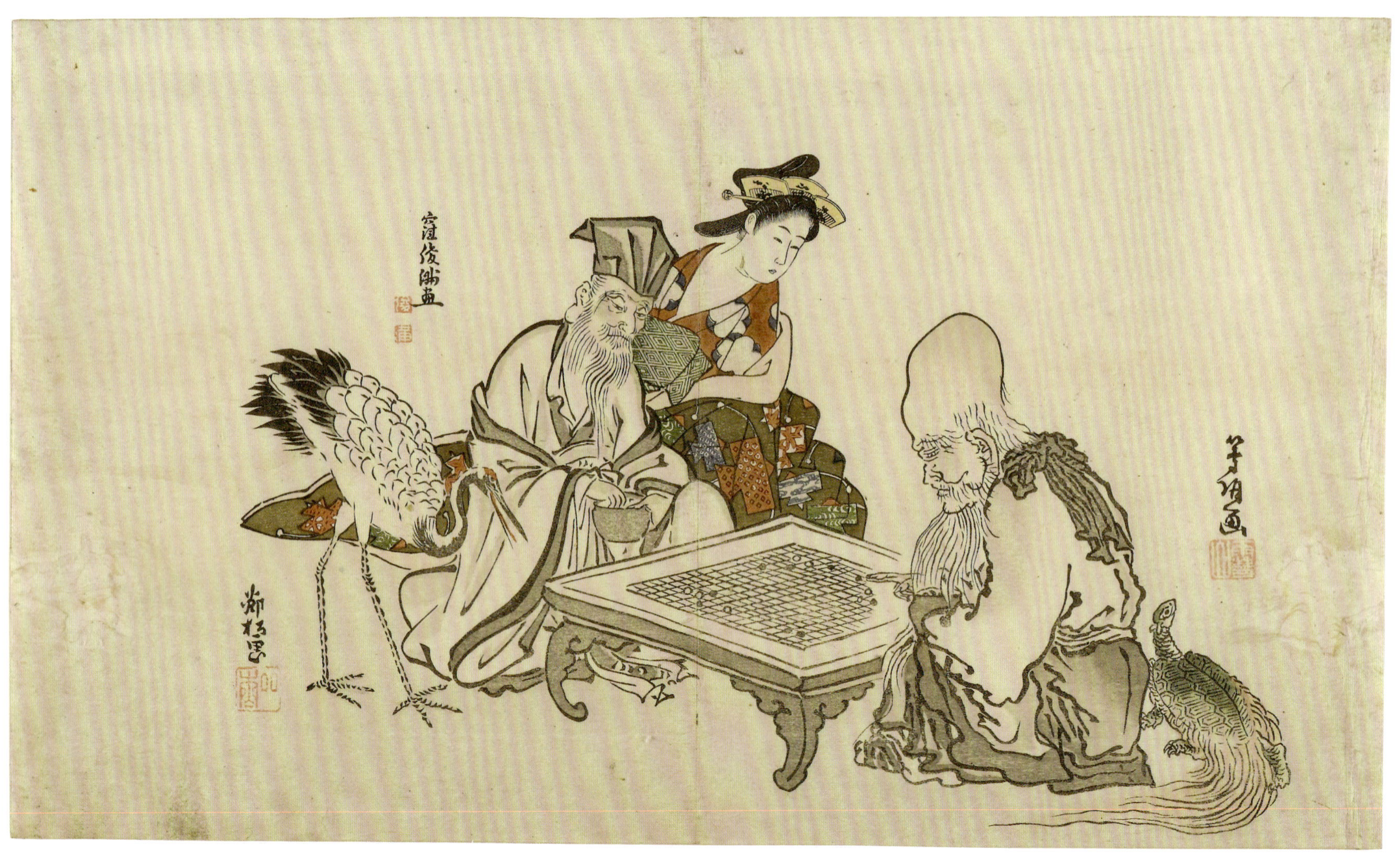

Fig.3 *A courtesan watching a game of go between the god Fukurokuju and the immortal Rinnasei.* A page from the book *Colours of Spring* (*Haru no iro*). 1794. EAX.4633

Surimono Poetry Prints – an Overview

Clare Pollard

A brief history of *surimono*

The literal meaning of '*surimono*' is 'printed thing' and the term originally referred to any kind of woodblock-printed material. By the Edo period (1603–1868), however, the term had come to be used for limited edition, single-sheet woodblock prints that were distributed as private gifts rather than sold commercially. *Surimono* were made for a variety of purposes, including announcements of musical and stage performances, the opening of new businesses or professional name changes, but the majority were commissioned by members of amateur poetry clubs to commemorate special poetry gatherings. These consisted of one or more poems with an accompanying image and can be thought of as a form of 'poetic presentation sheet', with the images an essential but secondary element.[1]

The practice of commemorating poetry gatherings by commissioning illustrated prints emerged in the late eighteenth century and derived from a long Japanese tradition of poetic exchange. The custom of presenting gifts of poetry in Japan, for both public and private reasons, dates back at least to the eighth century. Ceremonial sheets of hand-inscribed poetry, both in Chinese style (*kanshi*) and in the Japanese poetic form known as *waka*, were officially bestowed as offerings to shrines and imperial institutions, while poems were also privately exchanged by individuals. Works of classical literature, such as the eleventh-century *The Tale of Genji*, describe how refined courtiers of the Heian period (794–1185) would write poems and send them to each other in letters, taking great care to select the most elegant types of paper, ink, calligraphy styles and accompanying seasonal gifts.

The fifteenth century saw the emergence of *renga* or 'linked verse', in which several poets contributed connecting verses at poetry gatherings; these too were often ritually presented at shrines and temples. The New Year was a particularly important time for poetry presentation of all kinds. By the late sixteenth century *renga* practitioners had begun to compose short sets of three linked poems to present to shrines at the New Year; the practice was continued by *haikai renga* poets, who created linked poetry in a looser, less formal style. These short New Year poetic presentations were originally written in calligraphy, but from the mid-1630s they began to be woodblock-printed in greater numbers and presented to fellow poets. In due course illustrations came to be added to these poem prints, making them an important precursor for later *surimono*.

During the Edo period (1603–1868) poetry was an important part of everyday life, with all educated citizens writing poetry for special occasions. The poems adorning *surimono* were sometimes the 17-syllable *haikai* (familiar today as the one-verse *haiku*). More commonly, they were the 31-syllable poem called *kyōka*, literally 'mad' or 'playful' verse. *Kyōka* first appeared in the fifteenth century as a lighthearted alternative to solemn *waka* classical court poetry. *Kyōka* employed the same 5-7-5-7-7-syllable metre as *waka* poetry, but ignored many of its strict rules and conventions. The new style was characterised by its copious use of wordplay, puns and allusions to classical poetry. *Kyōka* poets aimed gently to subvert the classical poetry form and playfully to challenge the traditional canons of the past. At the same time. however, they sought to demonstrate their wit and literary knowledge by skilful use of those very same classical traditions.

Briefly popular at the end of the seventeenth century, the *kyōka* form was revived in the eighteenth century in the Kamigata region (Kyoto and Osaka), with the centre of activity shifting to Edo (modern Tokyo) in the 1760s. Some *kyōka* masters formed their own poetry clubs (*gawa*), which became extremely popular in Edo. Leading poetry clubs included hundreds of members, with sub-groups or 'circles' (*ren*) and affiliated groups in other cities and provincial towns throughout Japan. Poetry groups represented in the Ashmolean's collections include the Yomo-gawa and Go-gawa groups, and the Katsushika-ren, Hanazono-ren and Shippō-ren circles.

The poetry groups were composed of art-loving men and women from different social classes – mostly wealthy merchants, but also samurai, popular writers, professional artists, geisha and celebrated actors. During the Edo period Japan's ruling Tokugawa shoguns divided Japanese society into an official hierarchy of

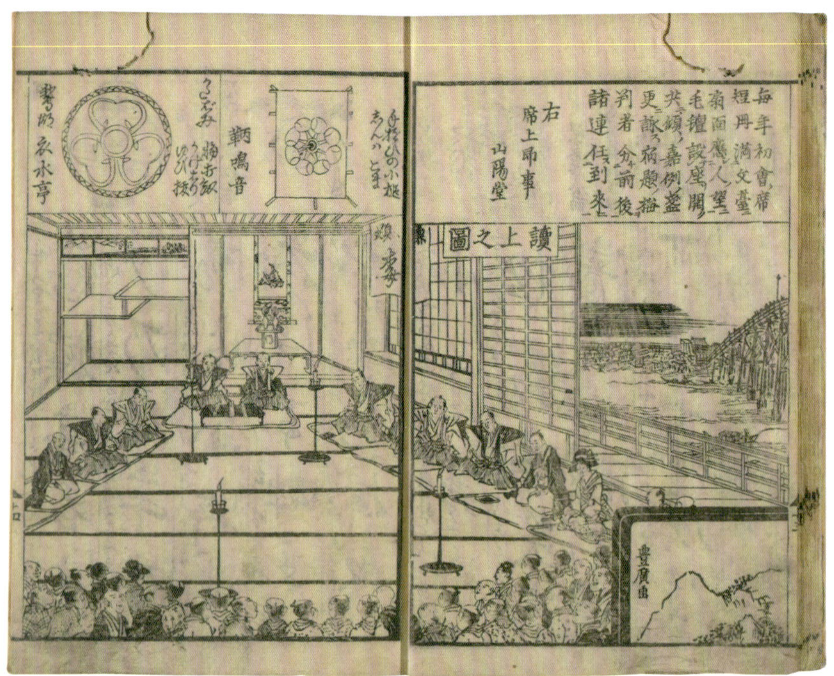

Fig.4 *A Picture of a Formal Poetry Recitation* (讀上之図). An illustration by Utagawa Toyohiro from Yomo no Utagaki Magao (ed.), *Playful Poems for Every Name, from the Yomo group* (*Yomo no tawamure utana zukushi* 四方戯歌名盡), 1809. National Diet Library, Tōkyō 京-263, info:ndljp/pid/2533900, Frame 17

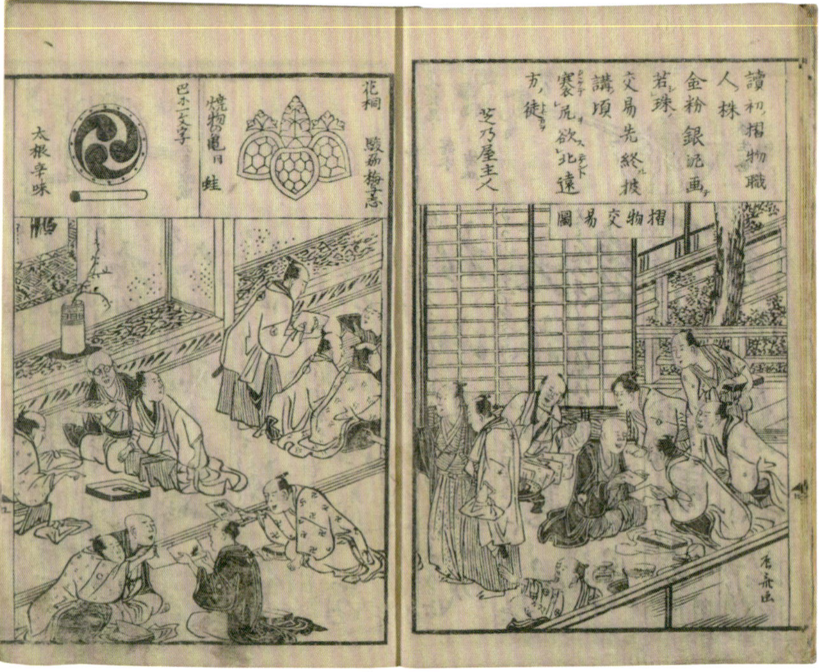

Fig.5 *A Picture of Surimono Exchange* (摺物交易図). An illustration by Ryūryūkyo Shinsai from Yomo no Utagaki Magao (ed.), *Playful Poems for Every Name, from the Yomo group* (*Yomo no tawamure utana zukushi* 四方戯歌名盡), 1809. National Diet Library, Tōkyō 京-263, info:ndljp/pid/2533900, Frame 8

four classes. The ruling samurai warrior class was placed at the top, followed by the farmers and peasants, then the artisans with the merchants at the bottom of the social scale. However, the long spell of domestic peace and growing urbanisation of the Edo period saw growing numbers of cultural 'salons' develop. Here townspeople from all classes could meet to pursue common cultural and intellectual pursuits.

Participation in poetry clubs was one opportunity to cut across traditional class lines, and members of these groups met periodically to compose and discuss verse. They often held poetry competitions (*kyōka-awase*); these were closely modelled on the centuries-old practice of court poetry contests (*uta-awase*), but usually took place in down-to-earth surroundings, such as fashionable restaurants or tea houses. At these *kyōka* contests – typically held at the New Year, but also to mark occasions such as weddings, professional name changes, retirements or death anniversaries – the poets composed verse on set topics, to be ranked by a judge, usually one of the leaders of the group (fig.4). The best poems were often selected for publication in woodblock-printed *kyōka* anthologies or single-sheet *kyōka surimono*, with accompanying illustrations commissioned from professional artists. These prints were exchanged among members of the group and distributed to acquaintances and friends (fig.5).

Most of the artists who provided designs for *surimono* artists were already well-established professionals in the field of commercially issued *ukiyo-e*. The renowned designer Katsushika Hokusai (1760–1849), for instance, was in great demand as a *surimono* artist. The exact nature of the relationship between poets and artists is not clear, but it appears that artists were given a good deal of freedom to create original designs in response to the poems. Some artists illustrated the verses quite literally, while others were more creative in their interpretations.

Many of the artists who designed *surimono* were themselves members of the poetry clubs for whom they made their designs; they took pleasure in creating images that brought a new and surprising layer of meaning to the words on a *surimono*, adding a pictorial puzzle to the cryptic wordplay of the *kyōka*. This interplay between text and image was one of the key features of *kyōka surimono*.

Also closely linked to the emergence of *kyōka surimono* was another form of private publication – the single-sheet illustrated 'picture calendar' (*egoyomi*). During the Edo period the ruling Tokugawa government strictly controlled the production of calendars, allowing only a limited number of licensed publishers to produce them. However, growing demand led a number of unlicensed publishers to produce unofficial calendars, often disguising calendar information within the designs or texts. By the mid-1760s it was fashionable for members of *haikai* poetry groups to commission private calendars to exchange at '*egoyomi* parties' over the New Year. These picture calendars were often lavishly illustrated using advanced colour printing technology. The popularity of these meetings undoubtedly influenced the production of *kyōka surimono* at the turn of the nineteenth century.

The production of *surimono* flourished during the first three decades of the nineteenth century. After the death of a number of its leaders in the late 1820s, however, the Edo *kyōka* movement gradually lost momentum. The extended Tenpō famine of 1832–6 and subsequent political reforms – including new laws that limited the production of elaborately produced prints – contributed to the decline of *surimono*. Although, as private publications, *surimono* were not subject to official regulation, the general mood of austerity still seems to have affected the production of these costly prints. The centre of *kyōka* composition returned to Osaka, where it had begun in earnest nearly a century before, and where artists of the painterly Shijō school continued to create *surimono* illustrations for both *haikai* and *kyōka* poetry groups.

The later nineteenth century saw a *surimono* revival of sorts. After Japan opened up to international trade in the mid-1850s, a craze for all things Japanese in the West led to a growing demand from European and American collectors for Japanese art of all kinds, including the beautifully produced *surimono*. Since supply could not meet demand, some commercial publishers cut new blocks to make facsimiles of early nineteenth-century *surimono*. The quality of these later *surimono* varies, but they often displayed many of the luxurious features of the originals, such as embossing and the use of metallic pigments. However, the paper is thinner than the original paper and discolours over time to a light brown. The Ashmolean collection contains several of these facsimiles.

Although *surimono* are characterised by the presence of images, they were not designed to be displayed. As poetry presentation sheets, they were intended to be viewed closely and in private. *Surimono* formats ranged from large folded sheets to tiny rectangular prints little bigger than a postcard (see figs 7–9 overleaf). Sizes mostly corresponded to subdivisions of a large, standard-size sheet

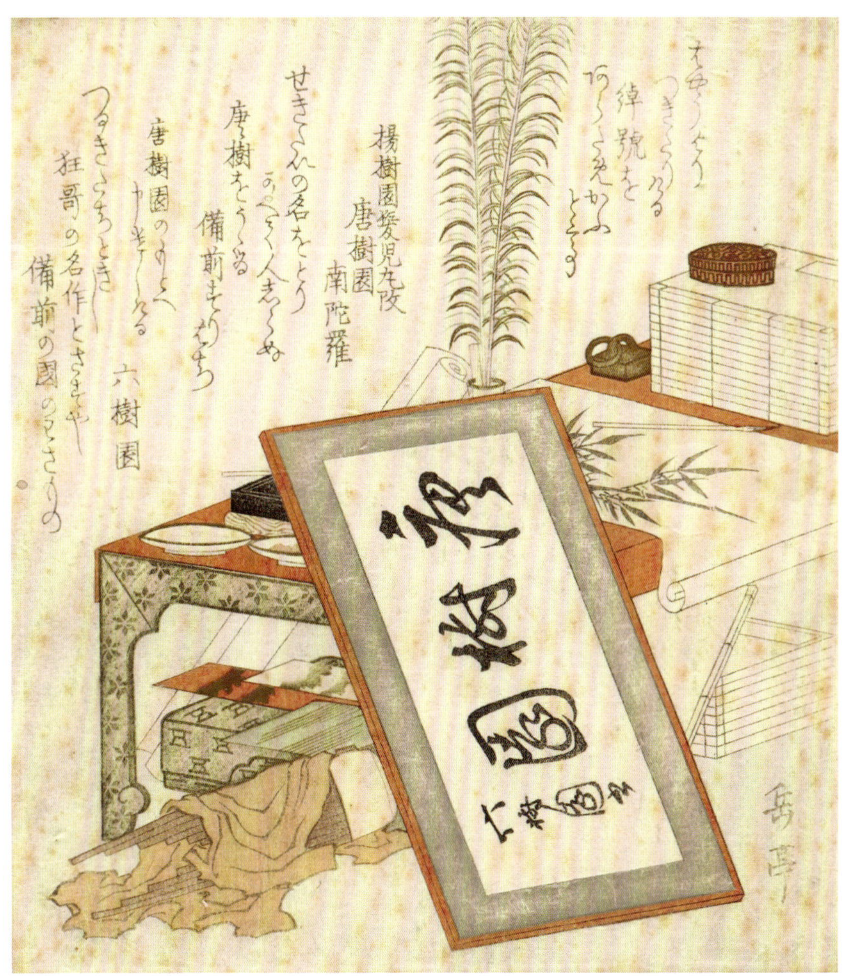

Fig.6 *A poet's writing table*. Originally issued by the poet Tōjuen Nandara to commemorate a change of pen name. Yashima Gakutei (*c*.1786–*c*.1855). Late nineteenth century (after an original of 1822). Colour woodblock print, with metallic pigments and embossing, 21.1 × 18.8 cm. Mrs E. M. Allan and Mr and Mrs H. N. Spalding, EAX.4562

Examples of different *surimono* formats

Illustrated at their relative sizes

Right:

Fig.7 *A Kabuki actor in the role of the strongman Asahina, with gourd and* sake *cup*. Commissioned by Sakuragawa Jihinari (1762–1833). Utagawa Toyohiro (1773–1828), 1809. 39 × 53 cm, *ōbōshozenshiban* ('large, full-sheet' format). EAX.4604. The dashed lines indicate the folds.

Below left:

Fig.8 *The calligrapher Tachibana no Hayanari*. Totoya Hokkei (1780–1850). From the series 'Four Companions of the Writing Studio for 1823', 1823. 21.4 × 18.8 cm, *shikishiban* ('*shikishi* poem sheet' format). EAX.4573

Below right:

Fig.9 *A woman playing with a young boy*. Attributed to Katsushika Hokusai (1760–1849), 1790s. 13.4 × 11.2 cm, *jūrokugiriban* ('sixteenth cut' format). EAX.4580b

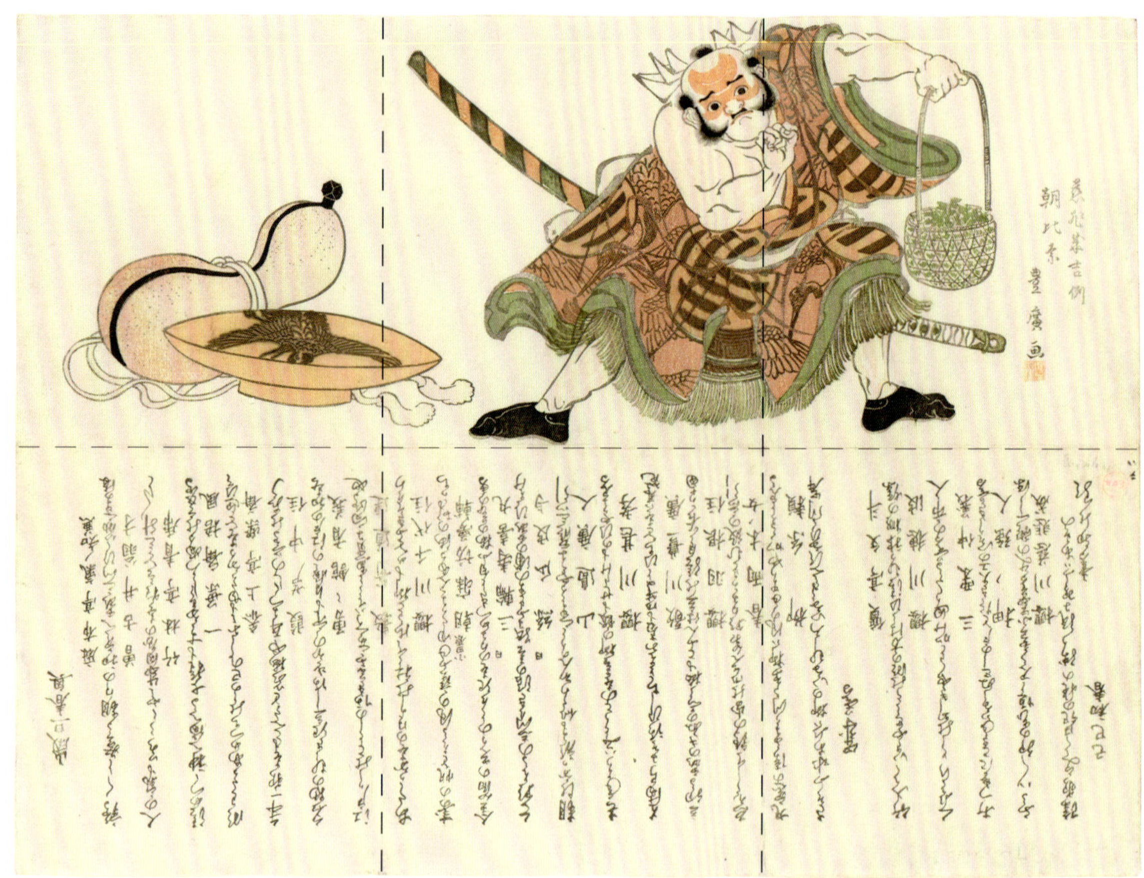

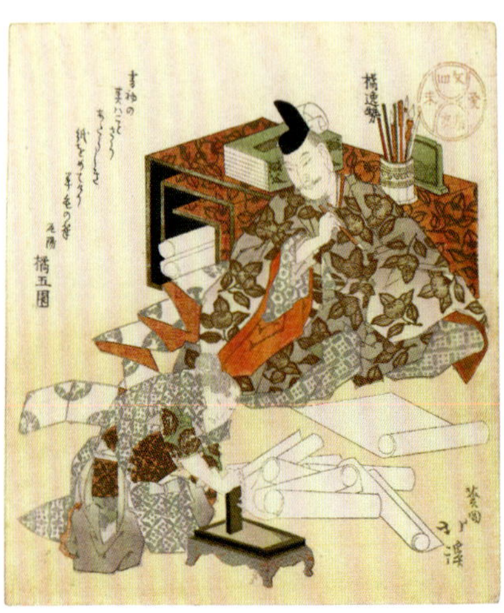

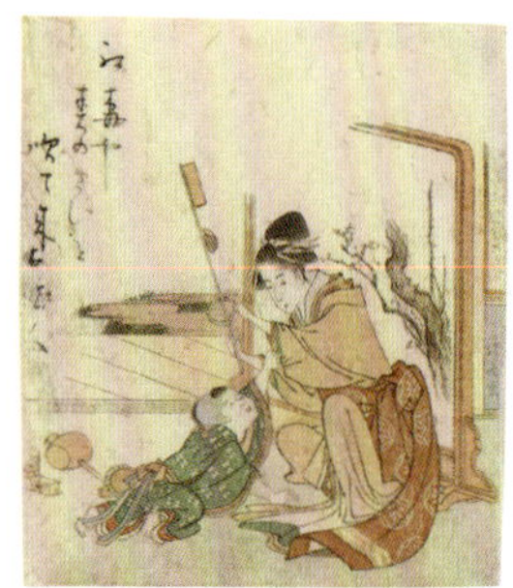

of high-quality paper known as *hōsho* (presentation paper), around 42 × 57 cm. *Surimono* produced to announce musical performances or other celebratory events were usually designed on a full sheet of *hōsho* paper. The relevant text – items on a programme, sponsors, performers or poems written by celebrities, friends and relatives – were written on one half. The other half of the *surimono* was reserved for the picture, which appeared upside down in relation to the text. The sheet was folded in half and then into thirds, so that just part of the picture was facing outward. The folded *surimono* was then placed in a paper wrapper. The *surimono* illustrated as fig.7 opposite, for example, commissioned by the poet and entertainer Sakuragawa Jihinari as a New Year's greeting, would have been folded so that at first only the *sake* cup and gourd flask were visible; viewers would have enjoyed opening the *surimono* to reveal the complete scene within. Many large *surimono* in Western collections have had their text sections trimmed off, presumably because the collectors were interested only in the images.

Larger formats were also used for sizeable gatherings of poets, when patrons wanted to include many poems. Most *kyōka surimono*, however, used smaller, more intimate formats (fig.9). From around 1808 the majority of *surimono* were made in the nearly square *shikishiban* (or *kakuban*) format, approximately 20 × 18 cm in size (fig.8). This was large enough to accommodate several poems in a legible size, but was considerably smaller and more intimate than contemporary *ukiyo-e* commercial prints. The format deliberately imitated the elegant poem cards from the Heian period (794–1185) known as *shikishi*, inscribed with verses by refined courtiers and pasted onto folding screens.

Techniques used in *surimono*

Surimono were usually made in small numbers – around 50 to 500 impressions, as opposed to several thousand for popular commercial prints. Because they were privately distributed, *surimono* were exempt from government censorship and therefore not affected by the government sumptuary laws that were regularly passed to limit extravagance in *ukiyo-e*. Nor were the patrons of *surimono* concerned with profit. Indeed *surimono* were a luxury product, specifically intended to display the wealth and taste of the individuals who commissioned them. They could therefore be as elegantly designed and as luxuriously printed as their wealthy patrons requested. The emergence of *surimono* in the late eighteenth century coincided with major advances in colour printing in Japan. *Surimono* artists were able to take full advantage of these, experimenting with new pigments and elaborate techniques. The exquisite prints that resulted were often collected and pasted into albums as personal memorials of friendships and shared events.

Traditional Japanese commercial prints (*ukiyo-e*) were produced by a team of highly skilled craftsmen, employed and directed by a publisher. The publisher commissioned an artist to produce an image, which was then carved onto wooden blocks by an engraver and finally inked and printed up by the printer. *Surimono* were made in much the same way, but the printing process was usually overseen by a specialist publisher, with the patron who commissioned the print remaining closely involved at each stage. The production of verse *surimono* also required the additional skills of calligraphers, as well as engravers who specialised in the carving of written texts. To create a *surimono*, a representative of a poetry club first commissioned an artist to create a design, leaving space around the image for the poetry. The outline of the design was copied onto thin paper that was passed to the block cutter, who pasted it face down onto a block of well-seasoned hard wood. Mountain cherry wood was often used because of its durability. The block cutter gently rubbed the back of the paper until only a fine layer of the paper remained and oiled it to allow the design to show through. He used a knife with an angled blade to cut around the lines of the design, and cleared away the wood and paper between the lines with a series of chisels and gouges. The artist's drawing was thus destroyed in the process. The carving on *surimono* was typically extremely delicate and precise.

The finished block, where only the lines of the pictures stood out, in a mirror image of the artist's drawing, was known as the 'key block'. The key block was sent to the printer to make several outline prints of the design. The printer placed a piece of dampened paper on top of the inked woodblock and rubbed the back of the paper in spiral movements with a flat tool called a *baren*. This was made of a coiled rope of bamboo fibre attached to a lacquered disc and covered with a bamboo leaf. In *surimono* the key block was often printed in a soft grey rather than in the strong black of commercial prints, giving the print as a whole a delicate, refined feel (see fig.13). The paper was often left unsized, which meant that it was highly absorbent, and so the resulting images were softer in appearance than *ukiyo-e*.

When the engraver had carved the key block a proof impression was sent to a professional calligrapher who inscribed the proof sheet with the poems. Poems were usually written in a visually appealing cursive or semi-cursive

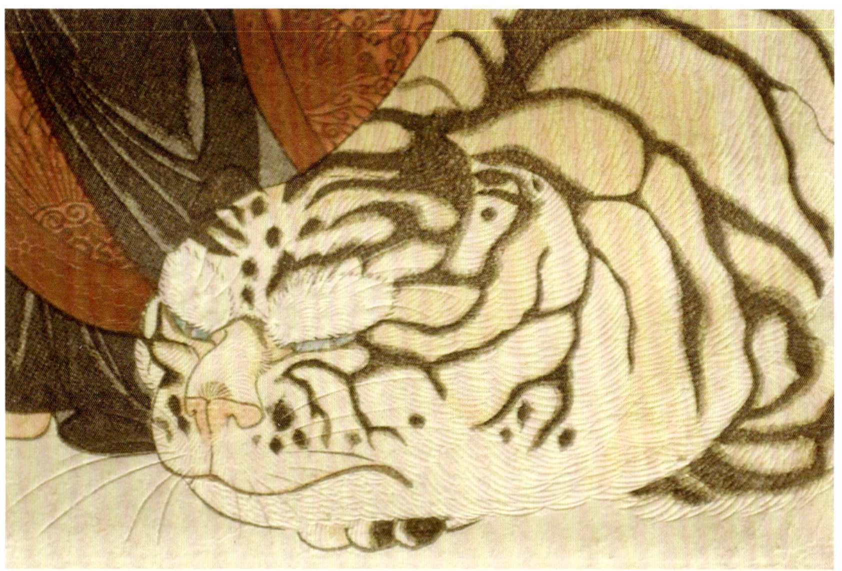

Fig.10 *Karazuri* embossing. EA1971.156 (see cat.5)

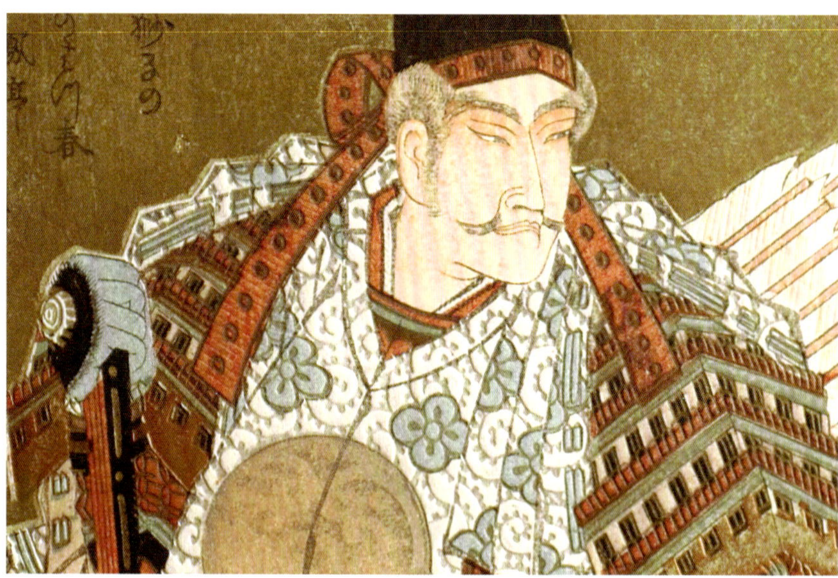

Fig.11 Metallic pigments, *karazuri* embossing and *bokashi* gradation. EA2014.35 (see cat.20)

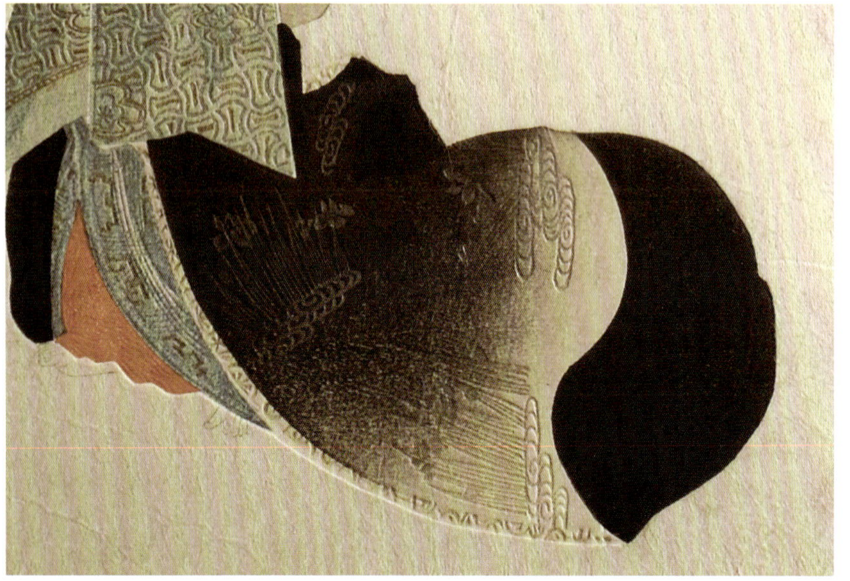

Fig.12 *Tsuyazuri* lustre printing, metallic pigments and *bokashi* shading. EA.2014.33 (see cat.31)

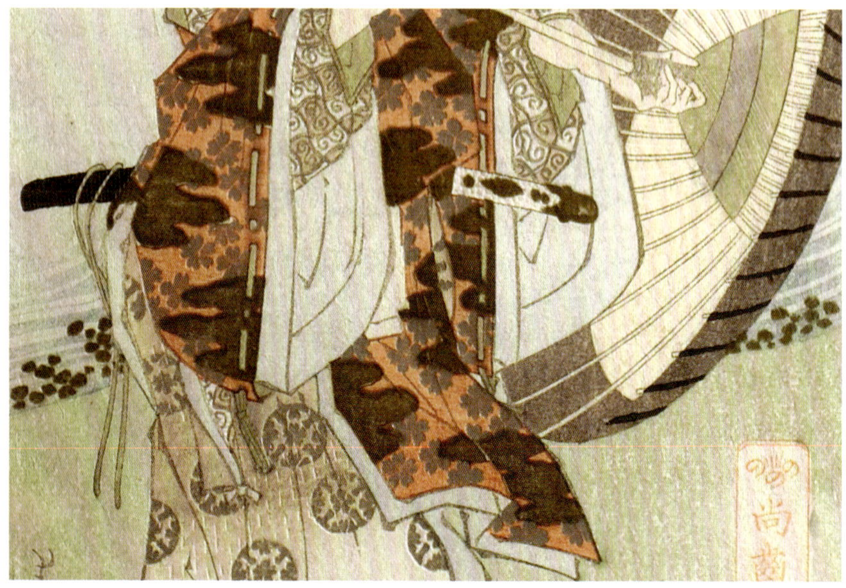

Fig.13 Soft colours, metallic pigments, *karazuri* embossing and grey outlines. EA2014.36 (see cat.17)

script. Different poetry groups favoured particular styles of script. The calligraphy on *surimono* issued by the Yomo-gawa poets, for instance, tended to be small and delicate, while Kabuki actors who commissioned *surimono* favoured strong, flamboyant calligraphy in keeping with their dramatic personae. *Haiku surimono* often contained far more verses than those published by the *kyōka* groups and these groups sought neat, compact calligraphy (see cat.40). Once the poet-patron had approved the design, it was sent it to a specialist calligraphy engraver to carve the text onto a separate block.

The paper used for *surimono* was typically the thick luxury paper known as *hōsho*. This was ideal for the addition of sophisticated printing techniques such as embossing (*karazuri*), in which the paper was impressed with carved but un-inked blocks to create texture. Embossing, or 'blind printing', was commonly used to create the effect of animal fur or fabric.

Each colour in a woodblock print was printed from a different woodblock. The printer began by printing the outline from the key block and then transferred the print to each of the colour blocks in turn to produce the final coloured image. The pigments were water-based and derived from vegetable or mineral pigments, such as red from safflower or white from powdered clamshells. The inks chosen for *surimono* were usually of the finest quality, allowing designers to create a wide variety of textures and a subtle gradation of colours, known as *bokashi*. In commercial *ukiyo-e* prints colours were generally applied evenly over large areas. *Surimono* printers, however, were highly skilled in varying colour intensity depending on the way in which they applied ink to the block and the amount of pressure they used during printing. Since the text and image were printed from separate blocks, the pigment colours and relative position of text and image often vary slightly from impression to impression. Blocks could be recycled and *surimono* were sometimes reissued with different poems or with changed image details.

Other luxury techniques seen on *surimono* were the application of expensive metallic powders, created from the filings of metal alloys, or dusting with mica powder or mother-of-pearl and a surface burnishing method known as *tsuyazuri* or 'lustre-printing'. In *tsuyazuri* animal glue was added to a pigment – usually black – that was polished after printing to give it the glossy appearance of lacquer or silk. This was often used on hair or on details of clothing such as collars or sashes. Many of these striking effects are only visible when the *surimono* is held in the hand and studied closely; they provide an element of surprise and thus enhance the viewer's enjoyment of the print. Just like the *kyōka* poems themselves, the images were designed to reward careful study and appreciation.

1 See McKee, 2008, for an extended discussion of this idea.

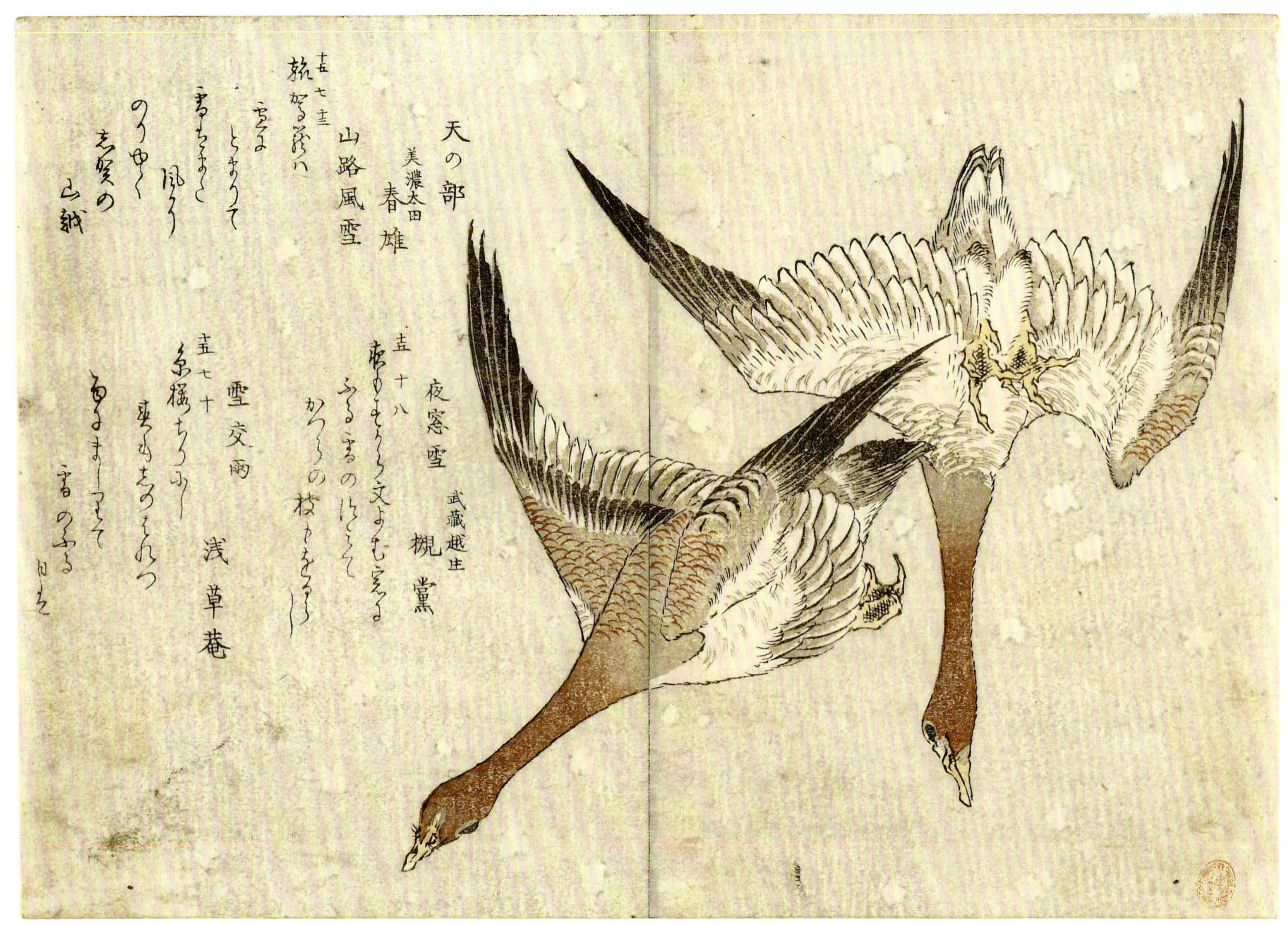

Fig.14 *Heaven*, Totoya Hokkei (1780–1850). From the book *One Hundred Verses on the Three Domains* (*Sansai hyakushu*). 1830. EAX.4645

Poetry and *Surimono*

Kiyoko Hanaoka

A brief history of *Kyōka*

The genre of Japanese woodblock prints known as *surimono*, characterised by the harmonious combination of poetry and image, belongs to a long Japanese tradition of unifying art and literature. From pictorial screens decorated with calligraphic poetry sheets in the Heian period (794–1185) through painted hand-scrolls of classical stories, such as the tenth-century *The Tales of Ise* and the twelfth-century *The Tale of Genji*, to Chinese-style literati hanging scrolls with poetic inscriptions in the eighteenth century, poetry has long been inextricably linked with art in Japan.

Poetry has always played an important role in Japanese culture and aesthetics. The significance of poetry within Japanese culture was famously described by the court poet Ki no Tsurayuki in 914, in his preface to Japan's first imperial poetry anthology, the *Kokin wakashū* (Collection of Ancient and Modern Japanese Poetry). The preface opens with the words '*yamato uta wa hito no kokoro o tane to shite yorozu no kotonoha tozo narerikeri*' ('Japanese poetry takes as its seed the human heart'): men and women speak of things they hear and see, giving words to the feelings in their hearts. Poetry has also traditionally been seen as more than simply a form of personal expression. In Japan's oldest existing poetry collection, the eighth-century *Man'yōshū* (Collection of Ten Thousand Leaves), the term '*kotodama*' appears. Literally meaning 'word-soul', *kotodama* was the belief that words themselves have a magical power to influence reality: the use of auspicious words brings about the realisation of good things and the use of bad words leads to unfortunate consequences. The idea of *kotodama* was handed down from generation to generation in Japan and its echoes can be seen in *kyōka surimono*.

The basic form of traditional Japanese poetry is *waka* (literally 'Japanese poetry'). *Waka* are rhymeless poems that consist of 31 syllables made up of lines of alternating five- and seven-syllable units in a 5-7-5-7-7 meter. First recorded in the eighth century in the *Kojiki* (Records of Ancient Matters) and the *Man'yōshū*, *waka* were composed according to strict rules governing subject, language, mood and poetic technique. Most *surimono* in this catalogue combine images with a type of poem known as *kyōka*, literally 'crazy poems' or 'playful verse', which developed out of this classical *waka* tradition. For this reason they are known as *kyōka surimono*. *Kyōka* used exactly the same structure and poetic techniques as *waka*, but dispensed with many of *waka*'s formal constraints of style and theme. The 'craziness' of *kyōka* 'crazy verse' lies not in any extreme eccentricity of expression, but rather in its witty, sometimes sarcastic wordplay and its subversion of the rules of classical *waka* poetry composition (see pp.24, 28–9 for further explanation of these poetry techniques). *Kyōka*'s manner of deviating from the serious orthodoxy of *waka* while remaining faithful to its basic conventions can be traced back to a poetry form called *haikaika*, meaning comic or unorthodox poetry. *Haikaika* poetry was first recorded in the *Kokin wakashū*. It followed the conventions of *waka*, but was composed with an emphasis on humour and playfulness that was later seen in *kyōka* poetry.

The term '*kyōka*' first appeared in 1191 in an entry by the poet Fujiwara no Teika in his diary entitled *Meigetsuki* (Record of the bright moon). Here he wrote that '*kyōka* were improvised after one hundred formal classical *waka* were composed at an *uta-kai* (poetry gathering)'. This implies that *kyōka* were composed freely without being restricted by the complicated rules of *waka*. However, it was not until the end of the fifteenth century that *kyōka* was acknowledged as a new art form – practised not just by aristocrats, but also by samurai, priests and high-ranking merchants. Emerging first in Kyoto, the imperial capital and centre of culture, this new form of *kyōka* soon became popular with the affluent merchant class in nearby Osaka, Japan's commercial centre. Here it was known as 'Naniwa *kyōka*', reflecting the old name for Osaka.

The late 1760s then saw a growth of interest in *kyōka* in Edo, the political capital of the country. The pioneers of the Edo *kyōka* movement were mostly low-ranking samurai poets such as Ōta Nanpo (1749–1823), better known in *kyōka* circles by his poetry name Yomo no Akara, Karagoromo Kisshū (1743–1802) and Akera

Kankō (1740–1800). These poets met regularly for *kyōka-kai* (*kyōka* gatherings) and they also held *kyōka-awase* (*kyōka* contests), based on the *uta-awase* (*waka* poetry contests) of the Heian court. In a *kyōka-awase* members of poetry clubs competed with each other to produce the best poems, evaluated by a *kyōka* poet acting as a judge (*hanja*).

From the late 1770s poetry groups began to publish their *kyōka*. In 1783 Yomo no Akara edited a *kyōka* anthology entitled *Manzai kyōkashū* (Collection of playful poems of ten thousand years), which included *kyōka* by both contemporary and seventeenth-century *kyōka* poets. This collection was hugely successful and served to boost the number of *kyōka* followers in the city – not only among samurai, but also among the urban commoner classes (*chōnin* or 'townspeople'). *Kyōka* meetings offered a place in which educated people could withdraw from everyday life and enjoy spending time together, regardless of their social class. Using poetic pseudonyms (*kyōmei*), as if assuming another persona or identity, samurai or *chōnin*, Kabuki actors, *ukiyo-e* artists, craftsmen and publishers, men and women met to discuss and compose poetry.

Yomo no Akara set up his own poetry club called the Yamate-ren (Yamate circle). It was soon followed by many other groups (*gawa*) and sub-groups or circles (*ren*), including the Go-gawa under the leadership of Ishikawa Masamochi (also known as Yadoya no Meshimori), the Katsushika-ren headed by Asakusa-an Ichihito, the Shippō-ren, affiliated to the Go-gawa, under Fukunoya Uchinari, the Hakuraku-ren under Tsuburi no Hikaru and the Mimasu-ren, also affiliated to the Go-gawa and consisting mainly of Kabuki fans. The fashion for *kyōka* quickly spread from the major cities and clubs were also established in provinces throughout the country.[1]

The Edo *kyōka* movement flourished in the liberal political climate of the 1770s and 1780s. It reached its peak during the Tenmei era (1781–9) and gave a great impetus to other fields of literature, art and theatre.[2] However, after a series of sweeping financial and social reforms in the final years of the eighteenth century, Yomo no Akara and his samurai peers were obliged to focus on their duties as government officials. The Edo *kyōka* movement continued to thrive until the late 1830s, but the leadership of the movement was taken over by wealthy merchants and other members of the *chōnin* class of urban commoners.

Throughout this period members of poetry groups continued to meet at restaurants and tea houses for monthly *kyōka* contests. The winning verses were often published in collections known as *kyōka-bon* (*kyōka* books).[3] The vogue for *surimono* coincided with a boom in the Edo publishing industry. Particularly significant in the history of *surimono* was the private production of *egoyomi* (single-sheet picture calendars), which included the first multi-coloured *ukiyo-e* prints to be made in Japan in the mid-1760s. *Egoyomi* prints began to be produced as New Year's greetings to distribute among members of *haikai* poetry groups (who had also been publishing illustrated *haikai surimono* since the early eighteenth century). This practice was taken up by *kyōka* poets and they soon began to add *kyōka* to the calendar pictures. Over time the calendar function of *kyōka surimono* became less significant.

From the 1780s *kyōka* poets began commissioning artists to illustrate their poems, either as single-sheet *kyōka surimono* with accompanying pictures or as illustrated books (*kyōka-ehon*).[4] The artists commissioned to supply pictures for *surimono* mostly belonged to the *ukiyo-e* school. Leading *surimono* designers included Kitagawa Utamaro, Katsukawa Shunshō, Katsushika Hokusai, and his pupils (Hokkei, Gakutei and Shinsai), Kubo Shunman, Utagawa Toyokuni, Utagawa Kunisada and Keisai Eisen. There were close links between poets and artists, and we can assume that when a *surimono* was commissioned there was some level of discussion between the poets – or at least the head of poetry club – and the artist. Most *ukiyo-e* artists of the time were themselves well versed in classical *waka* and *haiku* poems and drew on this knowledge when producing their designs. In fact many artists belonged to one of the *kyōka* poetry clubs and had their own *kyōmei* (*kyōka* poetry name). During the 1820s the poetry club that commissioned and contributed the greatest number of *surimono*, often in multiple series, was the Yomo-gawa group, headed by Yomo no Utagaki Magao, the successor of Yomo no Akara.[5] All the poetry clubs had their own distinctive emblems, often incorporated into the *surimono* they commissioned.

Most *kyōka surimono* were composed to commemorate New Year's poetry gatherings and were known as *shunkyō kyōka surimono*. The subjects of the poems and images on *surimono* are varied, with the most conspicuous themes including still-life subjects, Kabuki actors, zodiac animals, legends and literature. What was common to all New Year's *surimono*, however, was that they invariably carried auspicious imagery that conveyed messages of vigour, happiness, longevity, beauty and wealth. Both those sending and those receiving *surimono* would be suffused with the pleasure of anticipation of positive things to come. The sense of anticipating auspicious things for the New Year or on other occasions took the form of ritualistic prayers and events known as *yoshuku*.[6] These consisted of celebrating in advance the thing that was wished for and performing actions designed to imagine the actual realisation of that thing. The poems and images on *surimono* often performed a similar function. Thus the tobacco pouch in the *surimono* 'Pipe case and tobacco pouch with a *netsuke* and chain' (cat.37) represents fullness and happiness because it is fully packed with tobacco. The armour-tugging scene depicted in cat.30 is an auspicious scene as it implies the pulling in of auspicious things at the New Year, while the recipient of the *surimono* 'Daikoku with an abacus and a woman with a white rat' (cat.4) would be happy because the boxes of gold coins that it portrays act as a symbolic gift – the promise of untold wealth.

The appreciation of *surimono*

According to the book *Ukiyo-e ruikō* (Various Thoughts on *Ukiyo-e*) – a collection of commentaries and biographies of *ukiyo-e* artists compiled by Ōta Nanpo (Yomo no Akara) and others from the 1790s – the great print designer Hokusai is said to have stated that '*surimono* pictures are highly valued when they do not look like *nishiki-e* [commercial colour prints]'.[7] The makers of *surimono* were keen to differentiate them from commercial *ukiyo-e* prints in terms of format, themes, colours, materials and treatment of space. Unlike *ukiyo-e*, the texts on *surimono* were as important as the images. *Surimono* artists were thus careful to create designs that left the appropriate space for a number of poems. The poems to be commemorated were written by a calligrapher and carved onto a separate wood block, then printed on the space reserved for them. The flowing lines of calligraphic cursive writing used for the poems were usually beautifully executed to please the viewer's eye, as if looking at a piece of an abstract artwork. The wood block medium, unlike moveable type printing, was able to represent the texture of brush strokes and the form of characters as if they were hand-written in ink on the paper. The fact that the poems were carved on a separate block made it easy to change the poems used with a particular picture, or vice versa.

The pictures accompanying the poems reflected the tastes and ingenuity of the commissioners, who were erudite members of poetry clubs. Images were designed both for aesthetic enjoyment and to enhance the understanding of the poems. High-quality materials and sophisticated printing techniques were employed on *surimono*, especially from the 1810s onwards, with the copious use of embossing (blind printing), the addition of gold, silver and bronze metal powders to standard colour pigments and other novel refinements. Experimentation in *surimono* formats led in the early nineteenth century to the emergence of the square *surimono* that recalled the courtly *shikishi* poetry sheets used for poetry gatherings in the Heian period (794–1185).

The commercial *ukiyo-e* prints published at the same time as *surimono* were in demand because of their fashionable, contemporary subject matter. While *surimono* also often depicted scenes from everyday life, the Yoshiwara pleasure quarters or the Kabuki theatre, they also made a virtue of highlighting the past as often as they referred to contemporary life. Just as *kyōka* were packed with allusions to traditional courtly verse or historical events, so *surimono* commonly depicted scenes from Japanese or Chinese literature or prominent figures of the past. Often these venerated subjects were presented in a contemporary setting or represented by contemporary figures in a form of gentle parody called *mitate*. The members of *kyōka* poetry clubs took pride in their common cultural knowledge. According to the founder of the Yamate-ren poetry circle, Yomo no Akara, to be a proficient *kyōka* poet required knowledge of the 'Three Histories' and 'Five Classics' written in Chinese, *The Tale of Genji*, the *Man'yōshū* (Collection of Ten Thousand Leaves), the 21 imperial poetry anthologies and the work of famous *kyōka* poets of the past, as well as the ability to establish one's own style. This knowledge was put to the test in the appreciation of *surimono*, not just in reading the poems, but in establishing connections between poems and images.[8]

In some cases the link between the poems and pictures is obvious. In others the significance of the subject depicted is not easy to comprehend without the accompanying poems. For example, the meaning of the enigmatic group of objects in 'A vase with plum twigs and a crab on a court hat' (cat.38) can only be understood on reading the accompanying poems. The poems refer to the Battle of Dan no Ura of 1185, a famous conflict between the two warrior clans, the Heike and the Genji families. From this clue it becomes obvious that the fierce-looking crab depicted is a 'Heike crab', representing the spirits of the defeated Heike warriors, while the black court hat (*eboshi*) is a symbol of the noble rank of the Heike family. Similarly in 'The Divine Horse-grass' (cat.35) the poems inscribed all relate to horses, although the picture appears to have no link with horses whatsoever. The key lies in the title 'The Divine Horse-grass' (*jinmesō*), a type of seaweed that happens to contain the character for 'horse'. The word '*jinmesō*' derives from an ancient account of a horse owned by the Empress Jingū; the animal was fed with this type of seaweed, which thus acquired the name 'god horse seaweed'. The central straw-like bundle depicted in the image is made of dried *jinmesō* seaweed. Understanding the derivation of the word '*jinmesō*' allows the viewer to unravel the meaning of the *surimono*.

The changing spatial relationship between poetry and image

A *surimono* is composed from poems and an image, carved and printed from separate woodblocks. When the theme of a picture for a particular *surimono* was decided upon, we can presume that the artist would have had a preconceived idea of the treatment of space within that *surimono* and know how to strike a balance between the calligraphic text and the image. Over the decades from the 1780s until the 1830s, the half-century in which *surimono* flourished in Edo, this spatial relationship between poems and pictures changed substantially. So did the palette of colours used on the pictures, with the image assuming an increasingly dominant role. These changes are illustrated below with reference to *surimono* in this catalogue.

From the 1790s until the 1810s *surimono* were designed with ample space allocation for the poems next to or above the image. In the *surimono* shown on p.25, the images are designed so as not to interfere with the poems. On the *surimono* in cats 15 and 12, three and four *kyōka* poems respectively are inscribed in neat vertical lines in a reserved space set aside to the left of the image. The *haiku* poem found in the *surimono* cat.2 is written in four lines of bold calligraphy to one side of the image, the lines staggered to echo the tilted platter held by the monkey. Similarly the beautiful butterfly and moths in the *surimono* in cat.39 are carefully placed at the edges of the design to allow the three poems plenty of space at the centre. *Surimono* pictures of this early period were printed in pale red, purple, orange, yellow, green and blue hues, with the outlines executed in grey rather than in the black used for commercial *ukiyo-e* prints.

During the 1820s a subtle shift in the balance between text and image on *surimono* occurred, as the poems became more closely integrated with the images (see p.26). The subjects on *surimono* of this period are often more dynamic than earlier examples, and the poems tend to be inscribed in the space left around the pictures. The two poems in cat.7, for example, a *surimono* of a stylish woman with a kite, are slotted into the spaces on either side of the woman's head and shoulders. Similarly the three poems in the *surimono* in cat.8 are inscribed apparently at random to fill the space remaining to the left of the strong diagonal composition of the rearing horse. The name of the artist, placed next to the horse's rear left hoof, almost looks like part of the poetry.

Cat.30, with its bold triangular configuration, strong colours and gold background, is a typical example of a *surimono* from the late 1820s. The two poems are inscribed discreetly in the space in the upper left-hand corner of the *surimono*, whereas the name of the artist, written boldly and conspicuously, stands alone in the lower right-hand corner. This period saw increasing experimentation in the treatment of space, with the addition of decorative frames and patterned backgrounds (cat.23)and the occasional enclosure of poems within square or rectangular poem card-shaped cartouches. The colours used for the *surimono* in this period were generally brighter than those of earlier years, although the outlines remained grey.

By the 1830s the images on *surimono* had become an even stronger element of the design, with bold compositions and strongly coloured pigments, while the poems had become secondary in terms of the treatment of space (see p.27). The practice of enclosing poems within decorative cartouches, as illustrated in cats 26 and 27, became more common. In the innovative composition of cat.10 the poem and picture are each contained within a separate, overlapping cartouche.

Another striking development of this period was the use of imported Prussian blue pigment, also called *beroai* (Berlin blue). This distinctive blue pigment was also used to great effect by Hokusai and Hiroshige in *ukiyo-e* landscapes from the late 1820s, and by the early 1830s was commonly seen in *surimono* (as shown in the examples above). The dramatic depiction of the sky in cat.6, for instance, is enhanced by the effective use of the new blue while the poems, printed in silver pigment against the winding bands of cloud, seem little more than a decorative motif to emphasise the skyscape.

Poetic techniques used in *kyōka surimono*

The rhetorical techniques used in *kyōka* were all inherited from classical *waka* poetry, but were applied in a more light-hearted and playful manner.

Honkadori (literally 'taken from the original poem') is a technique in which distinctive phrases are borrowed from famous classical poems and incorporated into a new poem to impart an additional depth and elegance. In more formal types of Japanese poetry this process of literary quotation is done in a highly respectful manner, but in *kyōka* it is usually done with a degree of humour. In the *surimono* 'Kuronushiyama' (cat.19), for example, *honkadori* is used in the first poem by the poet Kikunoya no Magaki:

sasanami ya
shiga no yamaji ni
sodachi temo
uta ni taenaru
miyakodori

(continued on p.28)

Surimono of the 1790s – 1810s

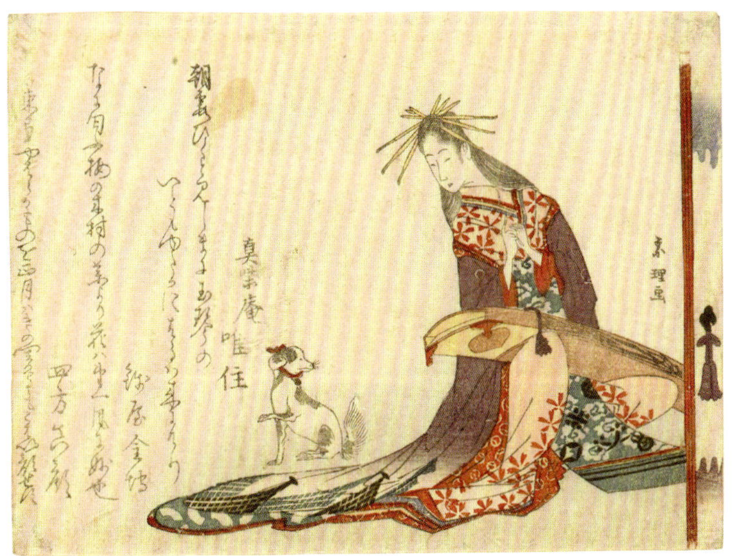

Cat.15, 1794–8

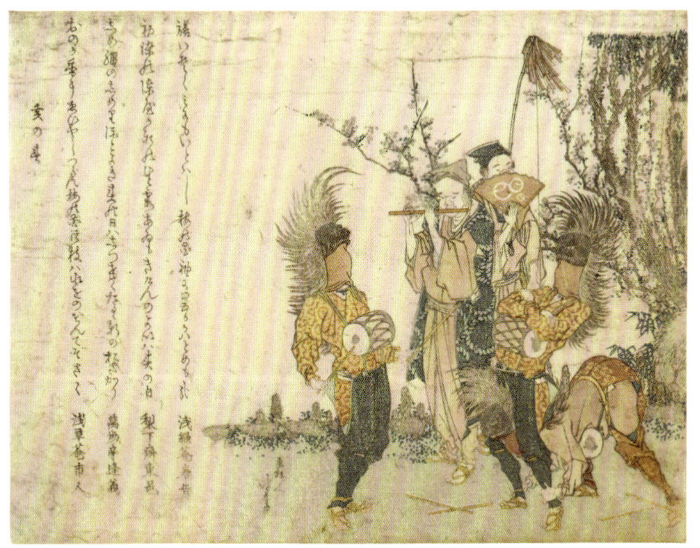

Cat.12, 1803

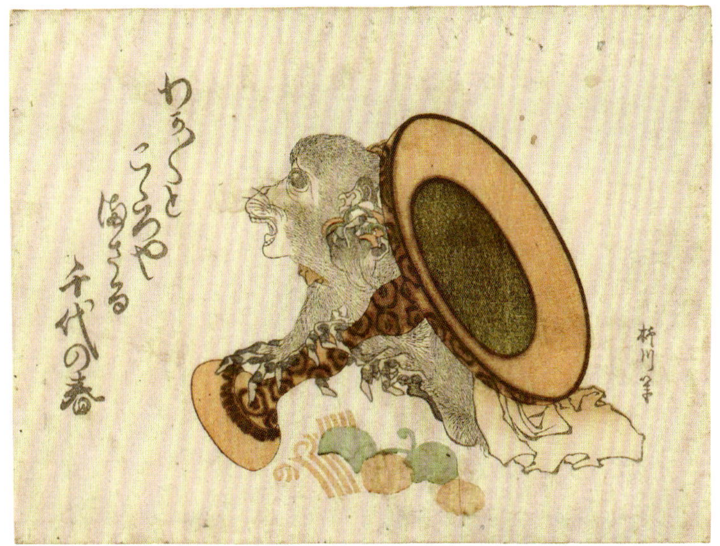

Cat.2, 1812

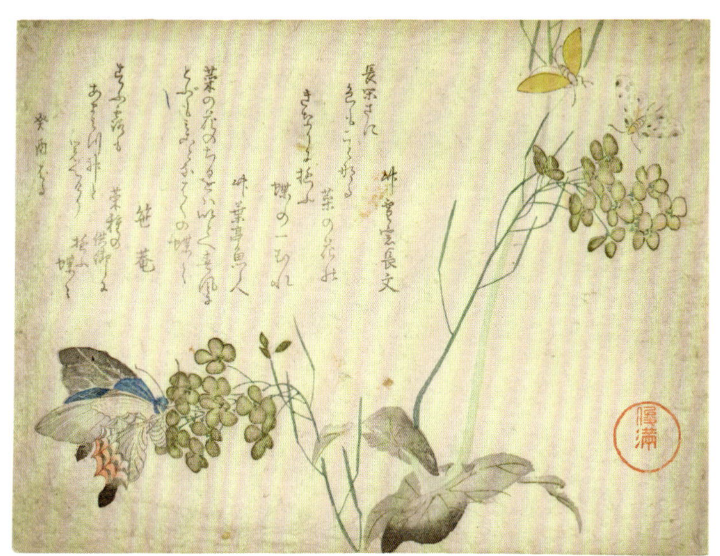

Cat.39, 1813

Surimono of the 1820s

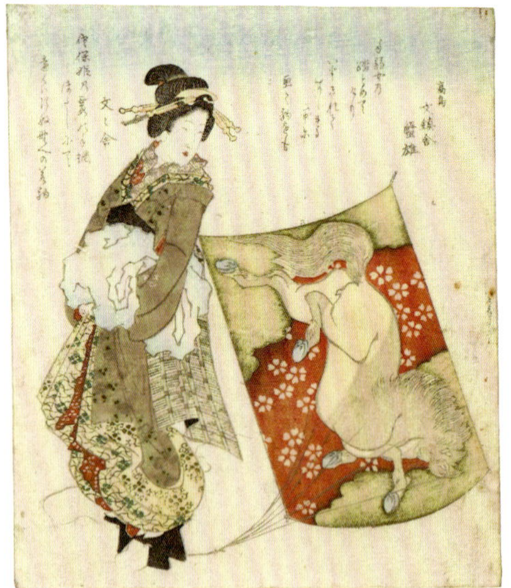

Cat.7, 1822

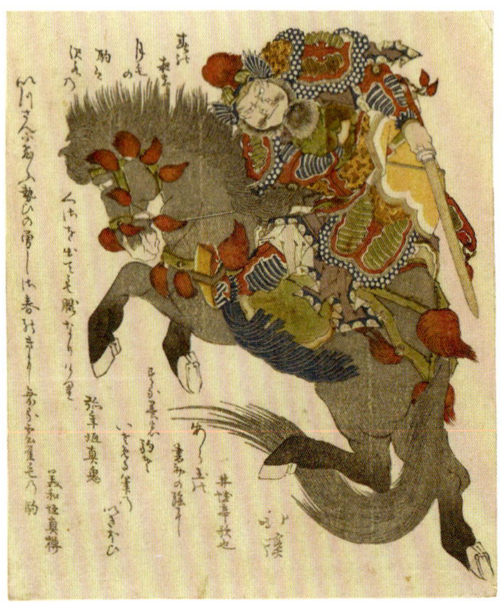

Cat.8, 1822

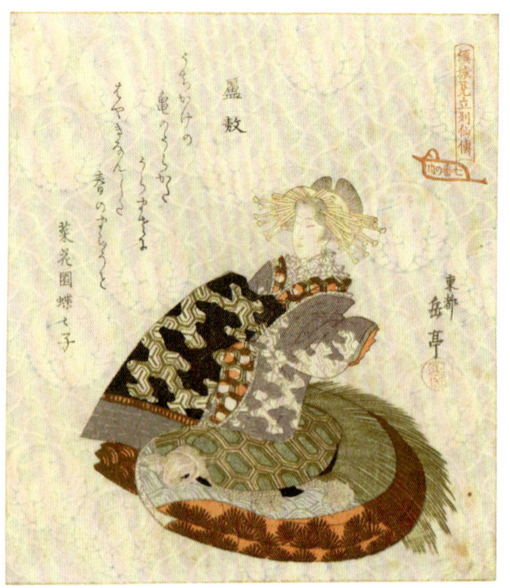

Cat.23, *c.* 1821–2

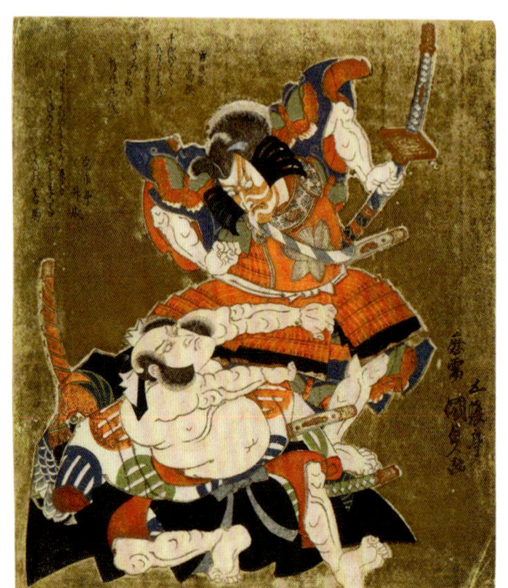

Cat.30, 1827

Surimono of the 1830s

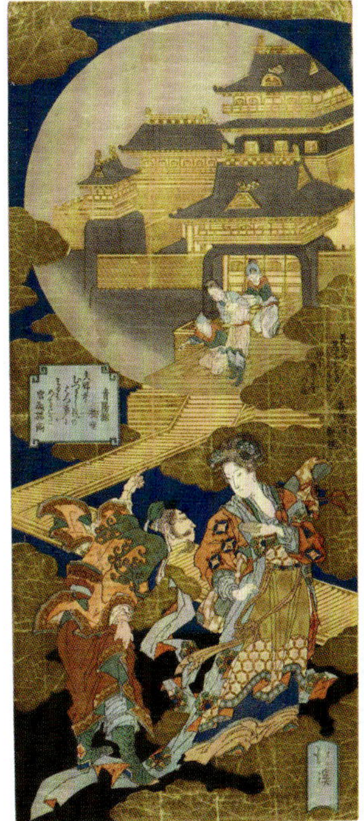

Cat.27, 1831

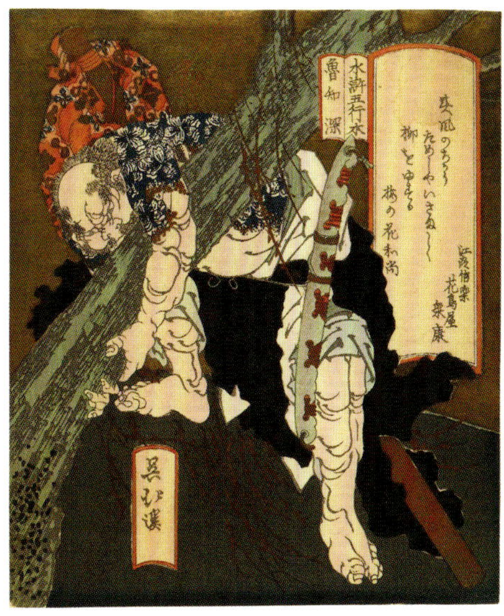

Cat.26, early 1830s

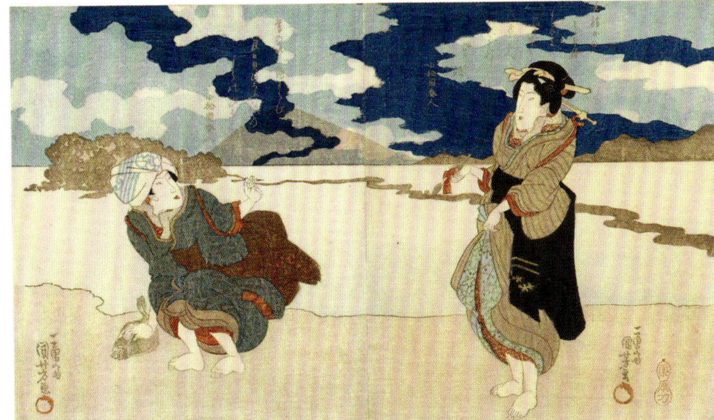

Cat.6, 1833

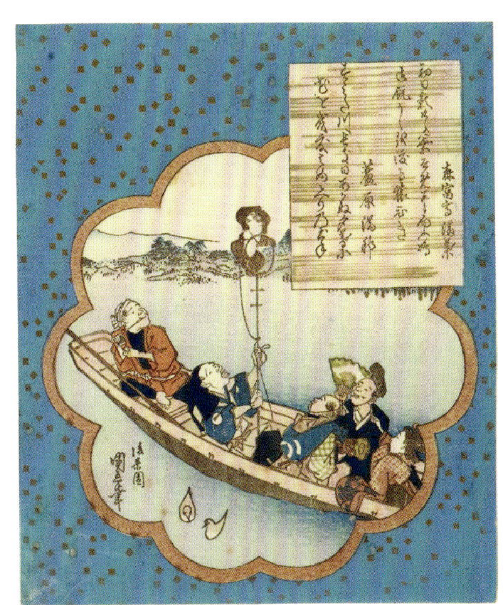

Cat.10, 1836

Although brought up
on the mountain paths
in Shiga of the rippling waves
– how exquisitely the capital bird sings!

This verse was composed in reference to a classic *waka* poem by the renowned poet Taira no Tadanori in the twelfth-century poetry collection *Senzaishū* (Collection of a Thousand Years).

sasanami ya
shiga no miyako wa
arenishio
mukashinagara no
yamazakura kana

The old capital at Shiga of the rippling waves
has become a ruin
but the mountain cherry blossoms on Mount Nagara
bloom as of old
(*Senzaishū* no.66)

The particular phrase '*sasanami ya shiga no*' in Taira no Tadanori's twelfth-century *waka* has been borrowed by Kikunoya no Magaki for his nineteenth-century *kyōka*. Magaki links the place name 'Shiga' to another classical poet, Ōtomo no Kuronushi, who was born in rural Shiga Province but moved to the imperial capital, Kyoto. Magaki borrows the word '*miyako*' or 'capital' from the earlier verse, within the word '*miyakodori*' or 'capital bird'. '*Miyakodori*' refers metaphorically to Ōtomo no Kuronushi, who became famous as one of 'Six Immortal Poets' in the capital, Kyoto (*miyako*). Viewers of the *surimono*, well versed in classical literature, would immediately have understood the reference. The fact that Magaki draws a parallel between a humble bird from the rural mountains of Shiga and the sophisticated court poet would have amused readers. In this way *honkadori* was used not only to link the past and the present, but also gently to mock the solemnity of the past.

Makurakotoba (literally 'pillow word') is a technique in which set epithets are used in association with certain words, in order to enhance the tone of those words. In the poem above *sasanami* ('rippling waves') is a pillow word to embellish the place name 'Shiga'. *Makurakotoba* were used only as decorative phrases in poems and carried no real meaning.

Kakekotoba (literally 'pivot word') is a type of pun. The device of *kakekotoba* takes advantage of the abundance of homophones in the Japanese language by using a single word to provide multiple meanings. It thus allows the poet a greater range of artistic expression within the short space of a 31-syllable poem. *Kakekotoba* are generally written in the Japanese phonetic alphabet (*hiragana*) to encourage ambiguous readings and are often coupled with *engo* (see below).

Engo (literally 'associated words') is a rhetorical device in which two or more semantically associated words are used in a poem for appealing effect. In *kyōka* poetry *engo* are often coupled with *kakekotoba* pivot words for humorous, sometimes even vulgar effect. In the *surimono* 'Surusumi' (cat.8) both *kakekotoba* and *engo* are used in the first poem by Seiatei Utanari:

aratama no
kakizome no e ni
suru sumi no
koma zo isameru
fude no ikioi

The first drawing of the New Year
is a picture of Surusumi
– a horse to be restrained
by the strength of a brush stroke

The word '*suru*' is a *kakekotoba*. When read with the previous words as '*e ni suru*' it means 'to make (*suru*) a picture (*e*)'; when read with the following word as 'suru *sumi*' it means 'to rub (*suru*) an ink stick (*sumi*)' on an inkstone to produce black ink for drawing. It carries a third meaning too, by referring to Surusumi, the name of a famous horse. *Engo* verbal association is to be found in the words '*sumi*' (ink, or ink stick) and '*fude*' (brush), which both relate to painting and calligraphy.

Utamakura (literally 'poem pillow') is the use of a specific place name to evoke a mood or atmosphere traditionally associated with that place. In the *surimono*

'The courtesan Komurasaki' (cat.31) the word 'Naniwa-e' in the first poem by Kesō Fumito is an example of *utamakura*:

ume min to
murekuru hito ni
ashi no kiri
tatsuru tokoro mo
naniwa-e no haru

Crowds of people
coming to view the plum blossoms
stand at Naniwa Bay in the springtime;
there is no space between them,
not even for a single young reed.

Naniwa-e (Naniwa Bay in modern Osaka Prefecture) was famous for its extensive reed beds, and so the use of 'Naniwa-e' in the *kyōka* evokes the image of a large marshy area covered in reeds. *Utamakura* are often place names mentioned in classical poems, serving to imbue a *kyōka* with the elegancy of an ancient *waka*.

1 Kobayashi, pp.45–6.
2 Carpenter 2005, p.170.
3 Makino, p.55.
4 Asano 1997, p.7.
5 Carpenter 2008, p.10.
6 Kishi, p.163.
7 Yura, p.139. At this stage Hokusai was using the pseudonym Sōri, rather than Hokusai.
8 Hasegawa and Hibbett, p.231.

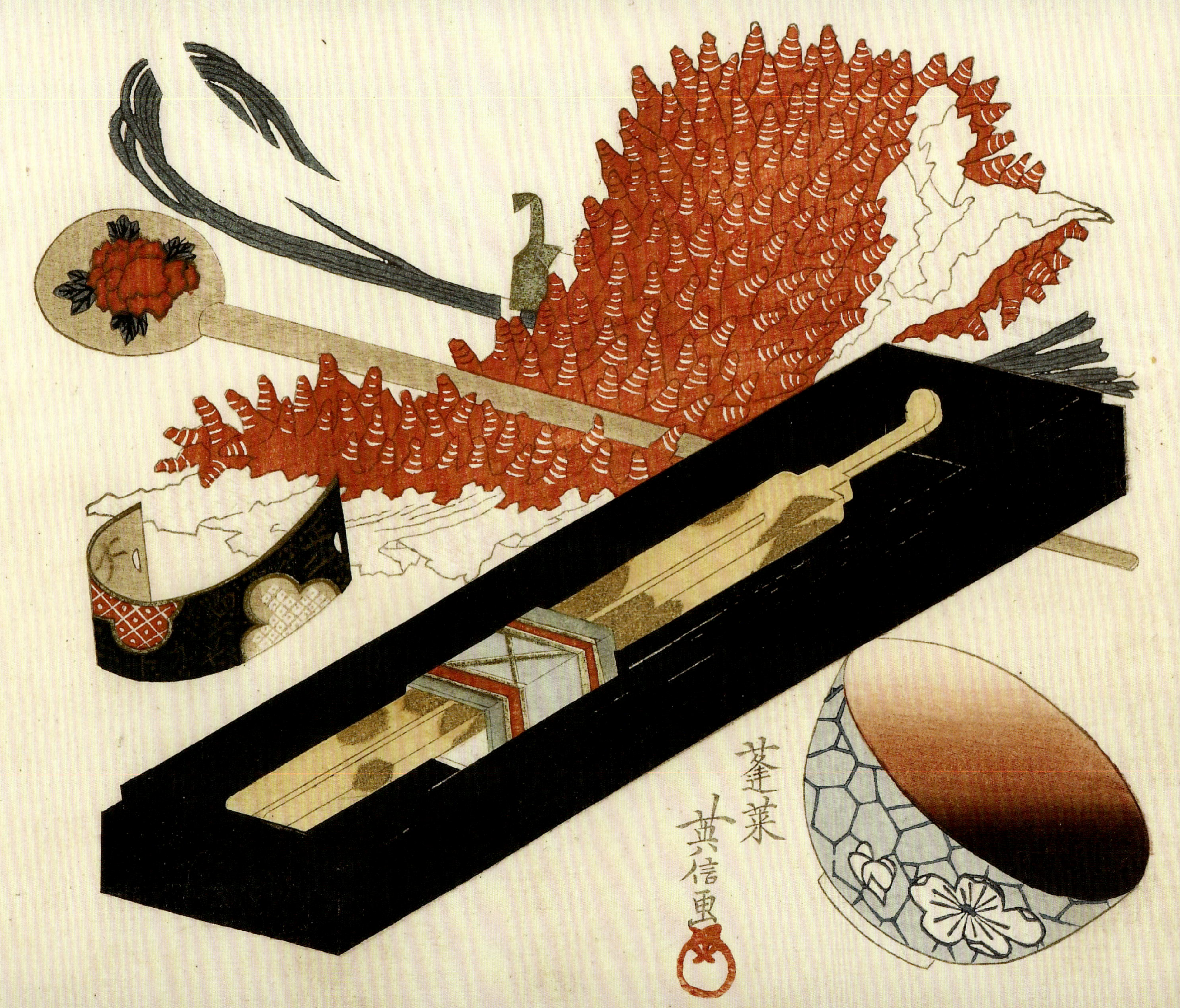
蓬莱
英信画

I

Picture Calendars

Until the adoption of the Gregorian calendar in 1873, the Japanese calendar was based on a lunar system in which a year was composed of twelve alternating long months (30 days) and short months (29 days). Since twelve lunar months are shorter than one solar (seasonal) year, every few years an extra month, called an intercalary month, was inserted to keep the lunar calendar in line with the solar cycle.

The sequence of long and short months varied from year to year. During the Edo period (1603–1868) this information was published in official public calendars (*koyomi*) ready for the Japanese New Year which, according to the Gregorian calendar, fell in mid-February. Some of these calendars were illustrated and known as '*egoyomi*', or 'picture calendars'. The publication of these calendars was strictly regulated by the ruling Tokugawa shogunate, and only a few publishers were licensed to produce them.

In the early eighteenth century, however, some publishers began surreptitiously to issue images that disguised the calendar information within the designs or accompanying texts. These commercially published (illegal) calendars fell out of production in the mid-eighteenth century, perhaps due to government crack-downs, but in the mid-1760s illustrated picture calendars began to be privately printed by wealthy sponsors to exchange with members of their literary circles. Initially made without poems, by the end of the century these *egoyomi* often included *kyōka* poems composed by members of the commissioning groups. The numbers of the long and short months were often hidden within the designs, ingeniously disguised as motifs on clothes or furniture or appearing as decorative elements on household objects. Viewers enjoyed the challenge of searching for these clues.

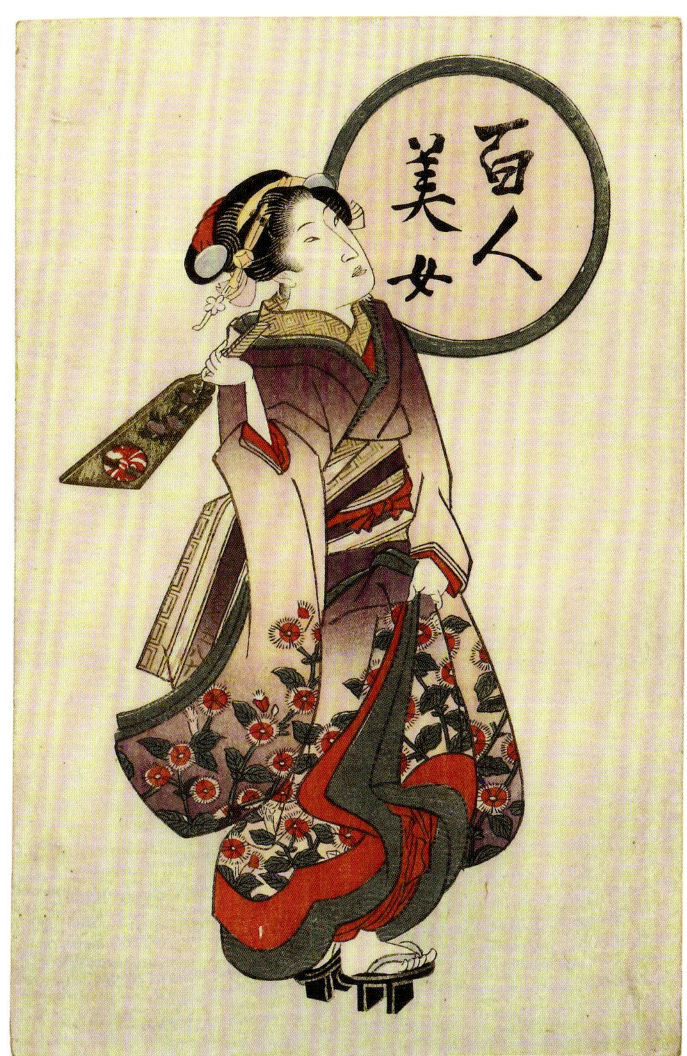

Right: Fig.15 *Woman with a battledore*, printed in *surimono* style. The calendrical information is hidden in the purple section of the bow at the back of her sash. Attributed to Utagawa Kunisada (1786–1864) 歌川国貞. Series: One Hundred Beauties (*Hyakunin bijo* 百人美女), *c*.1830s. Colour woodblock print, 35.8 × 24.6 cm. Presented by Mrs E. M. Allan and Mr and Mrs H. N. Spalding from the Herbert H. Jennings Collection, EAX.4661

1

A Korean cook on horseback, smoking a pipe

Artist unknown
1798 (Year of the Horse)
Colour woodblock print
19.1 × 9.9 cm, *koban* format
Presented by Mrs E. M. Allan and Mr and Mrs H. N. Spalding,
EAX.4649

This *egoyomi* picture calendar depicts a man wearing a traditional Korean hat and seated on a horse. He is holding a long pipe and blowing spirals of smoke from his mouth. On his lap is an open account book that displays the character *dai* 大 (long) and the numbers of the long months of the year to come: 2, 3, 5, 8, 11 and 12. The poem suggests that the information about the order of the long months encoded in this *egoyomi surimono* is sufficient for viewers of this print to deduce the short months too. This monthly configuration corresponds to 1798, the Year of the Horse, and the subject of the *surimono* has been chosen accordingly.

The horse is laden with a cook's equipment: a pair of chickens in a cage at the rear, a package wrapped in straw matting, an abacus and a wooden pail. A rope attached to the horse's bridle trails on the ground and disappears abruptly off the right-hand edge of the image, suggesting that the *surimono* might have been cropped from a larger original. In fact the image appears to have been copied from a design in a woodblock-printed book of 1770 entitled *Hanabusa Itchō gafu*. In this book the artist Suzuki Rinshō (1732–1803) reproduced earlier paintings by Hanabusa Itchō (1652–1724) and the second volume includes a strikingly similar image of a Korean cook on horseback, laid out across a double-page spread. On the right-hand page of the spread two men are shown standing next to the horse, with one of them holding the other end of the horse's rope. This right-hand section has been omitted from the *surimono* design (see fig.16, right). The original image is labelled 'Korean Cook (*makanai tōjin*)' and the figure may have been modelled on a member of one of the twelve Korean diplomatic missions sent to Japan between 1607 and 1811. The poem by Ranjatei Kaoru, however, refers to China, not Korea. In Edo-period Japan, the word '*tōjin*' was used to refer not just to Chinese people, but also to Koreans and other foreigners.

Ranjatei was an Edo tobacco merchant, and it is perhaps no coincidence that he chose an image of a man smoking to illustrate his poem.

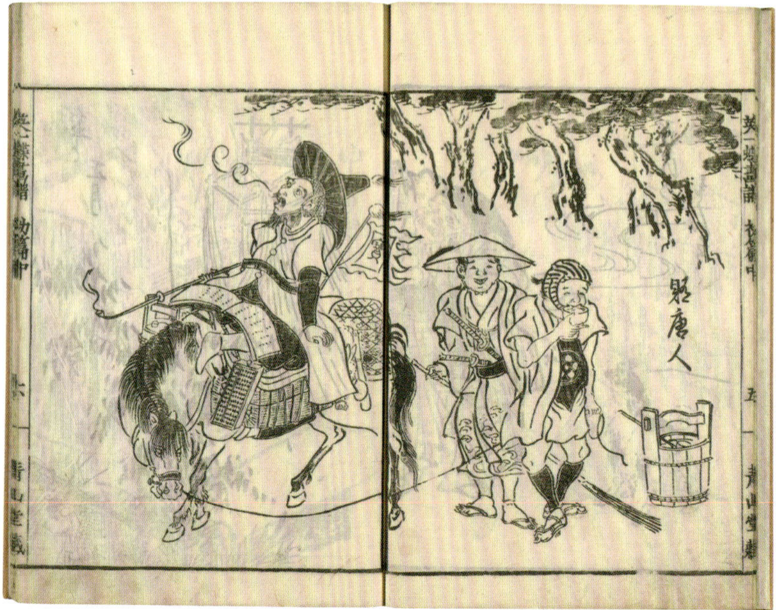

Fig.16 Illustration from *Hanabusa Itchō gafu* 英一蝶画譜, vol.2. Suzuki Rinshō (1732–1803), 1770. Woodblock printed book, 25.8 × 18.2 cm. National Diet Library Digital Collections, info:ndljp/pid/2554323 (frame no.8)

南京の
小き月も
わかるなり
大ミん国ハ
つうしいらすと

nankin no
chiisaki tsuki mo
wakaru nari
dai minkoku wa
tsūji irazu to

In Great Ming China, what is meant by 'short months' is understood without an interpreter, even in Nanjing.

RANJATEI KAORU 蘭奢亭 香ほる

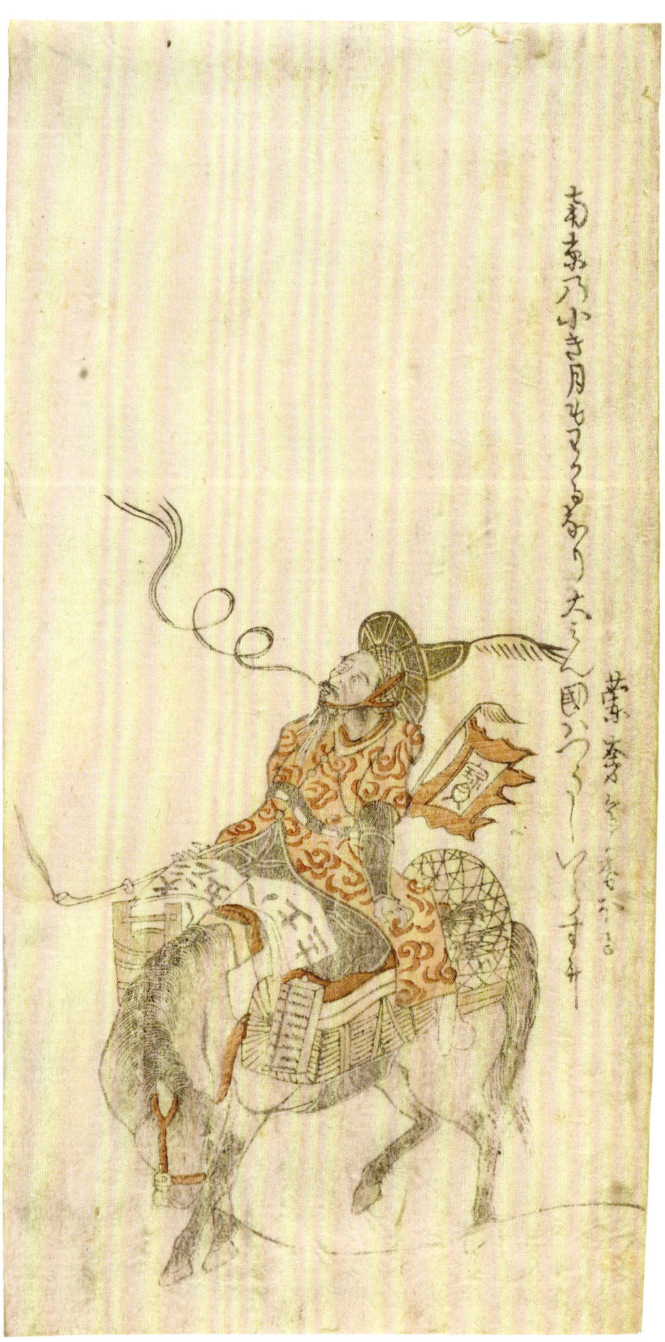

2

A monkey carrying off a platter of sweets

YANAGAWA SHIGENOBU (*c.*1787–1832)
Artist's signature: *Yanagawa hitsu* 柳川筆
1812 (Year of the Monkey)
Colour woodblock print, with metallic pigments and embossing
14.2 × 19 cm, *kokonotsugiriban* format
Presented by Mrs E. M. Allan and Mr and Mrs H. N. Spalding
from the Herbert H. Jennings Collection, EAX.4594

A monkey clasps a high-footed serving platter in his left hand, tipping the sweets that had been arranged on top on to the ground. The sweets are probably *aruheitō,* a type of moulded candy originally based on a Portuguese recipe. They had been placed on a piece of white paper, now shown crumpled beneath the platter. The image of a mischievous monkey knocking over a tray of New Year sweets illustrates the sense of springtime freshness and playfulness expressed in the poem.

This print is an *egoyomi* picture calendar for the Year of the Monkey, with the numerals for the short months of 1812 depicted in gold around the foot of the tray. The numerals are sadly rather blurred on this print, but we know from other impressions that the months indicated are 1, 3, 4, 8 and 12. The platter is decorated with a design of stylised plum blossoms, an appropriate motif for a New Year's calendar (bearing in mind that New Year was celebrated in the month we know as February, when the *prunus* trees were in bloom).

The *surimono* was designed by Yanagawa Shigenobu, a pupil of the famous print designer Katsushika Hokusai. Shigenobu produced many *ukiyo-e* prints and book illustrations as well as *surimono* (see cat.24). Shigenobu took his art name, Yanagawa, from the district where he lived in Edo. He was also an accomplished poet and may have composed the single anonymous *haiku* poem on this print himself.

The palette of colours used on *surimono* published in Edo changed significantly between the 1790s and the 1830s. Earlier *surimono* pictures such as this one were printed in pale colours, with the key block often printed in a pale grey. This was quite different from commercial *ukiyo-e,* in which the key block was usually printed in strong black ink. By the late 1810s the number of pigments used on *surimono* had increased and more of the paper surface was covered with colour. By the 1830s strong, bright colours were commonly seen on *surimono.*

わかゝゝと
こゝろやまさる
千代の春

wakawaka to
kokoro ya masaru
chiyo no haru

Anew! anew! My heart is exhilarated in this spring of a thousand years.

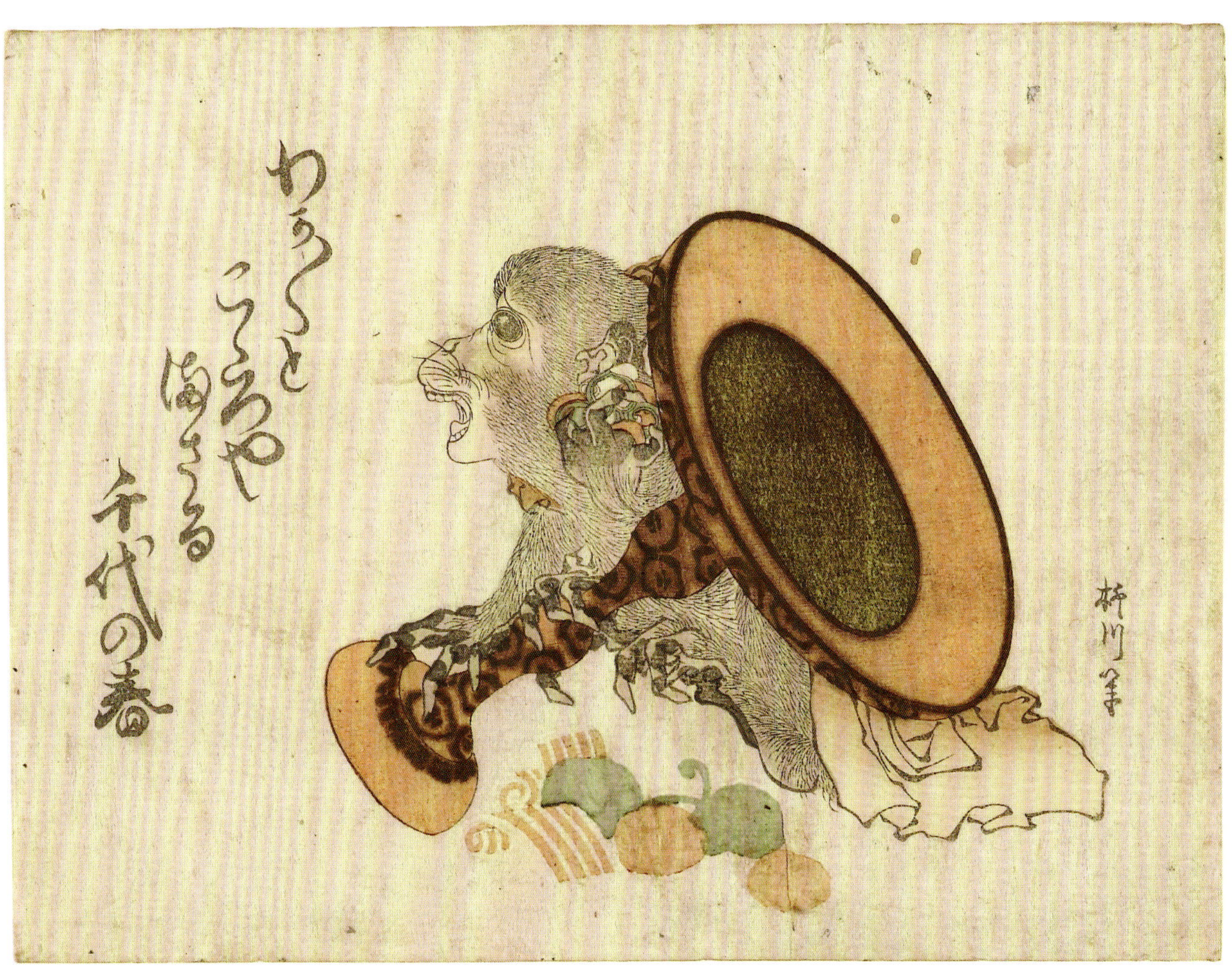

3

Still life with hair ornaments

After KIKUKAWA EISHIN (active *c.*1804–30) 菊川英信
Artist's signature: *Hōrai Eishin ga* 蓬莱英信画
Artist's seal: *Ei* 英
Early 1890s (after an original of 1818)
Colour woodblock print with metallic pigments and embossing
20.9 × 18.4 cm, *shikishiban* format
Presented by Mrs E. M. Allan and Mr and Mrs H. N. Spalding
from the Herbert H. Jennings Collection, EAX.4614

This *surimono* depicting a variety of fashionable hair ornaments is an *egoyomi* picture calendar. The character for 'long' (*dai* 大) is printed on the inside of the black flower-patterned barrette on the left of the print, while the numbers of the long months 1, 2, 4, 6, 7, 9 and 12 are printed on the outside of the barrette. This sequence of months corresponds to the year 1818.

The bundles of grey-green and white cords at the back of the composition would have been used to tie up the hair, while the red tie-dyed silk cloth was for decorating a chignon. Lying across the red cloth is an ivory hairpin decorated with a floral motif. In the black lacquer box is a tortoiseshell hairpin with an ear pick at one end. Hairpins and combs made of expensive imported tortoiseshell were greatly admired in the early nineteenth century, with only high-ranking courtesans or wealthy townswomen able to afford them. All the hair ornaments laid out here appear to be brand new, to delight a woman wearing them for the first time on New Year's Day.

Next to the ornaments is a small, pale blue porcelain cup featuring a design of plum blossoms and cracked ice. It contains lip rouge. In the Edo period lipstick was made from red pigment derived from safflowers; it was stored in small cups that were kept upside down to prevent the rouge from discolouring. To apply the rouge, a thin moistened brush was used to soften the surface of the rouge and then brush it onto the lips in layers.

Eishin's illustration clearly takes its cue from the three poems, all of which refer to a woman's appearance at the New Year. The first poem alludes to a well-known proverb: 'Even the mountain gods are horrified to see a woman wearing make-up in December' ('*shiwasu onna no keshō niwa yama no kami mo kowagaru*'). In the last month of the year women were expected to be so busy with household chores in preparation for the New Year that they should have no time for concerns about their appearance. The poem contains a type of pun called a 'pivot word' (*kakekotoba*) in the word *aratama*: '*aratama*' is a *makurakotoba* (pillow word) associated with the word 'spring' (*haru*), but when read as part of the expression (<u>*ara tama*</u>*getaru*) it means 'to be surprised'. 'Ara' is an exclamation of surprise that might be translated as 'oh!'.

The *makurakotoba* '*aratama*' also appears in the second poem, associated with the word 'year' (*toshi*). Again it works as a *kakekotoba*, this time in conjunction with the word '*kashira*' or head, which refers both to the beginning or 'head' of the year and to a courtesan's head decorated with hairpins. The third poem puns on the verb *sasu*, which means both 'to put on [lip rouge]' (*beni o* <u>*sashi*</u>) and 'to wear [a hairpin]' (*kanzashi… o* <u>*sashi*</u>). '*Sashi*' is a conjugated form of the verb *sasu*.

諺の
師走女も
見違えて
あらたまけたる
春の粧ひ

kotowaza no
shiwasu onna mo
michigaete
ara tamagetaru
haru no yosooi

In the last month of the year the woman from the proverb astonishes me – how surprising she looks all dressed up in her New Year's finery!

MUNAGAI NO HARANARI
鞁ノ腹成

唯一夜
あくれハ今朝ハ
あら玉の
年のかしらに
かさるかんさし

tada hitoyo
akureba kesa wa
aratama no
toshi no kashira ni
kazaru kanzashi

Just one night has passed and this morning I adorn my head with a jewelled hairpin for the New Year.

ISHIDŌRŌ NIWAZUMI
石燈楼庭住

棹姫も
玉のかんさし
くちへにを
さしかさりたる
春の粧ひ

saohime mo
tama no kanzashi
kuchibeni o
sashi kazaritaru
haru no yosooi

Even Saohime, goddess of spring, wears a jewelled hairpin and red lip rouge in her New Year's finery.

SANKYOKUSHA 杉旭舎

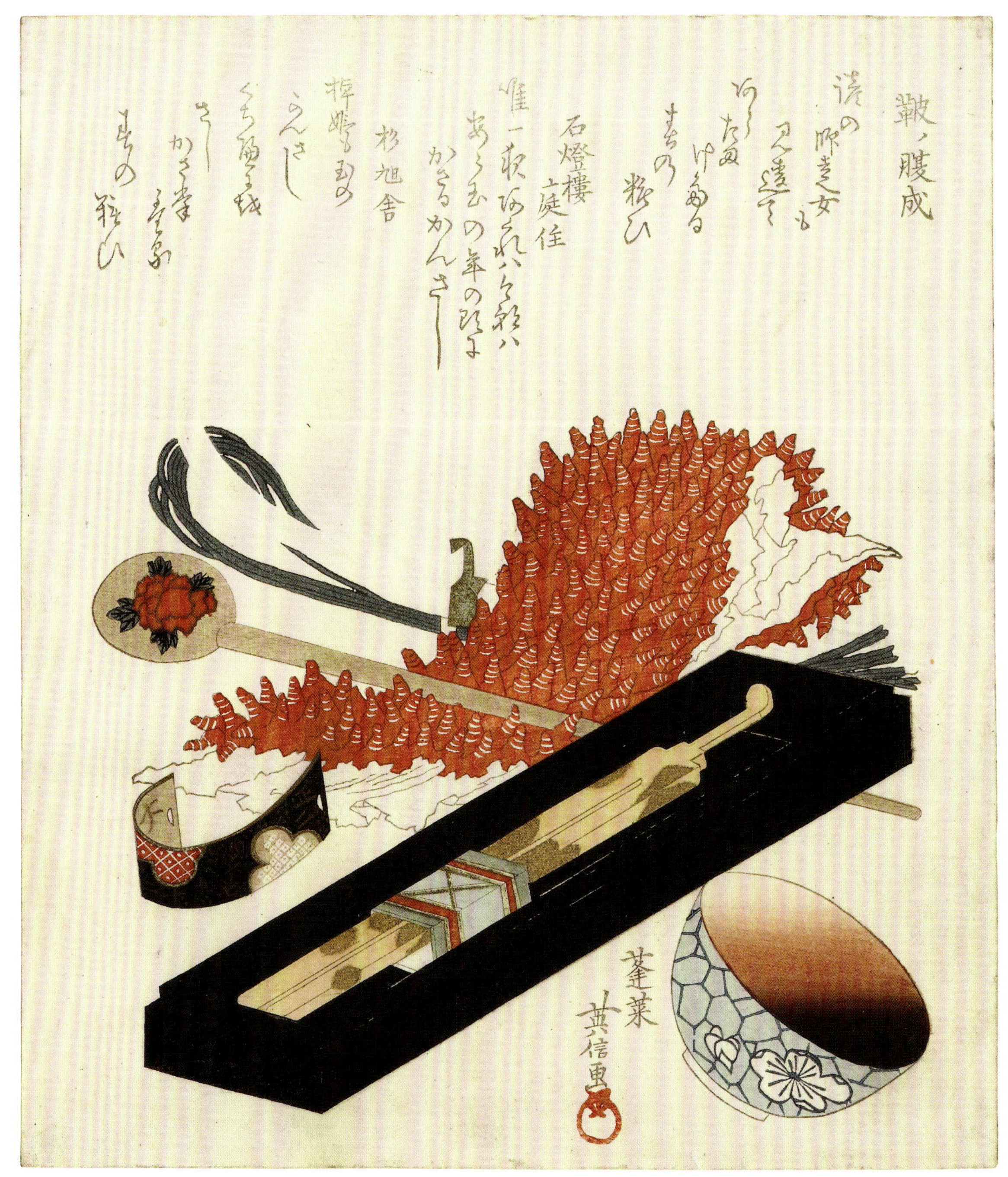

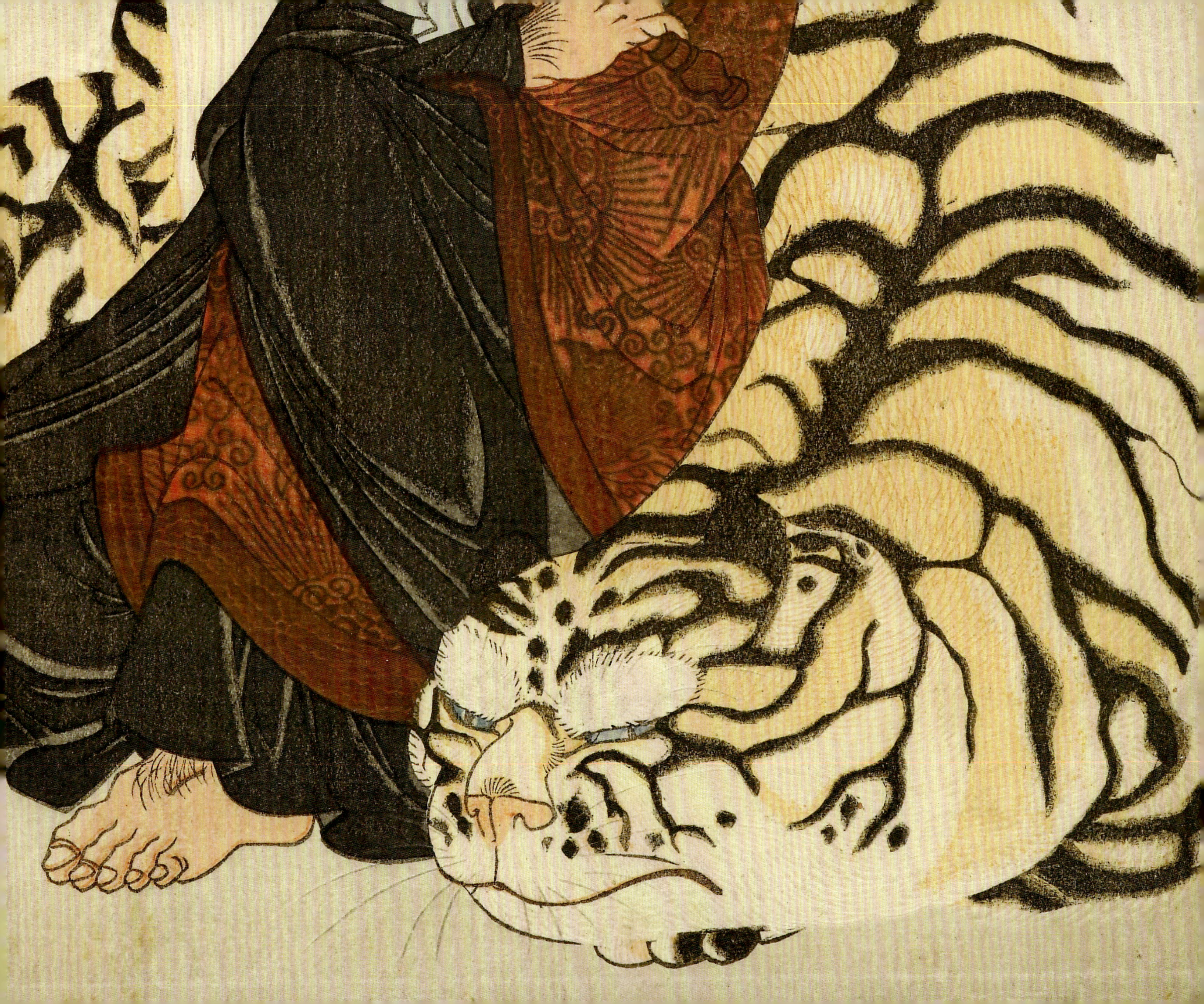

II

Zodiac Animals

The Japanese calendar was introduced from China via Korea in the sixth century and evolved over the following centuries into a highly complex system. Years were organised into a 60-year cycle of ten 'stems' (two for each of the five elements – wood, fire, earth, metal and water) and twelve 'branches', each represented by an animal. These twelve zodiac animals consisted of the rat, ox, tiger, hare, dragon, snake, horse, sheep, monkey, rooster, dog and boar.

Poets and designers alike often featured zodiac animals in their compositions, either directly or indirectly; they may be represented by a child's toy, for example, or by a figure or object closely associated with that animal. *Surimono* are rarely dated, but the presence of a specific zodiac animal, taken in conjunction with the dates of particular artists and poets, is usually enough to indicate the year in which a print was made.

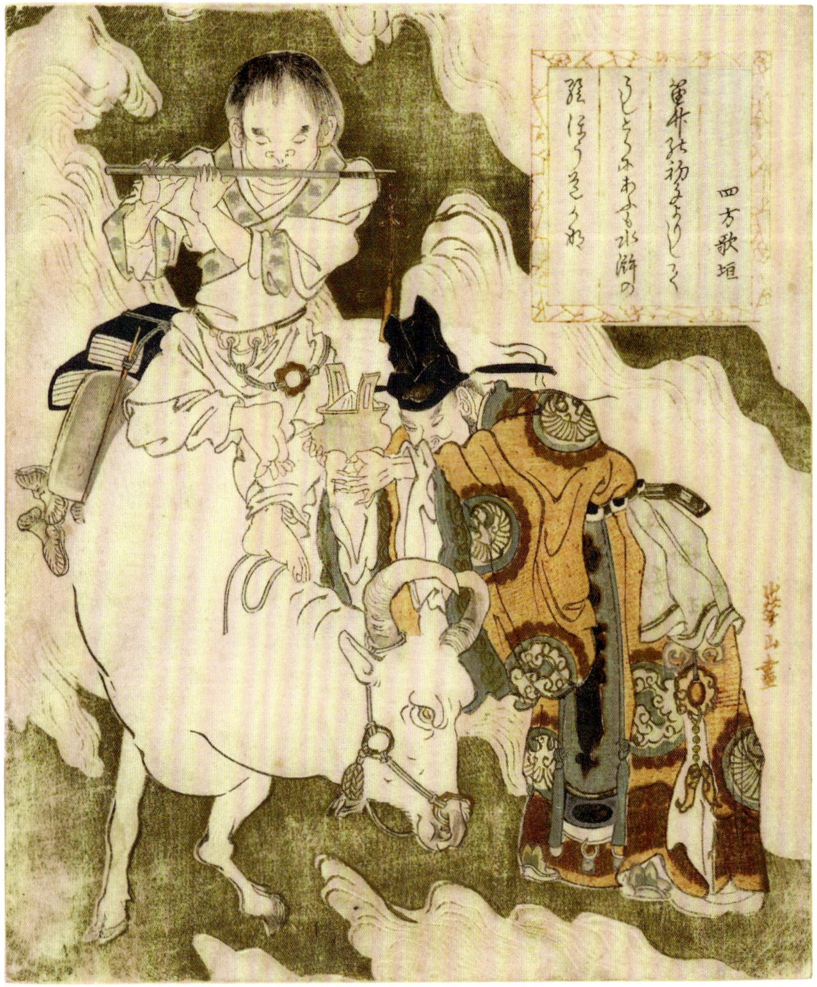

Right: Fig.17 *A messenger from the Emperor of China offers incense to a herd boy playing the flute.* From a series depicting scenes from the *Tales of the Water Margin* (*Suikoden*). Watanabe Kazan (1793–1841) 渡邊崋山
Artist's signature: *Kazan ga* 崋山畫. 1829 (Year of the Ox). Colour woodblock print with metallic pigment and embossing, 20.9 × 18 cm, *shikishiban* format. Presented by Mrs E. M. Allan and Mr and Mrs H. N. Spalding from the Herbert H. Jennings Collection, EAX.4581

4

Daikoku with an abacus and a woman with a white rat

*t*KEISAI EISEN (1790–1848) 渓斎英泉
Artist's signature: *Keisai* 渓斎
1890s (after an original of 1828, Year of the Rat)
Colour woodblock print with metallic pigments
20.8 × 18.2 cm, *shikishiban* format
Presented by Mrs E. M. Allan and Mr and Mrs H. N. Spalding
from the Herbert H. Jennings Collection, EAX.4609

This *surimono*, designed for the Year of the Rat, depicts Daikoku, one of the Seven Gods of Good Fortune. Daikoku, associated with wealth and prosperity and revered as a household deity in Japan, is usually represented standing on a pair of rice bales with a treasure sack over his shoulder and carrying a lucky, wealth-giving mallet in his right hand. Here the smiling Daikoku, wearing his distinctive floppy hat and his mallet on his back, is shown seated on a pile of wooden cash boxes and counting his money on an abacus. With so much money to hand, he has no need for his sack.

On top of the cash boxes behind Daikoku is an adonis plant, a typical New Year decoration symbolising wealth and longevity. In front of him sits a wealthy-looking young woman in an elegant kimono with a purple *bokashi* (gradation) design. Her left sleeve is tucked up, revealing a white rat running up her arm. The white rat is believed to be Daikoku's messenger and is regarded as an auspicious symbol of wealth. On the ground in front of the woman is a book entitled *Nezumizan*. This word – mentioned in both poems – has multiple meanings. Firstly it refers to a method of progressive calculation called '*nezumi-zan*', but it can also mean 'multiplying like rats'. A third reading of the title as '*nezumi-san*' means 'Mr Rat'.

Eisen's illustration also picks up on other references in the two poems. The cash box on which Daikoku is sitting is called a *senryōbako*, literally 'a box for a thousand gold coins', which relates to the first poem's 'spring of a thousand gold coins'. '*Kukudachi*' is a *kakekotoba*, or pun: the term '*kuku*' at the opening of the poem means multiplication tables, while '*kukudachi*' means 'overgrown stalk (*kuku*)'.

Above the poet's name on the second verse is a small circle. *Kyōka* were often composed at competitions (*kyōka-awase*) and it is thought that the circles were used to mark the best poems.

冨ハ潤ふ
去年の餘慶の
鼠算
月ゝふえる
千金の春

tomi wa uruou
kozo no yokei no
nezumizan
tsukizuki fueru
senkin no haru

The wealth earned last year from the rewards of virtue has multiplied like rats, month after month – Spring of a thousand gold coins.

The lay priest HARIHARA, formerly TŌYŌ, of Nobote in Ōita County
鍼原入道先東養大分上手

くゝだちの
草のはつかの
鼡さん
親ともに子を
ふやす春雨

kukudachi no
kusa no hatsuka no
nezumisan
oyatomo ni ko o
fuyasu harusame

In the overgrown grass, rats increase their progeny in the spring rain.

KYŌKADŌ 狂歌堂

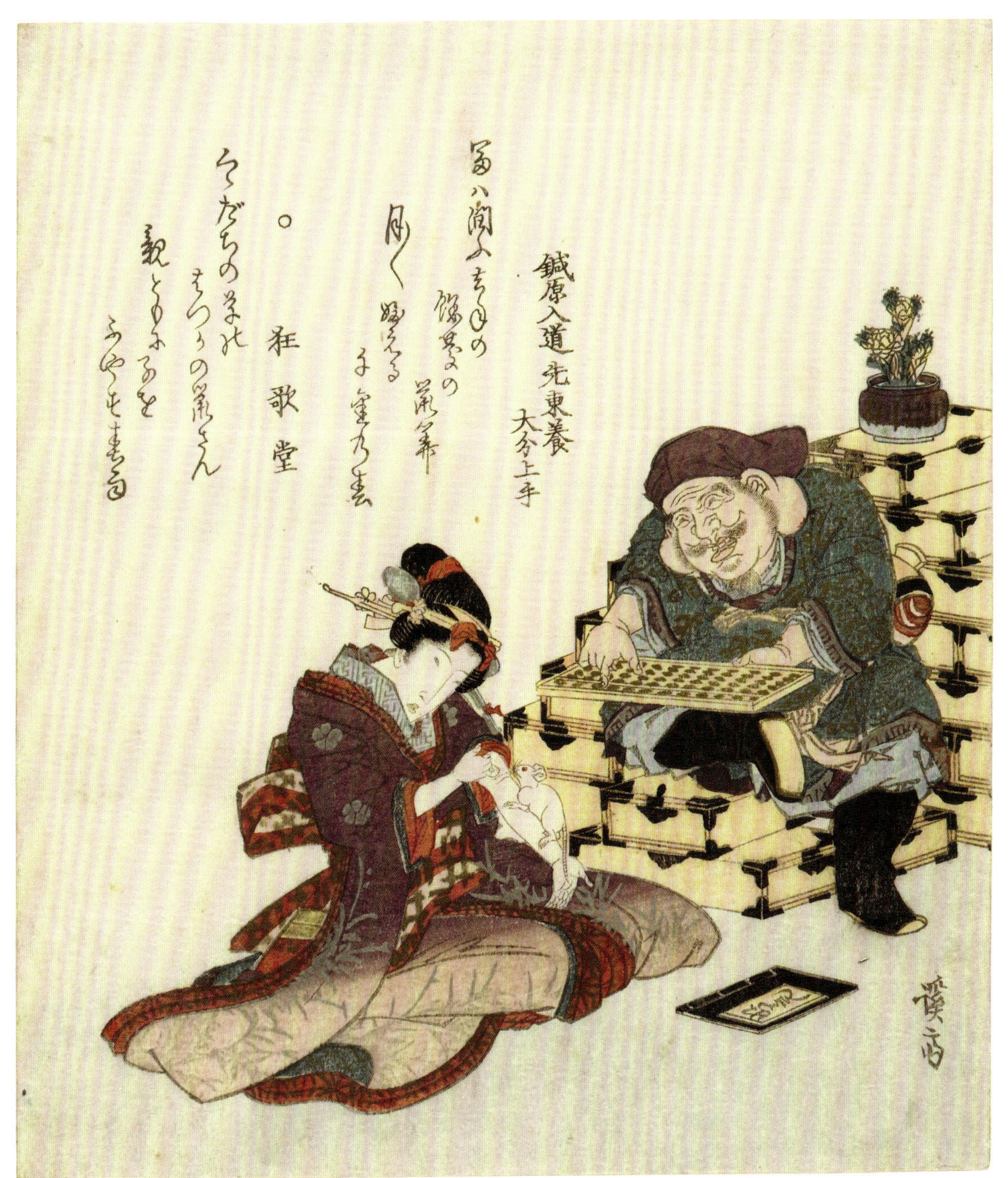

5

An *arhat* with a tiger

UTAGAWA KUNIYOSHI (1797–1861) 歌川国芳
Artist's signature: *Ichiyūsai Kuniyoshi ga* 一勇斎国芳画
1830 (Year of the Tiger)
Colour woodblock print with metallic pigment and embossing
21.1 × 18.5 cm, *shikishiban* format
Presented by George Grigs, Miss Elizabeth Grigs and Miss Susan Messer, in memory of Derick Grigs, EA1971.156

Both poems on this *surimono* seem to express a desire for the ideal Buddhist state of mind: freedom from any concerns of everyday life. It may be this Buddhist mood, and perhaps also the mountain setting of the second poem, that suggested the subject of an *arhat* to Kuniyoshi. The Sanskrit term *arhat* ('*rakan*' in Japanese) refers to a group of enlightened disciples of the historical Buddha – saintly ascetics charged with protecting Buddhist law on earth. In Chinese and Japanese Buddhism specific groups of *arhats*, such as the sixteen *arhats*, eighteen *arhats* and five hundred *arhats*, have long been venerated and depicted in paintings and sculptures. In Japan the sixteen *arhats* are particularly popular, especially in Zen Buddhism.

Arhats are typically depicted with intense, distorted faces and wearing simple monks' garments. They are usually represented with characteristic attributes and some are attended by animals, real or mythical. The *arhat* represented in this *surimono* sits leaning against a tiger with his left leg drawn up. He has a bald head and glaring eyes with long, bushy eyebrows and wears a reddish monk's vestment over his black robe. In his right hand he holds a fly whisk, symbolising the Zen master's authority to transmit the Buddha's teachings to others. The large tiger lying next to him appears relaxed and contemplative, with half-closed eyes and a mild expression. Since tigers are not indigenous to Japan, artists often referred to Chinese paintings or even to tiger skins when painting the animals. The resulting images often appear more like domestic cats than ferocious beasts.

The subject of this *surimono* could be one of two *arhats*. The seventh *arhat* Karika (Kālika in Sanskrit) is typically featured leaning against a pine tree, his left leg drawn up and his left hand patting a tiger (see, for instance, a fourteenth-century hanging scroll in the Freer Gallery of Art, no.F1904.301, and a painting in Komazawa University Library, no.188.82/289). Both are very like the composition of the *surimono* shown here. The sixth *arhat* Badara (Bhadra in Sanskrit) is also sometimes depicted sitting on a rock, with his right hand placed on the head of a tiger (for example, an eleventh-century painting in the Tokyo National Museum, no.A-10946).

The artist Utagawa Kuniyoshi, a highly successful designer of *ukiyo-e* commercial prints, was particularly known for his dynamic depictions of warriors and historical figures. He was noted for his innovative designs that adopted elements of Western perspective and shading. Kuniyoshi also occasionally designed *surimono*, and this is a good example of his distinctive style. The fur of the tiger and the strands of the fly whisk are cleverly enhanced through embossing.

今朝若起
水にこころに
藝もなく
青柳に
なふられている
雀かな

kesa wakaki
mizu ni kokoro ni
gei mo naku
aoyagi ni
naburarete iru
suzume kana

Early this morning, intoxicated by the first fresh water, a sparrow dawdles, surrendering to the teasing branches of the green willow tree.

山住や
暮れはくるる
としまかせ

yamazumi ya
kurereba kururu
toshimakase

Living in the mountain, just let the year advance entirely as it likes.

Both poems by BAIGETSUKAN SENREI 梅月舘沾嶺

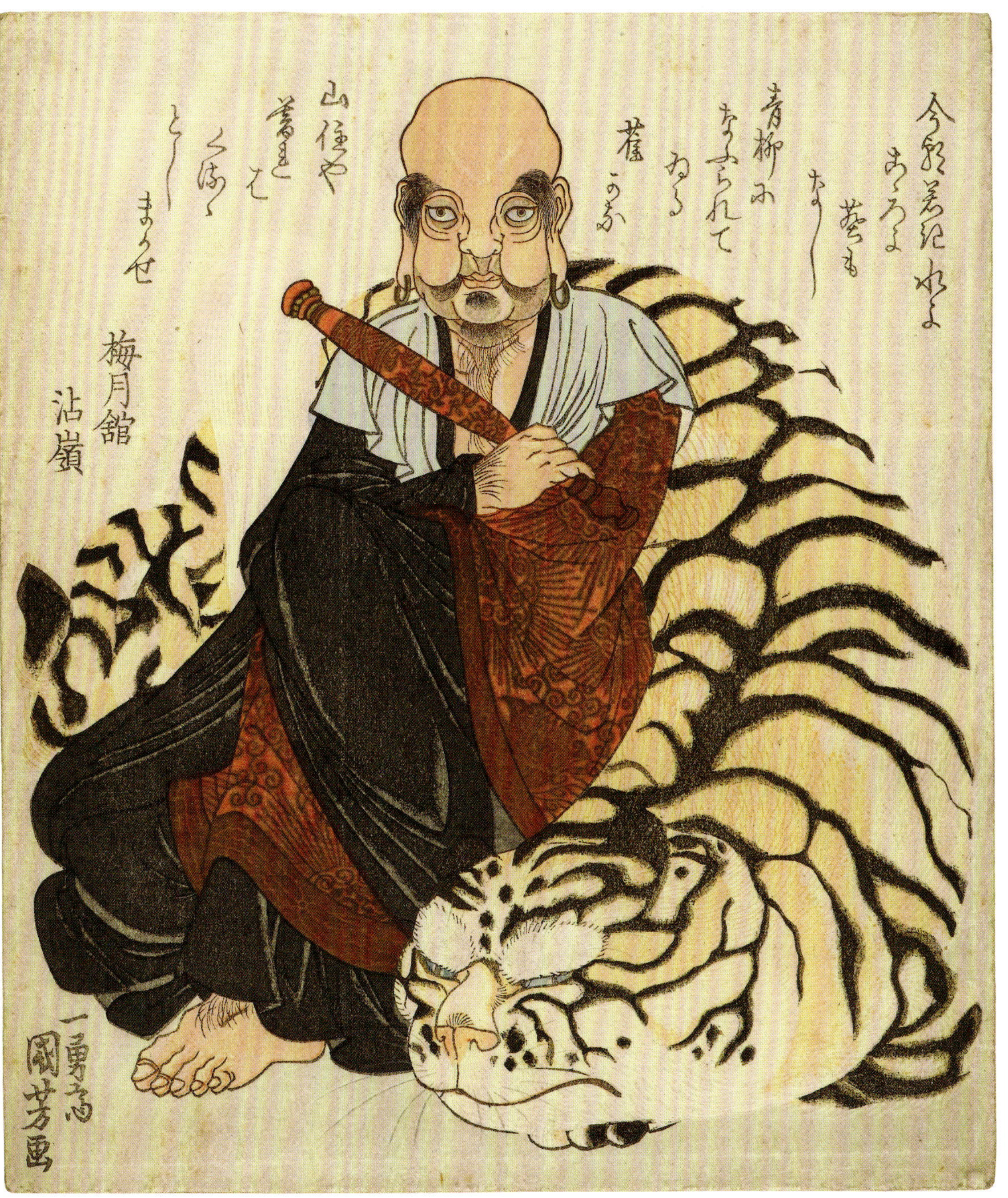

6

Two women on the beach at Enoshima

UTAGAWA KUNIYOSHI (1797–1861) 歌川 国芳
Artist's signature: *Ichiyūsai Kuniyoshi ga* 一勇斎国芳画
Artist's seal: *toshidama* seal on both pictures
Block cutter's seal: Tōu tō 棠雨刀 (in a gourd-shaped cartouche)
1833 (Year of the Snake)
Colour woodblock print with metallic pigments and embossing
20.5 × 17.5 cm (each sheet), *shikishiban* diptych
Presented by Mrs E. M. Allan and Mr and Mrs H. N. Spalding
from the Herbert H. Jennings Collection, EAX. 4763a–b

This charming two-panel *surimono* depicts a pair of barefooted women on the beach at Enoshima, a popular pilgrimage destination not far from the capital Edo and a common subject of woodblock prints in the nineteenth century. The island of Enoshima, seen in the distance on the left, is attached to the mainland by a narrow piece of land, accessible only at low tide. This winding, snake-like path was known as the 'ebb tide path' (*shiohiji*). Enoshima housed a shrine to Benzaiten (also known as Benten), the goddess of music and entertaiment. Her messenger was a white snake, and so it was common practice to commission prints depicting Enoshima for the Year of the Snake. This diptych *surimono* is thought to have been commissioned for the Snake Year of 1833.

Enoshima was a popular spot for shell gathering. The woman standing on the right of the print holds up her skirt in one hand, a pipe in the other. The second woman squats, trying to catch a flat fish that has been washed up on to the beach. Over the shoulders of each woman is a red strap known as a *tasuki.* Worn across the back, the *tasuki* was used for tucking up the sleeves up while working. Behind the women Mount Fuji can be seen in silhouette. The dramatic depiction of the sky and clouds shows the European influence on Kuniyoshi's work, and demonstrates the effective use of imported Prussian blue pigment. The undulating shapes of the clouds echo the winding, snake-like path. Two poems by the same poet are printed in silver against the sky, possibly in a reference to the colour of the white snake enshrined on Enoshima. Kuniyoshi also designed a five-sheet *surimono* with a similar design of women foraging at the seashore for the Hisakataya poetry group.

Both poems refer to the seashore. The *kujira-obi* mentioned in the first poem is a type of sash with a different colour on each side, like the black and white markings of a whale (*kujira*). The poem also contrasts the white foam of the waves and the dark colour of the path. The second poem continues the theme of colour contrasts. The 'saucer scallop' (*tsukihi-gai,* literally 'moon-sun shell') mentioned here is light yellow on one side, like the moon, and a reddish-orange colour on the other, like the sun. This reference links back to the first poem as the *kujira-obi* was also called a *chūya-obi,* literally meaning 'day and night' sash; this corresponds to the moon and sun of the saucer scallop.

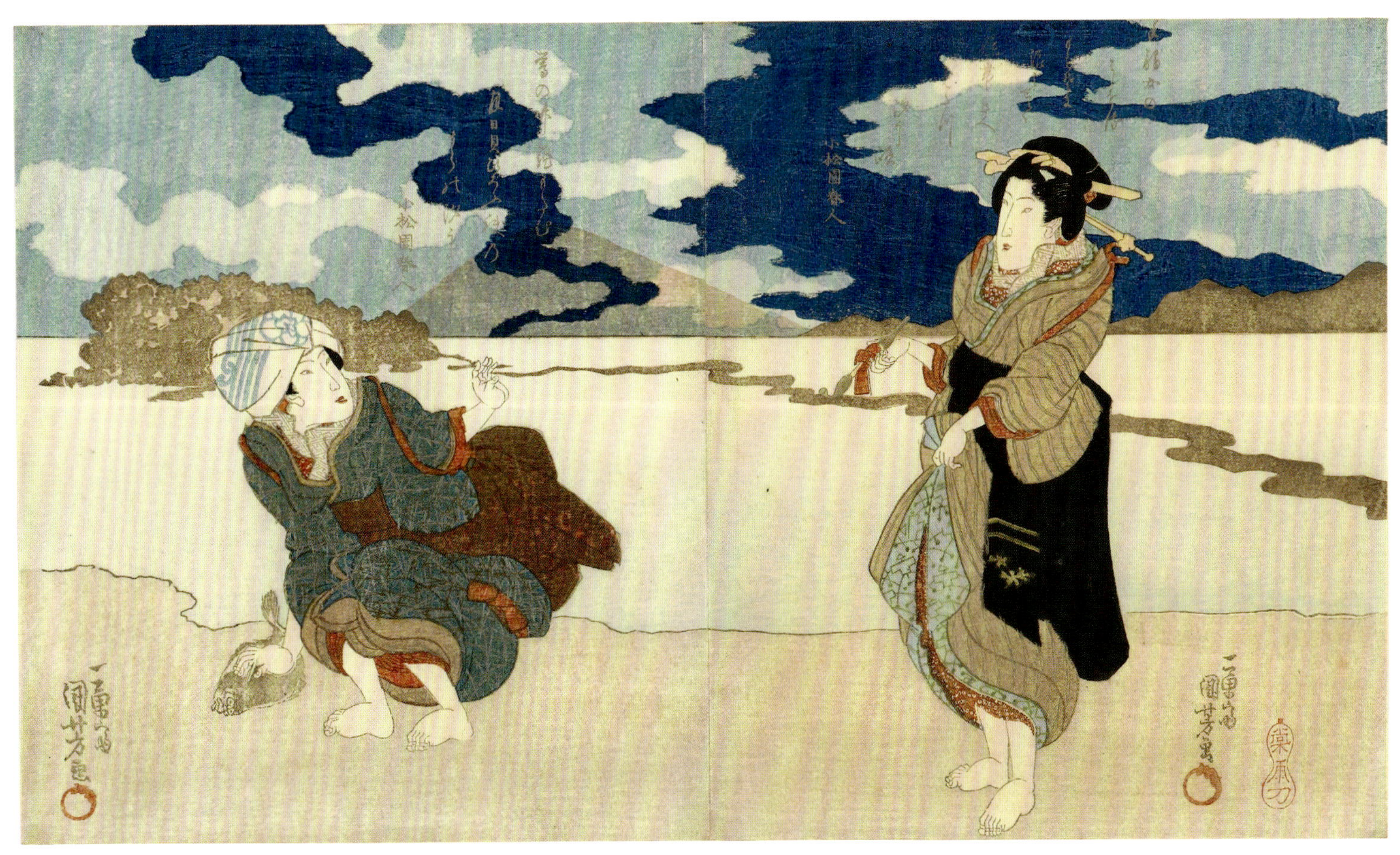

手弱女の
はしをるもすそに
浪みせて
鯨帯さへ
めたつ汐ひ路

taoyame no
hashoru mosuso ni
nami misete
kujiraobi sae
medatsu shiohiji

A graceful woman tucks up the hem of her *kimono*, revealing the waves, her *kujira* sash stark against the ebb tide path.

鶯の
竹籠もたん
月日貝
ひろう秋の
うらの汐ひに

uguisu no
takekago motan
tsukihigai
hirou aki no
ura no shiohini

I carry a warbler in a bamboo birdcage, while gathering saucer scallops at low tide on the seashore in autumn.

Both poems by KOMATSUEN HARUNDO 小松園春人

7

A courtesan as the strongwoman Okane

Commissioned by the Katsushika-ren circle
KATSUSHIKA TAITO II (active 1810–53) 葛飾戴斗 (Hokusen 葛飾北泉)
Artist's signature: *Beikadōjin Taito* 米華道人 戴斗
Possibly 1822 (Year of the Horse)
Colour woodblock print with metallic pigments
21.6 × 18.6 cm, *shikishiban* format
Presented by Mrs E. M. Allan and Mr and Mrs H. N. Spalding
from the Herbert H. Jennings Collection, EAX.4622

The figure depicted here represents the legendary strongwoman Okane, a courtesan from Takashima in Ōmi Province (modern Shiga Prefecture). The story of Okane is told in the *Kokon chomonshū* (Collected Anecdotes, Ancient and Modern), produced in 1254. She was said to have halted a runaway horse simply by stepping on its reins with her tall wooden clogs. In this *surimono* Okane is depicted as an elegant modern courtesan – an example of a form of gentle parody known as *mitate*, in which revered icons of history or literature are depicted in an everyday contemporary setting. Okane stops a kite portraying a prancing horse from flying away by treading on its strings with her black lacquered clogs.

The bundle of bleached white cotton fabric under the courtesan's left arm is another allusion to Okane, referring to a popular Kabuki dance based on a story about her. Entitled '*Sarashime*' or 'Laundry Maiden', it was first performed in 1813 at the Morita Theatre in Edo. In this dance Okane appears holding a wash basin full of white cotton cloth (*sarashi*) in both hands while she subdues a wild horse by treading on its reins with her clogs.

In the *surimono* the courtesan's stance, bending slightly backwards with her right hand holding the skirt of her kimono, reflects her femininity; yet she also wears a man's purple *haori* overcoat (now discoloured). The *haori* was originally worn only by men, until the famously free-spirited female geisha entertainers of the Tatsumi district in Edo took to wearing it in the late eighteenth century. To depict the courtesan wearing a *haori* may have been intended to demonstrate her strength and lack of inhibition.

The two poems make parallel comparisons. In the first the horse on a kite is immobilised by a woman as she steps on the kite strings. In the second another horse is tethered by a goddess using reins made of spring mists. The poet Bunchinsha Kanio (active 1820s–30s) was probably born in Takashima in Ōmi Province where the legendary strongwoman was said to have lived. He was a pupil of the *kyōka* poet Bunbunsha Kanikomaru (1780–1837), who composed the second poem. Bunbunsha was a leader of Katsushika-ren poetry circle, whose emblem was the character 'bun' 文. On the left sleeve of the courtesan's *haori* a motif composed of three of these characters can be seen.

手弱女の
踏とめてけりの
いと切れて
はしれる凧に
画く駒をも

taoyame no
fumi tomete keri
ito kirete
hashireru tako ni
egaku koma omo

An elegant woman stands on the broken kite string to stop the painted horse from running away.

BUNCHINSHA KANIO of Takashima
高島文鎮舎蟹雄

佐保姫の
霞の手綱
つけしにて
遠くは行ぬ
野への春駒

sahohime no
kasumi no tazuna
tsukeshi nite
tōku wa ikanu
nobe no harukoma

The Sahohime* attached her reins of mist to the young horse in the spring field, to prevent it from straying far away.

BUNBUNSHA 文々舎

*Also called Saohime

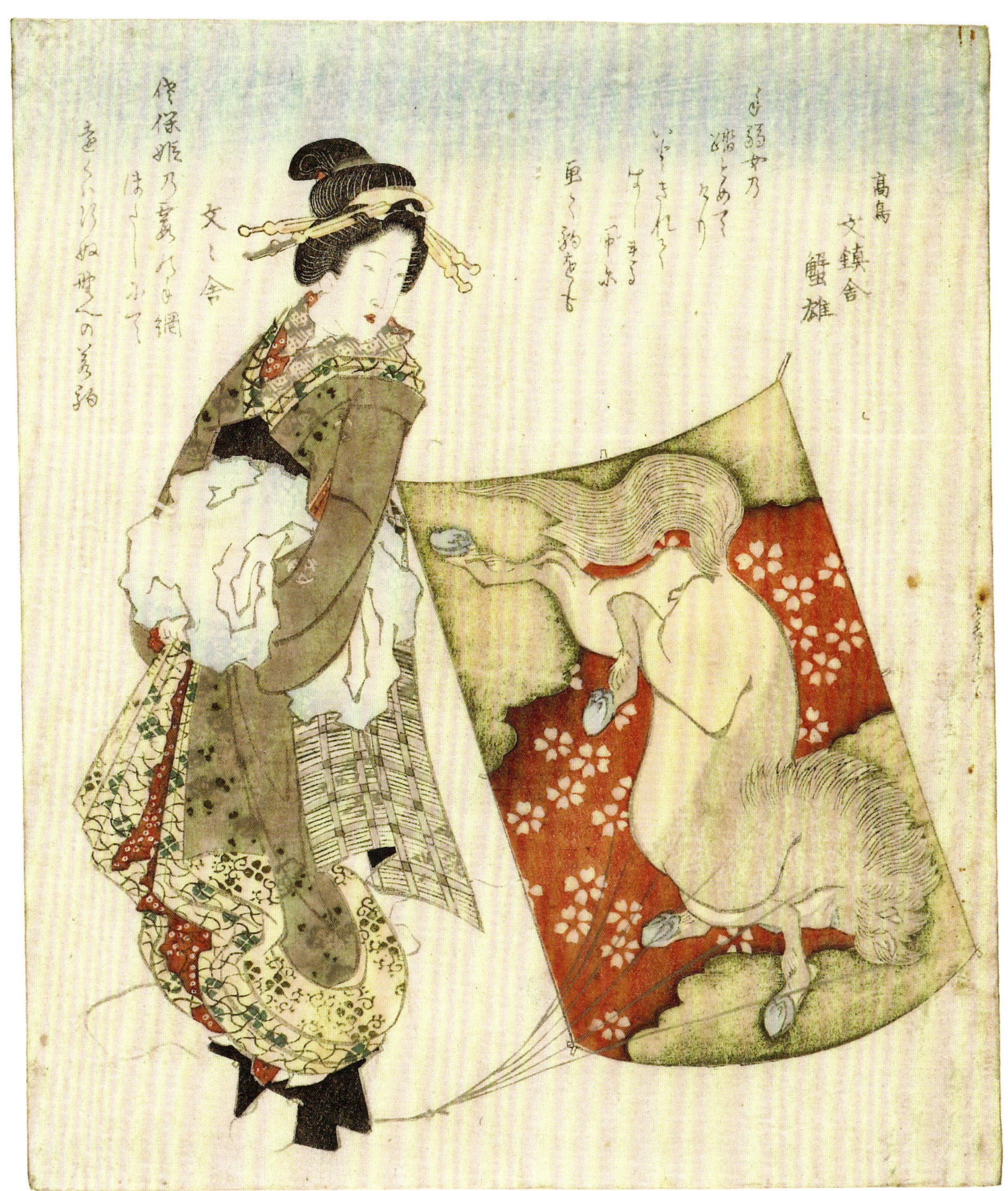

8

A Chinese warrior on a prancing horse

TOTOYA HOKKEI (1780–1850), active from 1799 魚屋北渓
Artist's signature: *Hokkei* 北渓
1890s (after an original of 1822, Year of the Horse)
Colour woodblock print with metallic pigments and embossing
21 × 18 cm, *shikishiban* format
Presented by Mrs E. M. Allan and Mr and Mrs H. N. Spalding
from the Herbert H. Jennings Collection, EAX.4646

A fierce-looking Chinese warrior rides a rearing horse, brandishing a sword in his left hand. The horse has a bridle, martingale and crupper decorated with red tassles. The image may refer to one of many stories of heroes and horses in Chinese historical fiction. Chinese works such as the *Annals of the Three Kingdoms* (*Sangokushi*) or *The Water Margin* (*Suikoden*) were translated into Japanese and became hugely popular in the late Edo period. Hokkei's teacher Katsushika Hokusai also created a number of designs of Chinese warriors on horseback.

Each of the three poems in this *surimono* describes a different horse. 'Surusumi' in the first poem was a horse described in the fourteenth-century warrior epic *The Tale of the Heike*, noted for his superb black coat and great strength. The words '*suru sumi*' can also mean the rubbing down of an ink-cake on an inkstone to make ink for drawing. The 'first drawing of the New Year' mentioned in the same poem was an annual event undertaken on the second day of the lunar calendar and another pun is contained in the word '*ikioi*', which means both the strength of a brush stroke and the speed of a horse. Thus Surusumi must be painted with a powerful brush stroke to prevent him from leaping out of the picture.

The word '*tsukige*' in the second poem means 'moon-coated' and indicates a Palomino horse. The poem elegantly links the colour of a hazy spring moon with that of the light-coloured horse. The third poem creates a different kind of spring atmosphere with its reference to skylarks. The word '*noru*' means both 'to ride [a horse]' and 'to follow [the spirit of spring]'.

あら玉の
書初の絵に
する墨の
駒そいさめる
筆のいきほひ

aratama no
kakizome no e ni
suru sumi no
koma zo isameru
fude no ikioi

The first drawing of the New Year is a picture of Surusumi – a horse to be restrained by the strength of a brush stroke.

SEIATEI UTANARI 井蛙亭歌也

春の夜の
月毛の駒は
沢水の
くさを出ても
朧なりけり

haru no yo no
tsukige no koma wa
sawamizu no
kusa o idete mo
oboro nari keri

In the spring night a horse the colour of moonlight emerges from the grass by the stream; the moon is still hazy.

IYATOSHIGAKI NO MAONI 弥年垣真鬼

いつさんに
飛ふ勢ひの
勇しさ
春のきに乗る
雲雀毛の駒

issan ni
tobu ikioi no
isamashisa
haru no ki ni noru
hibarige no koma

A plucky horse, the colour of a skylark, prances forward at great speed, following the spirit of spring.

MIWAGAKI MADARU 美和垣真樽

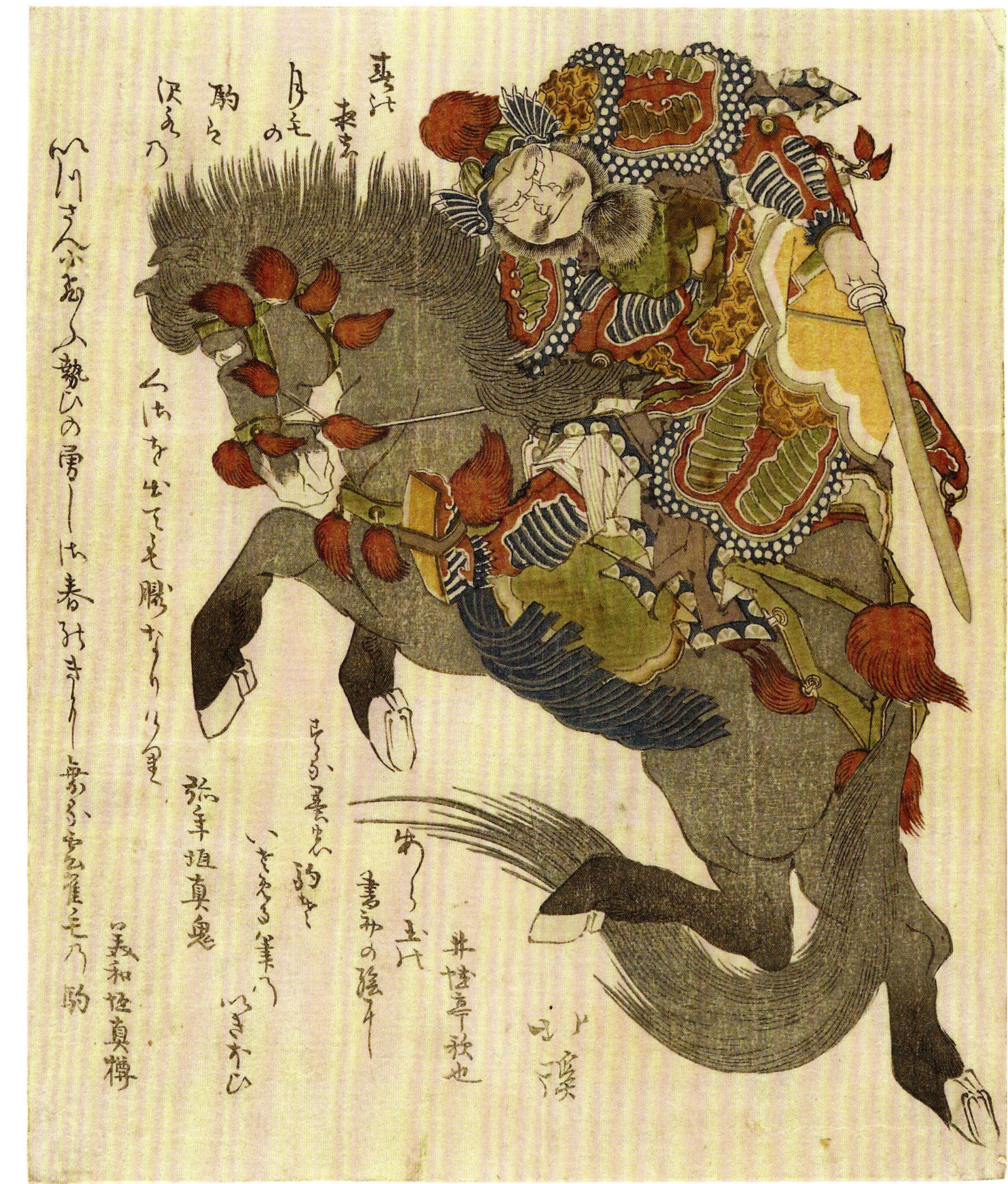

9

A courtesan in front of a screen depicting sheep

Probably commissioned by the poet Kitamado no Baikō (Madoya)
Attributed to UTAGAWA TOYOKUNI II (1777–1835) 歌川豊国 II (also known as Toyoshige 豊重)
Poet's signature: *Madoya* 窓屋 (on screen)
Poet's seal: *Kita* 北 (in a plum blossom cartouche on the screen)
1835 (Year of the Sheep)
Colour woodblock print with metallic pigments and embossing
21.4 × 18.1 cm, *shikishiban* format
Presented by Mrs E. M. Allan and Mr and Mrs H. N. Spalding
from the Herbert H. Jennings Collection, EAX.4671

A beautiful young courtesan in an elaborate kimono sits with her knees drawn up in front of a screen depicting two sheep. At first glance these appear to be goats, but we may assume that they are intended as sheep. As one of the twelve zodiac animals of the traditional Chinese calendar used in Japan, the sheep was a popular subject of *surimono* and *ukiyo-e* prints by Toyoshige and his contemporaries. However, sheep are not indigenous to Japan, and while Japanese people of the Edo period (1603–1868) were familiar with goats, they knew of sheep only through the Chinese zodiac or through imported Chinese picture books such as the *Sansai zue* (Chinese Pictorial Encyclopedia), imported in the seventeenth century and reproduced in a Japanese version in the eighteenth century. In China the character *yang* 羊 was used to refer to both goats and sheep, contributing to a blurring of distinction between the two animals in both countries.

The courtesan in the print gives a startled look over her shoulder as she crumples a piece of paper – possibly a love letter – in her hands. Perhaps somebody has just entered the room. Behind her is a large metal brazier, its three feet decorated with Chinese monster masks. She wears a green kimono decorated at the bottom with scattered pink plum blossoms, while her sash has a design of overlapping fans in dark red and blue.

Several elements in the design refer cryptically to people involved in the production of the *surimono*. On the right-hand side of the screen can be seen the signature Madoya 窓屋; below it is the seal Kita 北 within a plum blossom-shaped cartouche. These both allude to the pseudonym of the *kyōka* poet Kitamado no Baikō 北窓梅好 (also known as Tsurunoya Baikō). Baikō, who was based in Osaka and acted as a judge for the Go-gawa poetry group, wrote one of the two poems on this *surimono*. The character 'bai' 梅 of Baikō means plum and the plum blossom-shaped cartouche is a nod to this, as are the blossoms decorating the courtesan's kimono. The fan (*ōgi*) pattern on the courtesan's sash is probably a reference to the Osaka poet and publisher Ōgi-ya Risuke, who collaborated with Baikō to produce a number of *kyōka* books between 1831 and 1839. The pairing of the plum and fan motifs on the courtesan's garments may symbolise the close relationship between the two poets. Given the sheep motif and the period of collaboration between the two men, it is likely that this *surimono* was produced in the Year of the Sheep in 1835.

The first poem describes a traditional celebratory custom in which a young woman would wear a new kimono on the luckiest of the first three days of the New Year. '*Tomeki*' means to perfume a kimono with a fragrant wood burned in an incense-burner. The poet puns on the word *tome*, using it in the word for young woman (*otome*) and in the word for perfuming a robe (*tomeki*). Toyoshige includes the 'plum blossom patterns' of the poem as a motif on the courtesan's robe. The second poem alludes to the way in which wealthy men in the Edo period would typically wear many layers of expensive kimono, making their collars appear thick and ostentatious. A well-known phrase of the time '*eri ni tsuku*', literally meaning 'stuck to the collars' or 'attracted to the collars', meant 'to flatter a rich man'. In this poem, however, the idiom is used in the negative, indicating that this proud courtesan does not deign to flatter any patron, however wealthy.

おと免子か
とめきの衣の
きそはしめ
もやうの梅も
風にかをれり

otomego ga
tomeki no kinu no
kisohajime
moyō no ume mo
kaze ni kaoreri

A young woman, her new robe perfumed by burning incense, wears it for the first time in the New Year – the plum blossom patterns too send forth their scent on the wind.

MAN'NENTEI KIGŌ 萬年亭亀郷

うかれ女か
いきちを春の
風の手に
えりにはつかぬ
袖乃梅か香

ukareme ga
ikiji o haru no
kaze no te ni
eri niwa tsukanu
sode no ume ga ka

The courtesan's sense of honour is held high in the hands of a spring wind that transfers not the scent of plum blossoms from her sleeves to his collars.

MADONOYA 窓廼屋

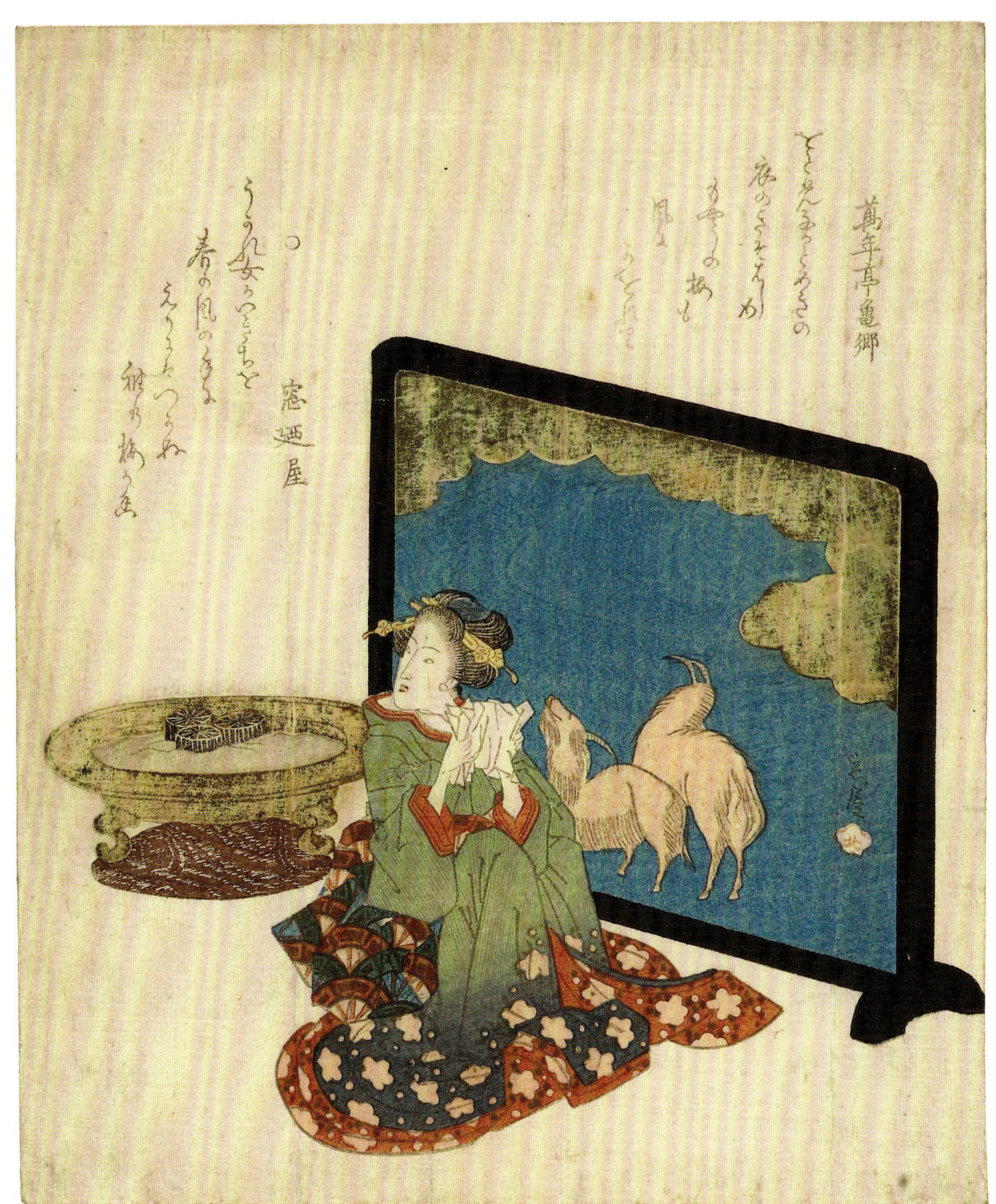

10

Left: Manzai performers with a monkey on a ferry boat on the Sumida River
Right: Manzai performer with a monkey in a *tayū* costume

UTAGAWA KUNINAO (1793–1854) 歌川国直
Artist's signature: *Kōsoen Kuninao hitsu* 後素園国直筆
Probably 1836 (Year of the Monkey)
Colour woodblock print with metallic pigments and embossing
Left: 19.6 × 17.2 cm; right: 19.7 × 16.8 cm, *shikishiban* format
Presented by Mrs E. M. Allan and Mr and Mrs H. N. Spalding
from the Herbert H. Jennings Collection, EAX.4582 and EAX.4583

These two prints are from a series of *surimono* featuring monkeys, each depicted within a lobed circular cartouche against a striking Prussian blue background embellished with gold leaf. Both these prints also represent Manzai street musicians, who travelled from house to house over the New Year singing and dancing. Manzai entertainers worked in pairs, with each performer wearing a distinctive costume. The singer was known as the *tayū* and wore formal clothing with a fan and an *eboshi* black hat. His companion was known as the *saizō* and wore plain clothing with a floppy hat of the type worn by Daikoku, one of the Seven Gods of Good Fortune. The *saizō* carried a hand drum and danced humorously to the *tayū*'s song.

In the right-hand print, a *saizō* beats time on a hand drum. The role of *tayū* is taken by his monkey, dressed up in an *eboshi* and holding a fan. In the left-hand print, a monkey trainer and a pair of Manzai performers, together with a young woman, are passengers on a ferry boat on the Sumida River in Edo. All eyes are on the monkey, who climbs to the top of the monkey trainer's pole, held by the *saizō*. The monkey trainer, identifiable by the cloth bag on his back, looks on. The *tayū* holds the *saizō*'s hand drum on his lap as he waves his fan and cheers the monkey on. The woman on the far right points up at the monkey while the ferryman takes a break from punting the boat and smokes his pipe as he enjoys the monkey's antics.

In Japan monkeys were traditionally thought to have the power to keep horses healthy, and monkey trainers were originally employed to conduct ritual prayers in front of stables. It was not until later centuries that monkey trainers earned money by making their monkeys perform in public. The poet has cleverly embedded an allusion to this history with his reference to the Onmaya embankment, which literally means 'the bank of the stables'.

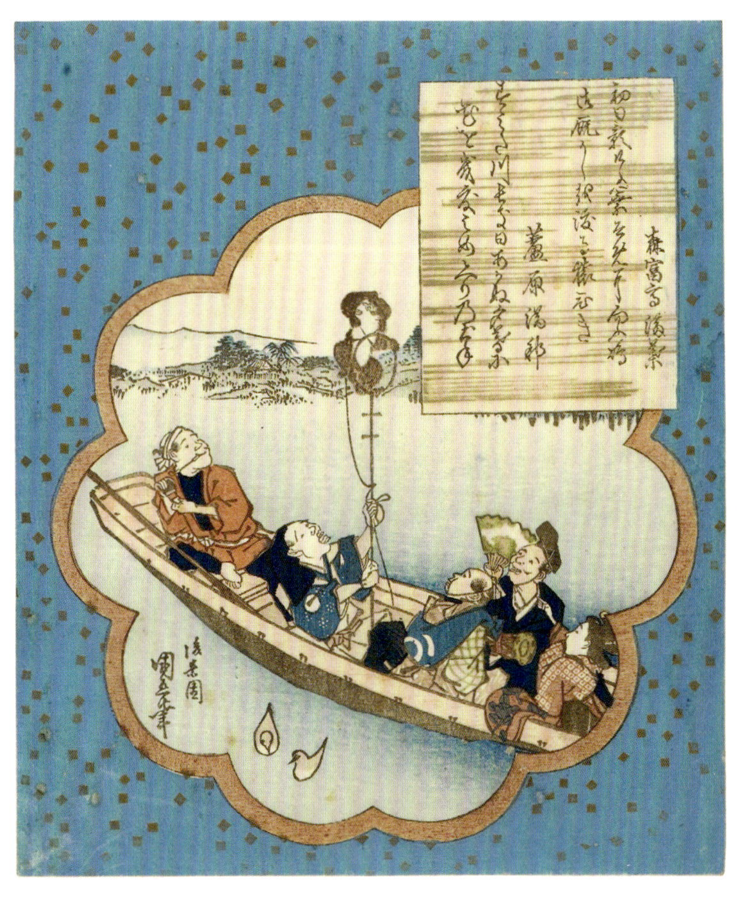

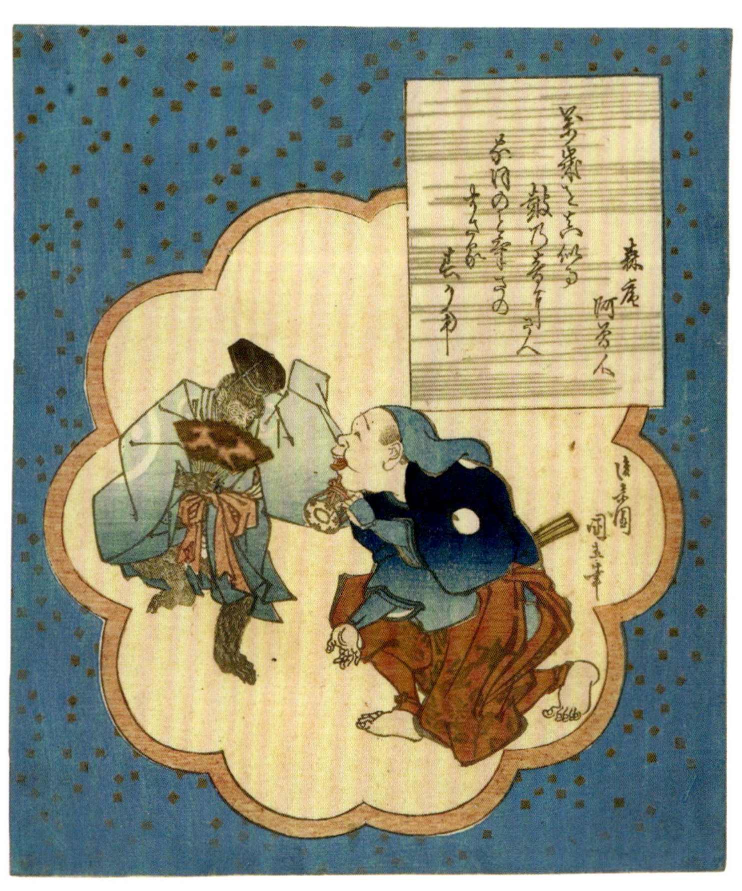

初日影
きょう乗そめに
向こう嶋
御厩かしを
渡る猿ひき

hatsuhikage
kyō norizome ni
mukōjima
onmayagashi o
wataru saruhiki

Today, at the New Year's sunrise, the monkey trainer takes his first boat trip of the year, crossing from Mukōjima to the Onmaya embankment.

SHINPUTEI MITSUBA 森富亭満葉

すみた川
長き日あらぬ
夕暮れに
花を幾度
みめくりの土手

sumidagawa
nagaki hi aranu
yūgure ni
hana o ikutabi
mimeguri no dote

On evenings after long busy days, how often we went to see the cherry blossom on the banks of the Sumida River at Mimeguri.

ASHIWARA MITSUKUNI 蘆原満那

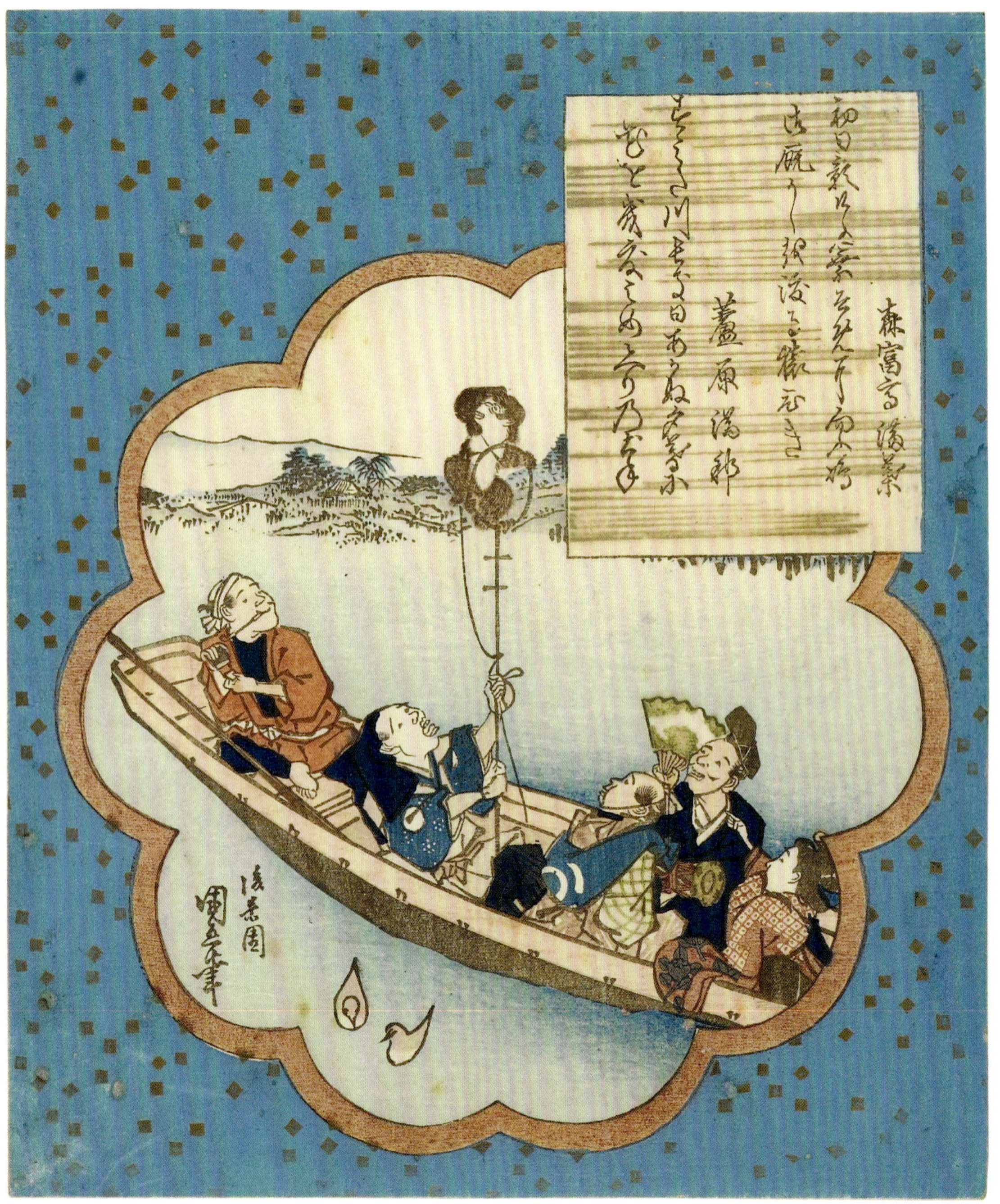

萬歳を
まねる鼓の
音にさえ
なほのとほさの
まさる春かな

manzai o
maneru tsutsumi no
oto ni sae
nao no tōsa no
masaru haru kana

Playing a hand drum in imitation of a Manzai performer; even the beating sound is still far from the coming of spring.

SHIN'AN ASOTO 森庵阿曾人

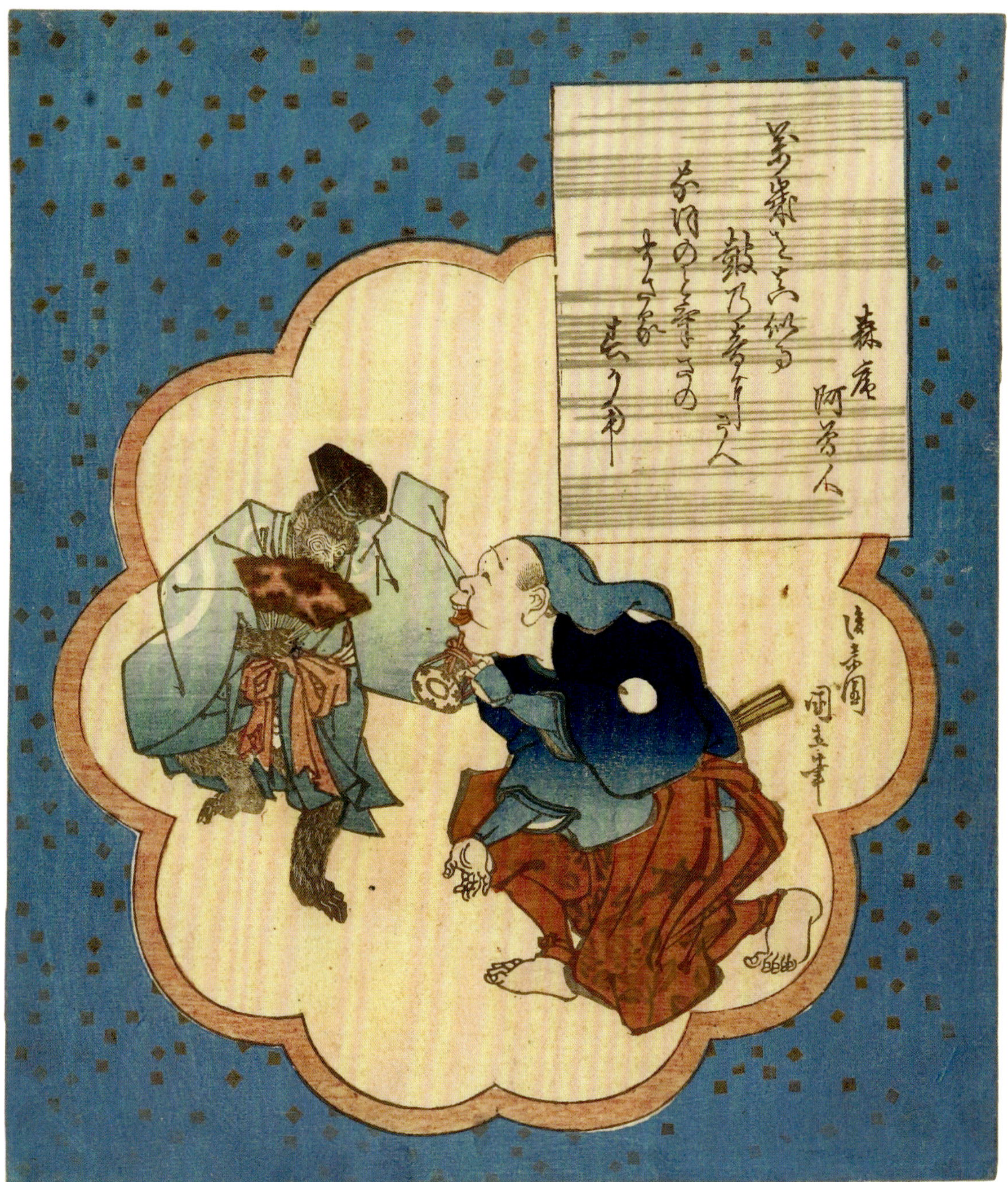

11

A mother with her two children feeding chickens

KEISAI EISEN (1790–1848) 渓斎英泉
Artist's signature: *Keisai* 渓斎
1825 (Year of the Rooster)
Colour woodblock print with metallic pigment
19.9 × 17.6 cm, *shikishiban* format
Presented by Mrs E. M. Allan and Mr and Mrs H. N. Spalding
from the Herbert H. Jennings Collection, EAX.4610

The picture portrays a happy scene of a mother and her children feeding chickens in their garden at the New Year, a blossoming plum tree behind them. It seems to be a wealthy Edo merchant's family. The mother wears smart yellow robes for the New Year, with a green sash tied at the back in the *hitotsumusubi* (tied and draped) style. She holds up the skirt of her kimono in her left hand while supporting her smiling younger son on her back with her right hand. The child points towards a pair of chickens that are being fed by his elder brother, who holds a birdcall whistle in his mouth. Both boys wear their hair in the Chinese *karako* style.

The first verse alludes to the poet Hamabe no Akehito's 61st birthday. A 61st birthday celebration – known in Japan as *kanreki* – always coincides with the zodiac year in which one was born (after five 12-year cycles). According to the traditional Japanese system of age reckoning (*kazoe-doshi*), people were born at the age of one and added a year to their age each New Year's Day. After Western-style age reckoning was adopted in Japan in the late nineteenth century, *kanreki* was celebrated at the age of 60. In Hamabe's case he was born and turned 61 in the Year of the Rooster. The word *kaeru* means both 'to return' and 'to hatch', and so '*hina ni kaeru*' means both 'hatching a baby bird' and 'returning to a baby bird'. The poet also puns on the word '*tori*', which means both 'growing old (*toshi wa tori*)' and 'bird' or 'rooster (*tori no haru*)'. Considering the chicken imagery of all three poems in conjunction with the lifespan of the third poet, Kyokadō Magao (1753–1829), the print was most likely produced as a New Year's gift for the 1825 Year of the Rooster.

The humorous use of onomatopoeic clucking sounds in the second poem ('*koko koko koko*') lends a light-hearted mood to the *surimono*. The third poem mentions a family visit to a shrine. The custom of visiting a shrine located in an auspicious direction to wish for happiness in the New Year was called '*ehōmairi*'. The auspicious direction differed every year. Above the name of the poet of this final verse is a small circle, which signifies that it was judged the best poem in a poetry competition.

The print designer Keisai Eisen was celebrated for his distinctive *ukiyo-e* prints of beautiful women (*bijin-ga*). He also produced a number of *surimono* and in this image he portrays the woman in an elegant and sensuous manner typical of his style.

またひとつ
年はとりしか
酉の春
かへりてひなの
ここちこそすれ

mata hitotsu
toshi wa tori shika
tori no haru
kaerite hina no
kokochi kososure

Yet again another year has come, growing older in the spring of the Year of the Rooster; returning to the year of my birth, I feel like a baby bird just hatching.

HAMABE NO AKEHITO 濱邊朱人

春ハ今
とひ来しおらん
我宿の
こゝこゝこゝと
いはふ庭鳥

haru wa ima
toi kishioran
waga yado no
koko koko koko to
iwau niwatori

Now spring has come with a visitation to our yard; the chickens celebrate spring with clucking sounds – cluck, cluck, cluck.

HAMABE NO MATSUSHIGE
濱邊松重

幸ひを
恵方参りに
親も子も
揃ふて年を
酉のはつ春

sachiwai o
ehōmairi ni
oya mo ko mo
sorōte toshi o
tori no hatsuharu

For good fortune the mother and her children go together to worship at the shrine in the most auspicious direction, in the spring of the Year of the Rooster.

KYŌKADŌ 狂歌堂

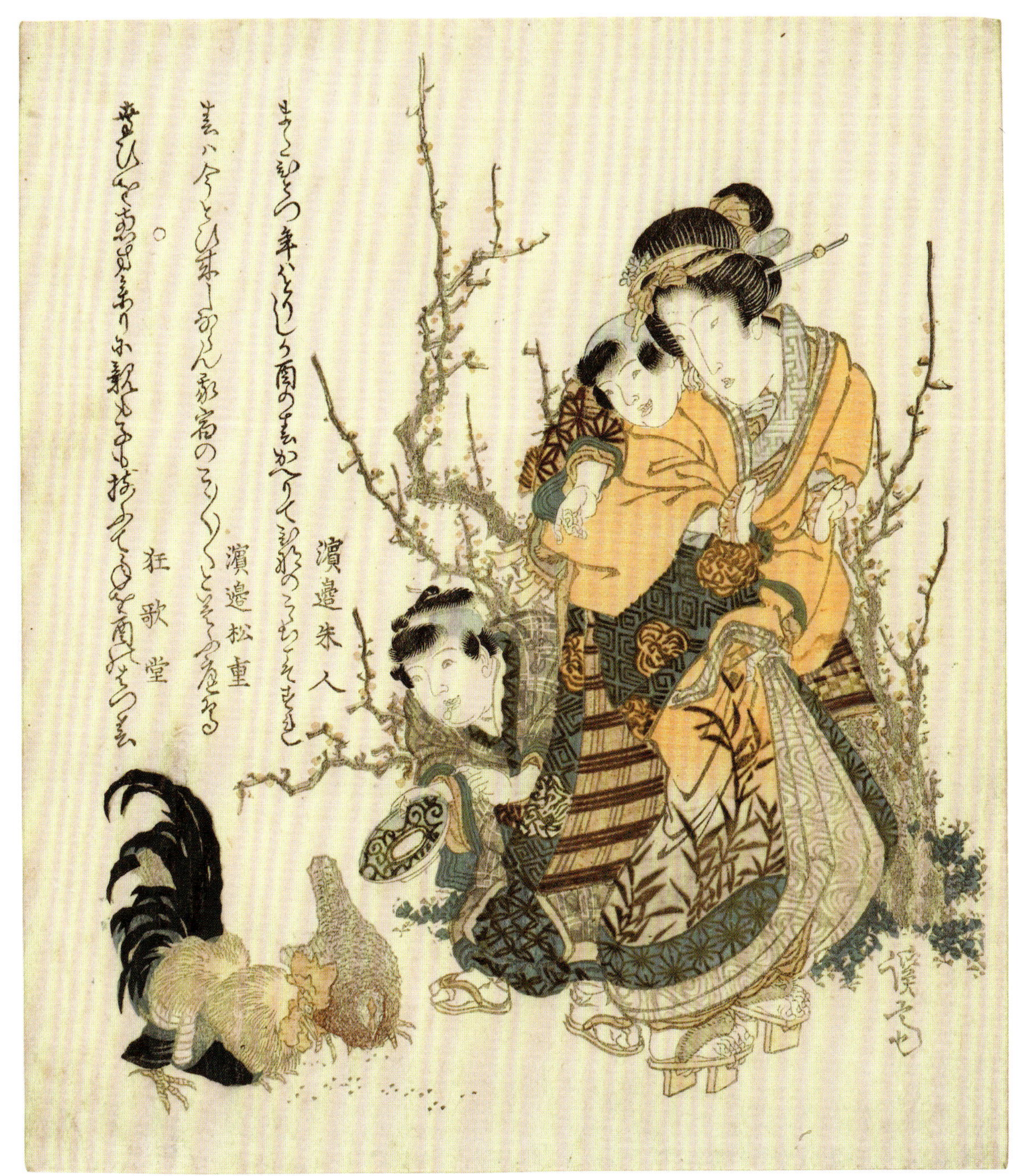

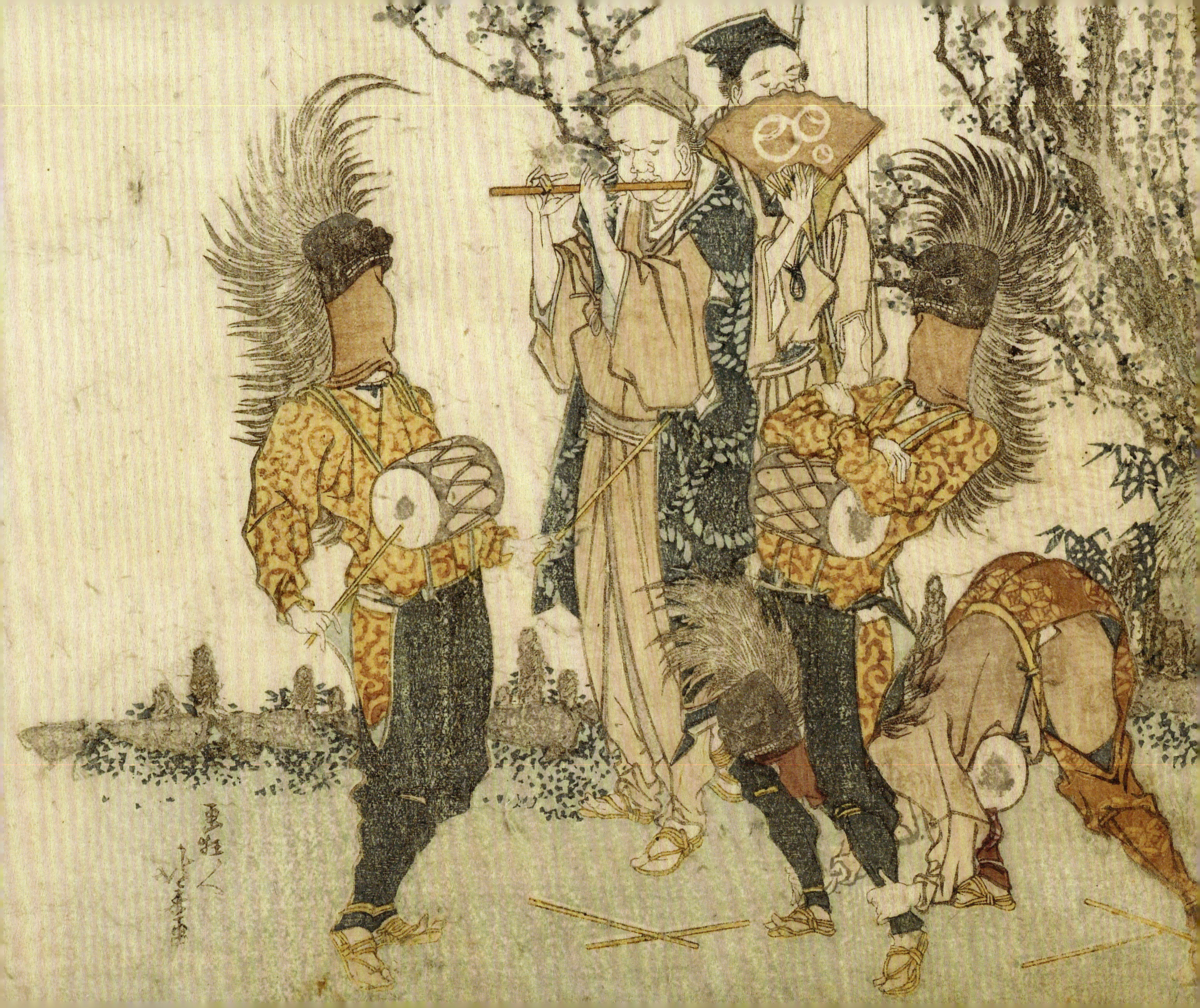
画狂人
北斎

III

New Year's Symbols and Activities

The majority of *surimono* were given with good wishes on the first day of the lunar New Year, which usually fell in what we know as mid-February. These New Year *surimono* were known as *shunkyō kyōka surimono* (*surimono* for celebrating spring). The New Year was the most important event in the Japanese festival calendar, marking the rebirth of nature in springtime. It was also a fresh start after setting one's affairs and house in order at the end of the previous year (through the settling of debts and cleaning).

Over the festive period special food and drink were consumed and homes adorned with New Year's decorations. A number of activities connected with an auspicious beginning to the year also took place, of which a series of ritual 'first things' (*kotohajime*), intended to set a good pattern for the rest of the year, was particularly important. The 'first things' included writing the first calligraphy, dyeing the first cloth of the year and playing a musical instrument for the first time. *Surimono* made for the New Year often reflect customs and objects associated with these festive days. Other New Year's activities included visiting the shrine, wearing new clothes and watching the sunrise.

The New Year was also a time to re-establish personal relationships, either by a direct visit or by sending greetings. Exchanging *surimono* was one means of reaffirming these social ties. Modern commentators have often compared *surimono* to Christmas or New Year cards, but *surimono* were more than a simple celebratory greeting. Since the first Japanese texts were written in the eighth century it was believed that words, especially in poetry, contained a spiritual power known as *kotodama,* and that it was possible to encourage good fortune through the use of auspicious words and imagery. *Surimono,* in both words and pictures, were packed with references to harmony, long life, good health and wealth, as well as to the plants that flourished in springtime, as a way of presenting good fortune to the recipient. These positive messages were also beneficial to the senders. *Surimono* can thus be seen as a woodblock-printed version of a long tradition of exchanging New Year's greetings.

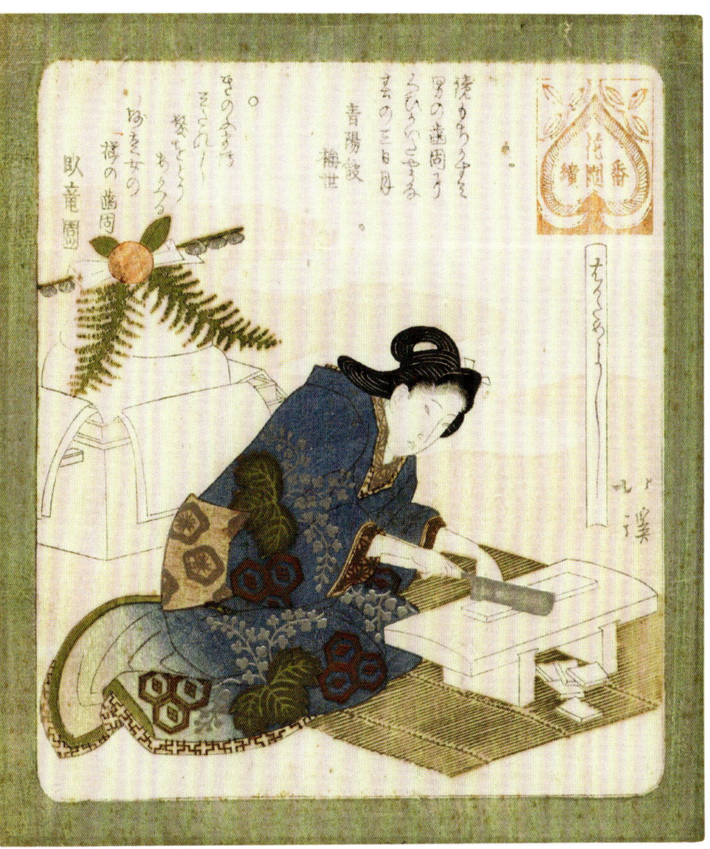

Fig.18 *It is favourable to harden one's teeth* (cutting a New Year's rice cake). Series for the Hanazono poetry circle (*Hanazono bantsuzuki* 花園番續). Commissioned by the Hanazono circle. Totoya Hokkei (1780–1850). Artist's signature: *Hokkei* 北溪. *c.*1824. Colour woodblock print with metallic pigments and embossing, 20.3 × 18 cm, *shikishiban* format. Bequest of Mrs Florian (Winslow) Carr, EA2007.133

12

A group of travelling entertainers

Commissioned by the Tsubo-gawa group
KATSUSHIKA HOKUSAI (1760–1849) 葛飾北斎
Artist's signature: *Gakyōjin Hokusai ga* (画狂人 北斎畫)
Spring 1803 (Year of the Boar)
Colour woodblock print with metallic pigment and embossing
19.5 × 25.8 cm, *yoko-chūban* format
Presented by Mrs E. M. Allan and Mr and Mrs H. N. Spalding from the Herbert H. Jennings Collection, EAX.4651

This *surimono* shows a group of five itinerant street entertainers known as *kakubējishi*, who travelled around performing lion dances, music and acrobatics. *Kakubējishi* were one of several kinds of strolling musicians who visited door to door during the New Year celebrations, making them a suitable subject for a *surimono*. This type of performance originated in Echigo Province (modern Niigata Prefecture) in the mid-eighteenth century and may have been named after a craftsman, *Kakubē*, who carved the masks worn by the acrobats.

The group consists of two adult musicians – a flute player and a singer – and three masked acrobats, each carrying a hand drum. The acrobats, usually young boys of around seven to fifteen years old, wear headdresses consisting of a *shishi* lion dog mask, red fabric neck piece and long cockerel feathers to represent a lion's mane. The acrobat on the left plays his drum while the two on the right prepare for a joint stunt, their drumsticks placed on the ground in front of them while they perform. The singer at the back holds a fan decorated with the jar-shaped emblem of the Tsubo-gawa group (Jar group) based in Asakusa in Edo, which commissioned this print. The composer of the fourth poem, Asakusa no Ichihito, was the leader of the Tsubo-gawa group which was also known as the Asakusa-gawa group. In the background Hokusai has depicted three plants particularly associated with the start of the New Year: pine, bamboo and plum. These plants were traditionally known in China as the 'three friends of winter' because they flourish during that season.

The four verses in the *surimono* do not refer to *kakubējishi*, but rather to plum blossoms and the arrival of spring; Hokusai's image, apparently inspired by the first poem's description of always being on the move, adds a fresh and unexpected element to the *surimono*. The first poem creates a sense of refinement, conveyed by the image of a traveller willing to appreciate the lingering fragrance of plum blossoms on his sleeves, however busy he might be. The word '*tome*' (to stop) is a *kakekotoba* 'pivot word', referring both to the scent of the plum blossoms 'lingering' and to the traveller 'stopping' his hurried journey. The second poem explores the image of dyeing threads for kimono in the New Year. The words '*hatsuzome*' (first dyeing), '*someya*'(a dyer) and '*ai*' (indigo) are associated theme words (*engo*). It is perhaps no coincidence that Hokusai chooses indigo blue for the colour of the flute player's robe and the acrobats' trousers in his illustration.

The words '*haru no hi*' (a spring day) and '*noki*' (eaves) of this second poem are used again in the third poem, which describes the rain dripping from the eaves at the beginning of spring. '*Osagari*' is a specialist term used to refer to rain or snow falling during the first three days of the New Year; this was believed to symbolise a gift from heaven and to presage a good harvest in the year ahead. The poet plays on the similarity between the words '*shimenawa*' (sacred straw rope) and '*shimeri*' (be moistened). The fourth poem continues the imagery of water and refers back to spring plum blossoms once again.

旅いそく
みにもいとハし
梅の花
袖に四五日
かハとめも哉

tabi isogu
mi nimo itowaji
ume no hana
sode ni shigonichi
ka wa tome mo kana

Always on the move, but I do not care; the scent of plum blossoms lingers on my sleeves for four or five days.

SENROKUAN HARUTSUGE 浅緑菴春告

初染の
染屋か軒の
ひと霞
あゐもきけんの
よいハ春の日

hatsuzome no
someya ga noki no
hitogasumi
ai mo kigen no
yoi wa haru no hi

The first dyeing of the year; just a single wisp of spring mist under the dyer's eaves – the indigo is also bright on this spring day.

RIKASAI TŌYŪ 梨下斎東邑

しめ縄の
しめりほとよき
春の日ハ
しつけくたるゝ
軒のおさかり

shimenawa no
shimeri hodo yoki
haru no hi wa
shizukeku taruru
noki no osagari

The sacred straw rope is being gently moistened on a spring day as the rain drops quietly from the eaves.

MANZAITEI HŌGI 萬歳亭 逢義

おのか香に
ゑひやしつらん
梅の花
片枝ハ水を
のそんてそさく

onoga ka ni
ehi ya shitsuran
ume no hana
katae wa mizu o
nozonde zo saku

The plum blossoms are intoxicated by their own fragrance; the many branches on one side of the plum tree thirst for water as they flower.

ASAKUSA'AN ICHIHITO 浅草菴市人

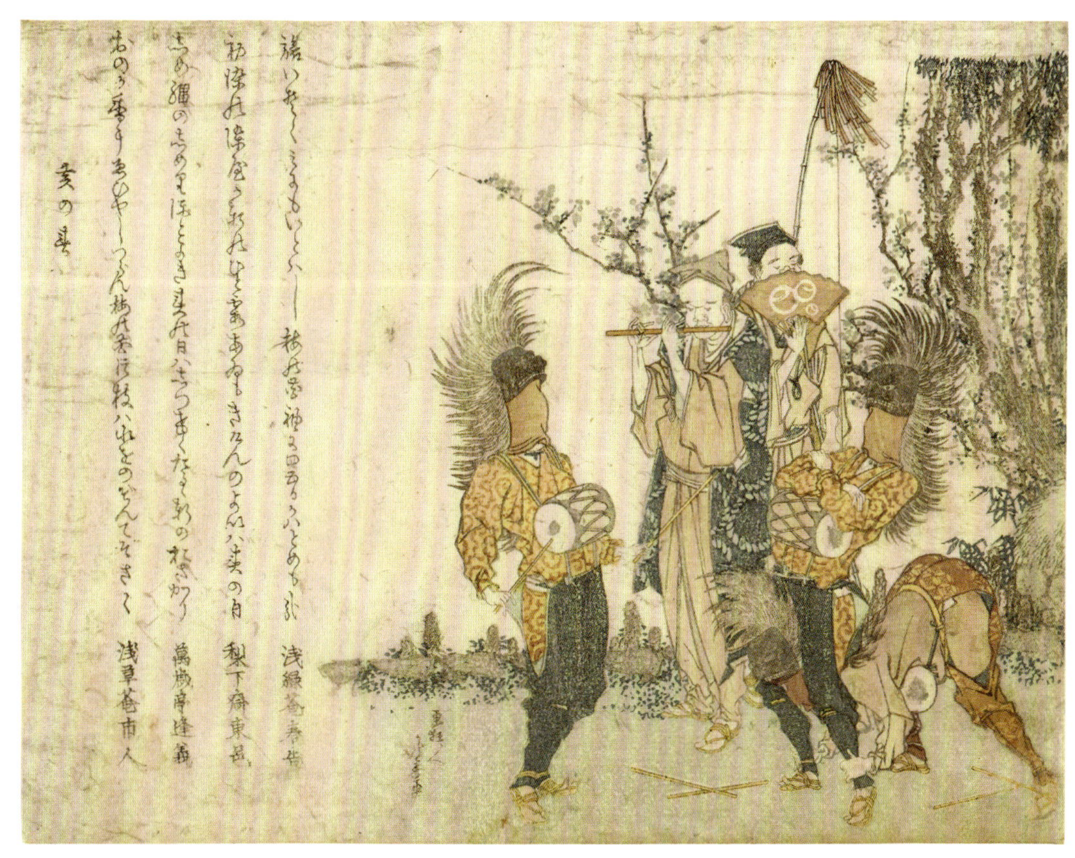

13

First bath of the New Year (*Hatsuyu* 初湯)

Series: A Set of The Seven Gods of Fortunes (*Shichifuku-zoroi* 七福揃)
HISHIKAWA SŌRI III (active 1797 – *c*.1813) 菱川宗理
Artist's signature: *Sōri ga* 宗理画
c.1800
Colour woodblock print with embossing
11.1 × 12.7 cm, *koban* format
Presented by Mrs E. M. Allan and Mr and Mrs H. N. Spalding
from the Herbert H. Jennings Collection, EAX.4576

This *surimono* is one of a set of prints representing Japan's Seven Gods of Fortune (*Shichifukujin*). In the Edo period the Seven Gods of Fortune were associated with the New Year, when it was believed that they arrived on their treasure ship to deliver gifts of luck and happiness. The figure on the left is Hotei, the God of Contentment and guardian of children. Thought to be based on an eccentric Chinese Zen monk called Budai, he is typically shown as a jolly man with a huge belly, carrying a large alms sack. This sack is the derivation of his name Hotei, which means 'cloth bag'. In this *surimono* Hotei carries a towel with a pattern of wish-fulfilling jewels (*hōju*) instead of a bag; he also wears wooden clogs, as if on his way to the bath house for his first bath of the New Year. He smiles down rather bashfully at the elegant young woman walking next to him, who carries her child on her back.

The boy is holding a fan, one of the attributes associated with Hotei and said to be a wish-giving fan. The child's hair is in the *karako* ('Chinese boy') style, introduced from China in the late eighteenth century. During the Edo period paintings depicting Hotei with playful Chinese boys clambering happily over his plump body became extremely popular. These were sometimes used as talismans for safe childbirth, probably because of the association between Hotei's big belly and that of a pregnant woman. The print title '*Hatsuyu*' may refer both to the first bath of the New Year and also to the first bath of a new-born baby.

The hand-written poem on this *surimono* is a *haiku* rather than a *kyōka*. *Haiku* poems consist of seventeen syllables (5-7-5) and conventionally contain a seasonal reference; here the image of plum blossom evokes the spring. In Sōri's illustration the scent of the plum blossoms is represented by the beautiful young woman; Hotei, walking next to her, is full of joy.

The print designer Hishikawa Sōri III was an early pupil of the celebrated artist Katsushika Hokusai, who used the art name 'Sōri' himself from around 1794 to 1798. He then passed the name on to his pupil Sōji, who became 'Sōri III'.

むめか香や
嬉しく今日の
野辺道

mumegaka ya
ureshiku kyō no
nobe no michi

Walking today
in a field full of joy
the scent of plum blossoms.

FUJŪ 布拾

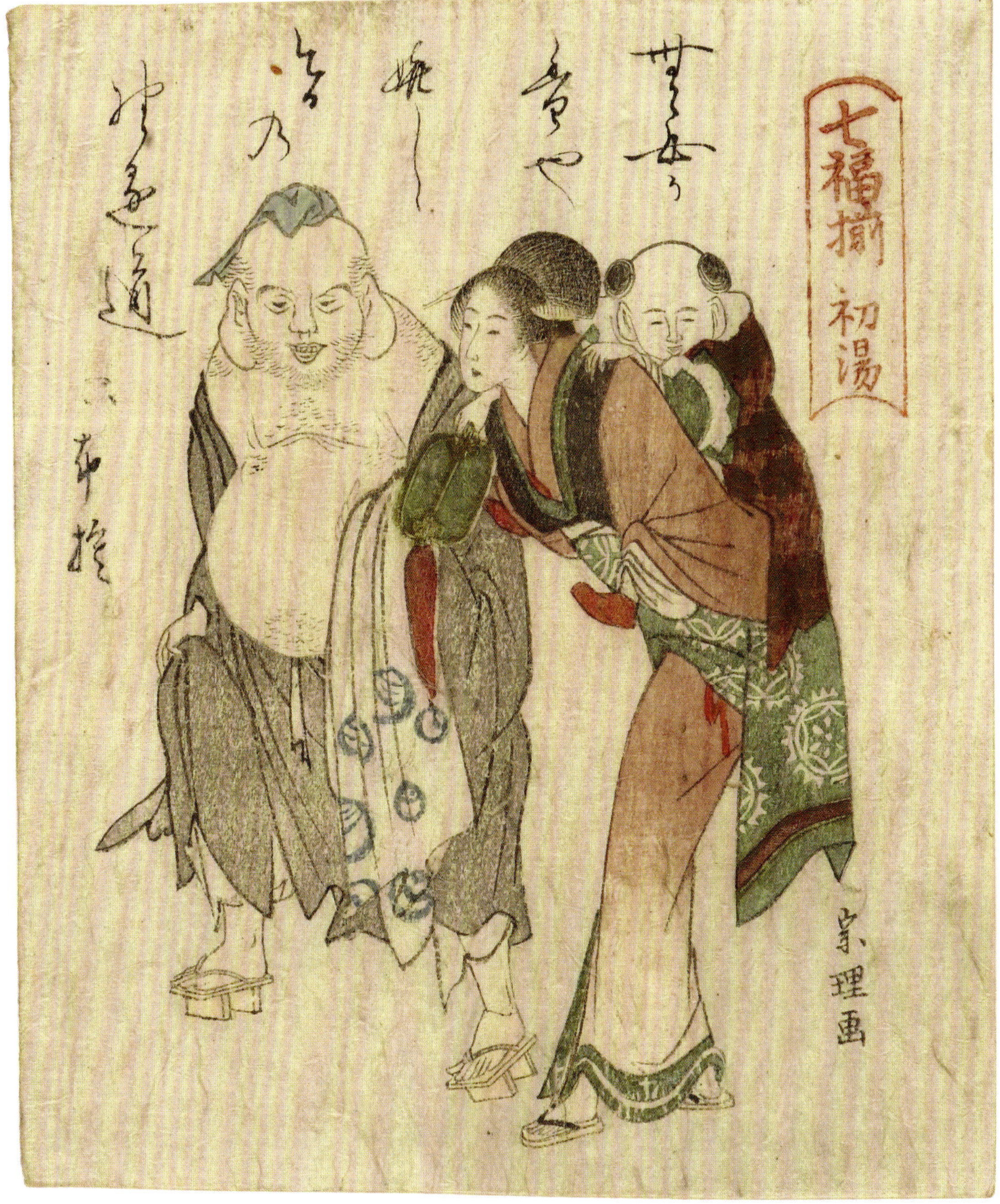

14

Rat calculations (*Nezumizan* 鼠算)

Series: Twelve Treasures of the Rat (*Nezumi-zukushi jūnihō* 鼠盡十二寳)
KEISAI EISEN (1790–1848) 渓斎英泉
Artist's signature: *Keisai* 渓斎
1890s (after an original probably of 1828, Year of the Rat)
Colour woodblock print with metallic pigments and embossing
20.9 × 18.1 cm, *shikishiban* format
Presented by Mrs E. M. Allan and Mr and Mrs H. N. Spalding
from the Herbert H. Jennings Collection, EAX.4607

This *surimono*, now sadly faded, is from a series of prints commissioned by an unknown poetry group for the Year of the Rat. During the period when the artist Eisen was active, this corresponds to either 1828 or 1840. It shows a scene of a family life, probably in the household of a wealthy merchant in Edo at the New Year. The season is indicated by the two-fold screen in the background, decorated with the spring motif of blossoming plum trees, and the pot containing a yellow adonis plant, typically cultivated for the New Year period. An old man sits on a cushion by a brazier; a cloth covering his head and neck and a shawl around his shoulders keep him warm. He is teaching a young boy, perhaps his grandson, how to use an abacus, using his long pipe as a pointer.

The subject of the print is suggested by the third poem, which describes a child being given an abacus lesson at the New Year. The poem seems to refer to the custom called *kotohajime* (the start of things for the New Year), in which people traditionally began activities at which they wished to improve. On the auspicious second day of the New Year skills such as calligraphy, abacus work, sewing or playing musical instruments would be taken up. The boy in the *surimono* works diligently as a young woman brings a teacup on a lacquered saucer for the old man. She wears a long-sleeved kimono, a sign of her youth, with a black satin sash tied in the fashionable long draping style. A black satin collar is attached to her kimono to protect it from staining.

All four poems on the print link images of children and the increase of progeny with mathematical calculations and increasing wealth. In the first poem '*nezumizan*' (rat calculations) is the term for a type of geometrical progression. It is linked with the word '*kodakara*', which conflates the words for 'children' and 'treasure' ('children who are treasures'). The rat is traditionally regarded as a messenger for Daikoku, the God of Wealth, and is also a symbol of fecundity – thus the idea of producing children in geometrical progression connects to that of progressively accumulating wealth. The second poem continues the mathematical theme of rat calculations with the term '*kameizan*', a special method of calculating on the abacus invented by Momokawa Jihē in 1645. In the third poem the word '*megane*' is a pun (*kakekotoba*) meaning both 'spectacles' and also 'being acknowledged by [a parent]' (*megane ni kanau*). Eisen has illustrated the spectacles in his design, lying on top of a book on the floor. The fourth poem refers obliquely to the Year of the Rat, the first year of the zodiacal calendar. The use of associated words – here terms referring to multiplying and prospering – is another example of the poetic technique known as '*engo*'.

月ゝに
増子宝も
ねつみ算
きのうのふゆや
千代の初春

tsukizuki ni
masu kodakara mo
nezumizan
kinō no fuyu ya
chiyo no hatsuharu

Precious offspring multiplying monthly, like rat calculations; winter belongs to yesterday and here comes the spring of a thousand years.

ANCHŪTEI MUCHIMARU of Sendabori, Shimofusa Province (modern north Chiba Prefecture)
下総千駄堀 安忠亭無智丸

玉の春
霞の棚や
鼠算
引てかけるハ
亀井さんかも

tama no haru
kasumi no tana ya
nezumizan
hiite kakeru wa
kameizan kamo

Spring, the jewel of the year! The racks of clouds increase like rats, subtracting and multiplying like *kameizan* calculations

RINRINSHA RYŌON of Tsukazaki, also from Shimofusa
同 塚崎 林々舎涼音

一芸と
子に磨せる
十露盤も
親の目かねの
玉の初春

ichigei to
ko ni migakaseru
soroban mo
oya no megane no
tama no hatsuharu

A parent instructs his child in the abacus, a skill to master; the child measures up to his expectations in the spring, the jewel of the New Year.

SHŪFŪDŌ OBITAKE of Fujigokoro, also from Shimofusa
同 藤心 秋楓堂帯丈

さちハいを
えとのかしらや
月も数
なれも十二の
子たからそうむ

sachiwai o
eto no kashira ya
tsuki mo kazu
nare mo jūni no
kodakara zo umu

Happiness – in the first year of the zodiac, twelve precious rat offspring born each month

SHŪCHŌDŌ of Tōto (modern Tokyo)
東都 秋長堂

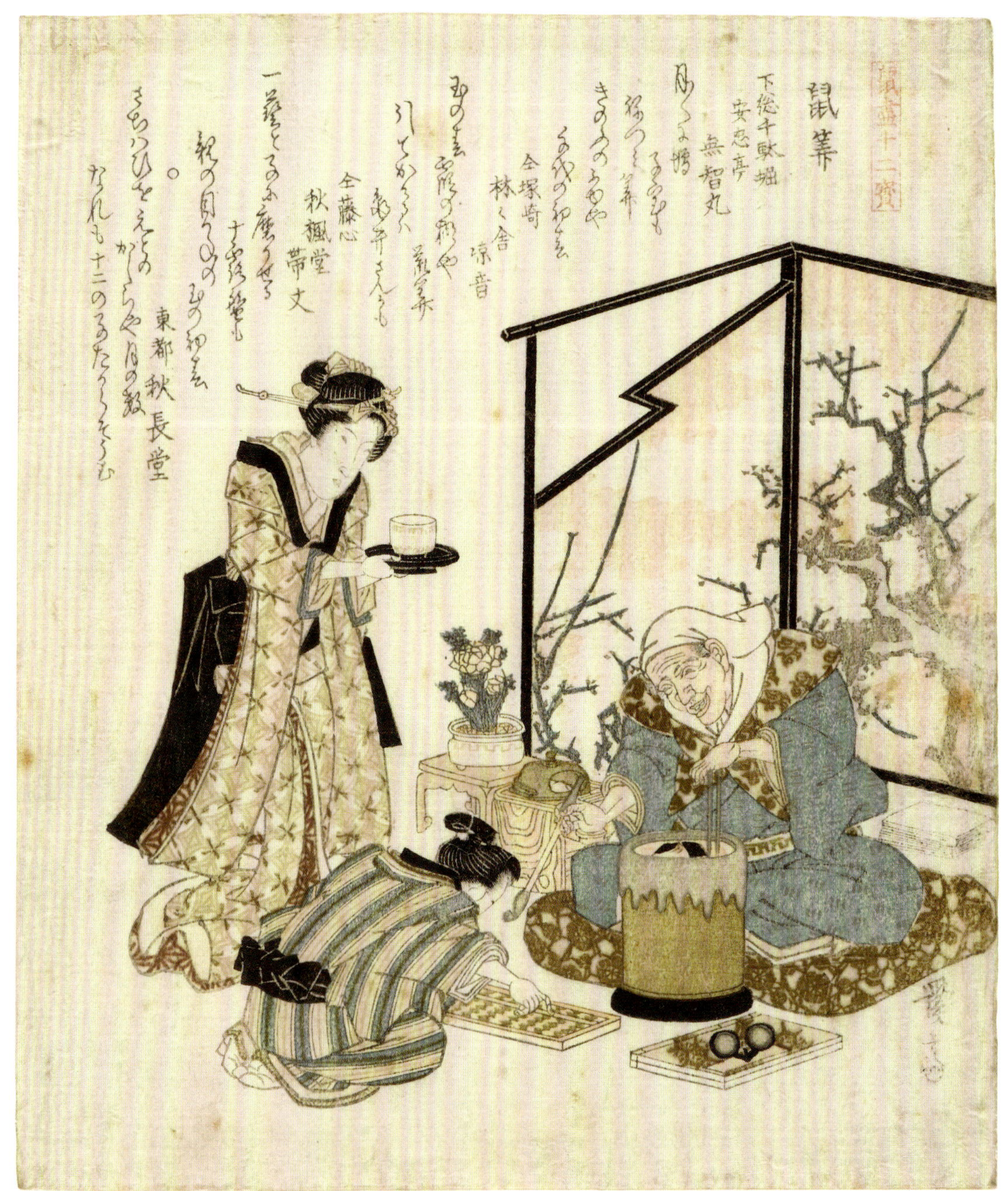

15

A courtesan with a *koto* and a dog

Commissioned by the Tsubo-gawa group
Attributed to KATSUSHIKA HOKUSAI (1760–1849) 葛飾北斎
Artist's signature: *Sōri ga* 宗理画
1794–8
Colour woodblock print
17.1 × 12.4 cm, *kokonotsugiriban* format
Presented by Mrs E. M. Allan and Mr and Mrs H. N. Spalding from the Herbert H. Jennings Collection, EAX.4575

An elegant courtesan looks fondly down at her pet dog as she prepares to play the *koto* (a traditional Japanese stringed musical instrument similar to a zither) on her lap. The first poem suggests that she might be playing for the first time in the New Year. She has already attached a plectrum to her right forefinger and holds another plectrum ready to place on her right thumb, but appears to have been distracted by the dog, which turns towards her. The courtesan seems to be enjoying some personal leisure time, and the way in which Hokusai has depicted the edge of a *fusuma* sliding door on the far right of the picture draws the viewer into this intimate scene, as if peeping inside her private quarters. The placing of the subject of a print beyond an object cropped in the foreground was a compositional device commonly employed by Hokusai and his contemporary Hiroshige.

The emblem of the Tsubo-gawa poetry group, which commissioned this *surimono*, is visible on the courtesan's orange under-robe. The emblem resembled a wide-mouthed jar, hence the name 'Tsubo-gawa' (Jar group). The courtesan's long, purple overgarment is edged with a design of drying fishing nets. The swooping triangular shapes of the nets echo the carefully designed triangular composition of the scene as a whole. Hokusai is known to have experimented with the use of geometrical forms within his designs. The courtesan wears her long hair loose in the traditional style known as *sagegami* (literally 'hanging-down hair'), elaborately decorated with long hairpins. Unadorned loose hairstyles had been worn by Japanese women since ancient times; during the Edo period (1603–1868), however, while aristocratic women continued to wear the old-fashioned *sagegami*, fashionable women of the commoner classes adopted a wide variety of hair styles and elaborate hair accessories. The hairstyle shown here, with its cluster of hairpins in the front, was a variation on the traditional *sagegami* worn only by courtesans, perhaps in imitation of courtly ladies of the past.

The first poem uses the poetic term *tamagoto*, or 'jewel-like *koto*', to describe the stringed instrument, and is the inspiration for Hokusai's illustration. Two puns are included in the poem. Firstly the word *hiku* refers both to 'lifting' (of mist) and 'playing' (of a *koto*). Secondly the word *ito* means 'string' (of a *koto*) and also acts as an intensifier, emphasising the splendid nature of the *koto* and of the music being played. The second poem alludes to a famous medicine produced and sold in Umenoki-mura (Plum tree village) in Gōshū (modern Shiga Prefecture). Many shops sprang up in Umenoki selling ineffective imitations of the original medicine, hence the poet's suggestion that the mere sight of plum blossom would be a better cure. The poet has chosen to mention this village because of its appropriately spring-like name, suitable for a New Year's poem. The third poem refers to a warbler, a symbol of spring frequently mentioned in *kyōka*.

朝霞
ひくと見しまに
玉琴の
いともゆたかに
はるは来にけり

asagasumi
hiku to mishimani
tamagoto no
ito mo yutaka ni
haru wa kinikeri

As the morning mist lifts a jewel-like *koto* is splendidly played – spring has come.

MASHIBA'AN TADASUMI 真柴庵 唯住

なに匂ふ
梅の木村の
薬より
花は第一
目に妙也

nani niou
umenoki-mura no
kusuri yori
hana wa daiichi
me ni myō nari

A scent floats in the air; the exquisite sight of plum blossoms is more effective than the medicine from Umenoki village.

ZENIYA KINRATSU 銭屋金埒

手束弓
やはらかものを
正月は
きの鶯も
こはい顔せす

tazukayumi
yawaraka mono o
shōgatsu wa
ki no uguisu mo
kowai kao sezu

He holds a bow yet he wears his fine silk garments at the New Year; the warbler in the tree is unafraid.

YOMO NO MAGAO 四方真顔

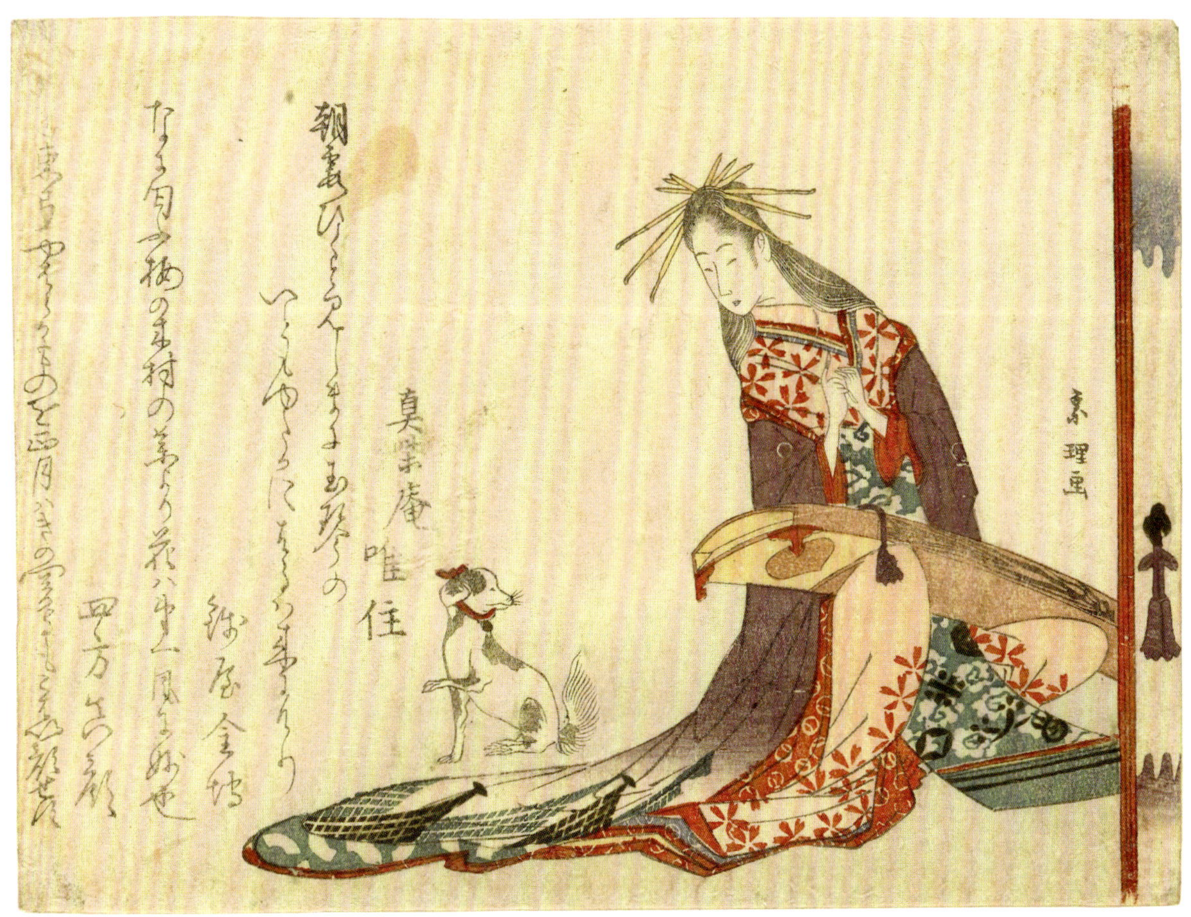

16

Butterfly (*Kochō* 胡蝶)

Series: Five Prints for the Katsushika-ren circle: Textiles Dyed the Colours of the Dawn of Spring (*Katsushika goban: haru no akebono-zome* かつしか五番春のあけほの染)
Commissioned by the Katsushika-ren circle
YASHIMA GAKUTEI (*c.*1786–*c.*1855) 八島岳亭
Artist's signature: *Gakutei* 岳亭
*c.*1830
Colour woodblock print with metallic pigment and embossing
21.4 × 18.4 cm, *shikishiban* format
Presented by Mrs E. M. Allan and Mr and Mrs H. N. Spalding from the Herbert H. Jennings Collection, EAX.4653

When women are depicted in *surimono* they are typically shown engaged in some kind of activity associated with the New Year, often doing something for the very first time that year. This *surimono*, issued by the Katsushika-ren circle, is one of a series of five designs showing women engaged in various domestic activities, from drinking tea to smoking a pipe. Each of the five women is shown seated against a densely decorated background with the pattern corresponding to the title of the print – in this case butterflies. The title of the series, '*Akebono-zome*', refers to a textile dyed to look like a dawn sky, with the colour gradually becoming lighter towards the edge of the fabric.

The butterfly imagery is continued throughout the print. The young woman holds a butterfly-patterned book in her hands and turns her face to the side, as if interrupted. She sits at a lacquered desk with a butterfly motif on the sides. Her *obi* (sash) and *akebono-zome*-dyed *kimono* are patterned with butterflies of different sizes and colours. Her hair is adorned with a silver hairpin in the form of a butterfly and tortoiseshell pins in her forelock. In Japan the butterfly symbolises womanhood and two butterflies together represent marital harmony. The elaborate hairstyle and long sleeves depicted here imply that this is a young unmarried woman from a wealthy Edo merchant family.

The three poems, set within a large, fan-shaped cartouche, are all associated with butterflies. In the first verse a graceful woman sports a hairpin adorned with a butterfly. In the second the face powder of Sahohime, Goddess of Spring, is as pale as white butterflies. The final verse describes a purple kimono decorated with butterflies and made in the *surihaku* technique. This textile technique, in which stencil-patterned gold or silver foil was pasted on to silk fabric, was often used for Nō costumes or sumptuous courtesan's robes. The artist Gakutei has illustrated the poem faithfully in his illustration, although the purple pigment in the print has sadly now faded severely. Gakutei, a prolific producer of *surimono* and picture book illustrations during the early nineteenth century, was noted for the way he used elaborate patterning to frame his *surimono* designs. Here he uses a repeated butterfly motif.

たをやめか
かさしの蝶は
結わけの
梅のあふらの
かをやしたへる

taoyame ga
kazashi no chō wa
yuiwake no
ume no abura no
ka o ya shitaeru

A delicate woman styles her hair with a pin adorned with a butterfly, drawn to the scent of plum blossoms that perfume her hair oil.

HAKUJITSUEN IWANUSHI
白日園岩主

佐保姫か
柳のかみも
夕化粧
紅さすそらに
蝶のおしろい

sahohime ga
yanagi no kami mo
yūgeshō
beni sasu sora ni
chōno oshiroi

The goddess Sahohime, her tresses like willow fronds; for her evening make-up she wears rouge like the red-tinged sky and face powder the colour of butterflies.

KEIMEISHA DADAMORI
鶏鳴舍忠守

色あせぬ
かすみのきぬの
むらさきに
春のもやうや
蝶のすり箔

iro asenu
kasumi no kinu no
murasaki ni
haru no moyō ya
chō no surihaku

The robe of silk purple mist that has not faded is embellished with the spring design of butterflies in *surihaku* foil.

HAKUMŌSHA (Manmori) 白毛舍

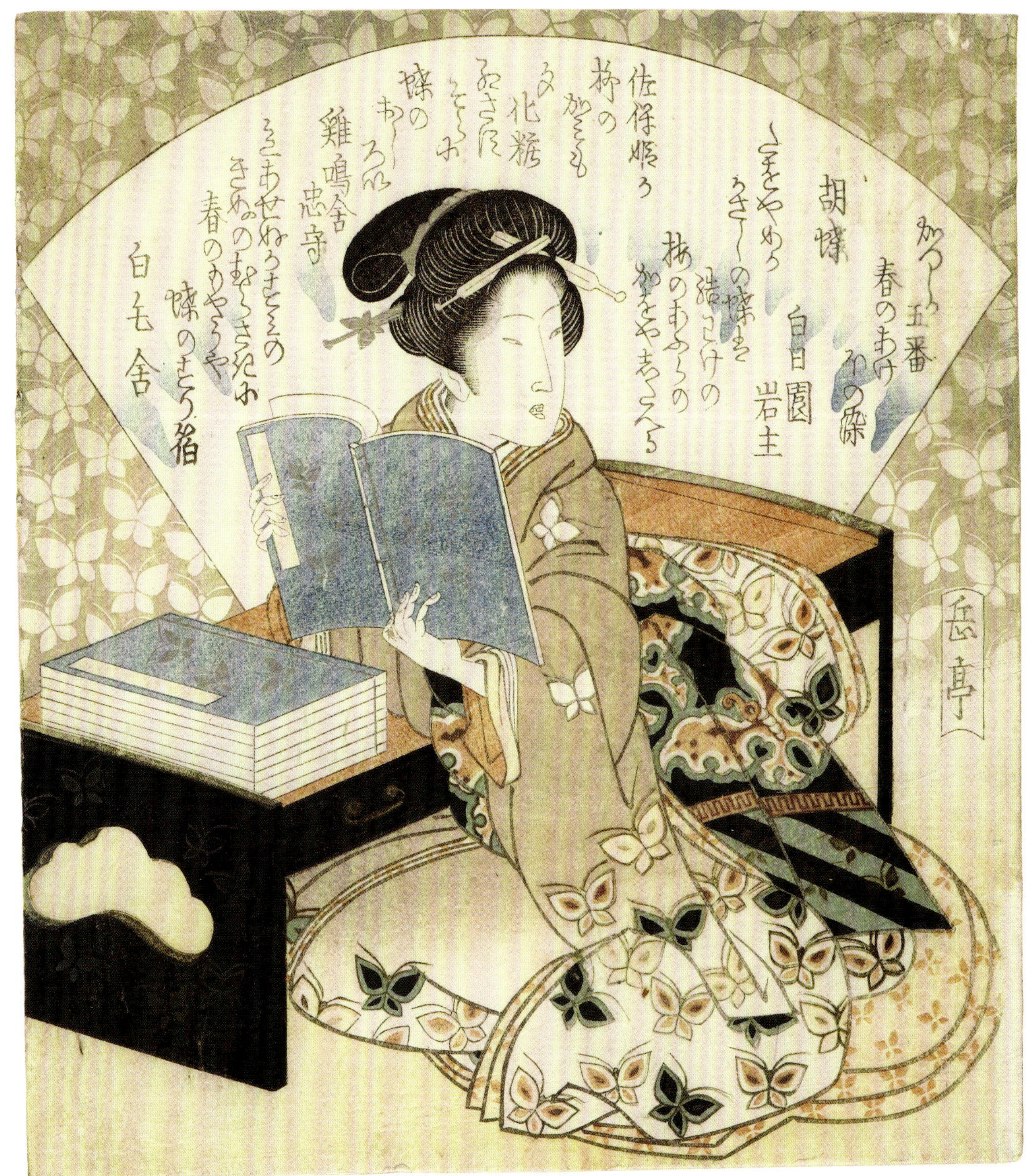

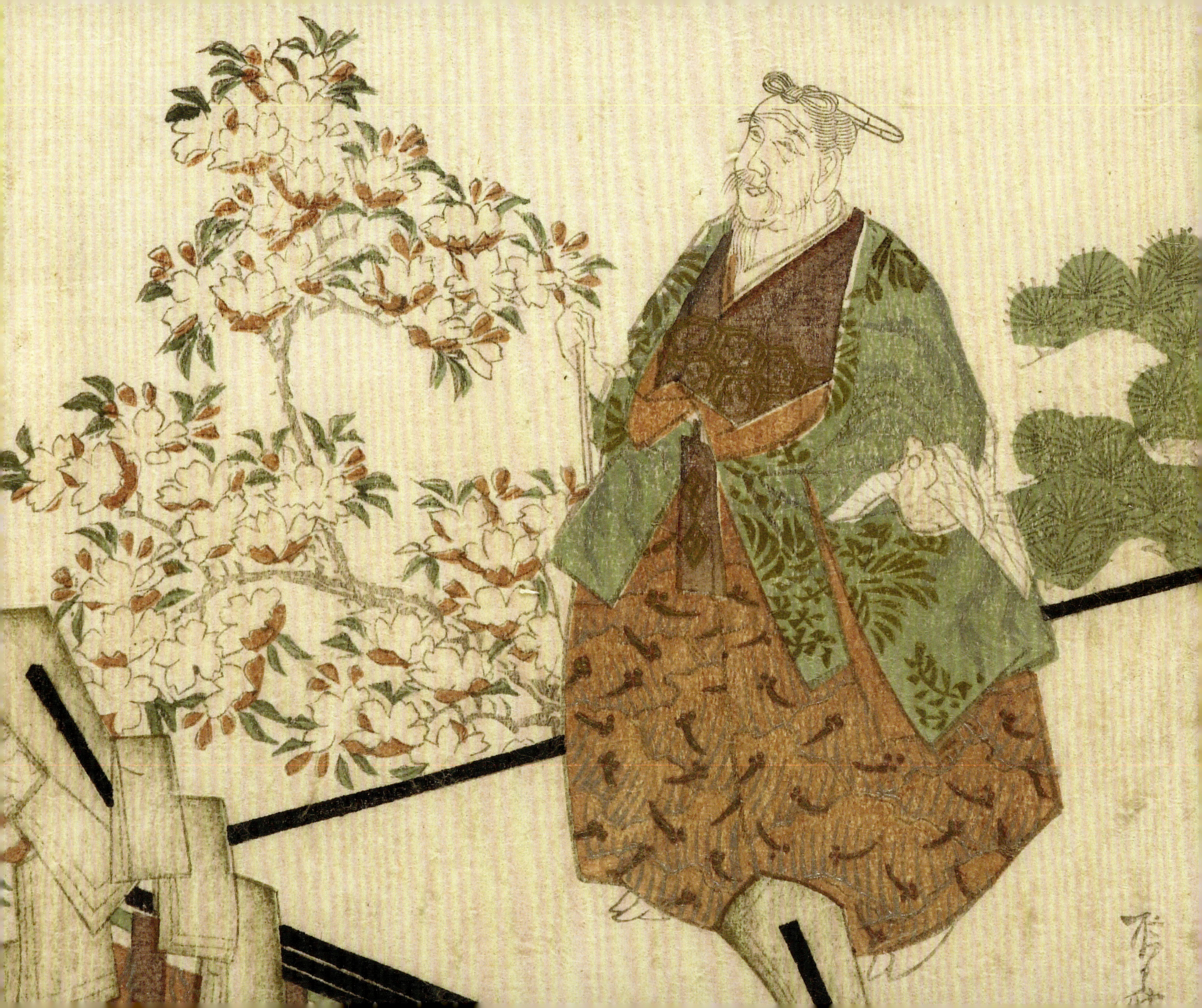

IV

History, Legend and Literature

The members of *kyōka* poetry clubs were extremely well read. They possessed extensive knowledge of Japanese and Chinese history, literature and culture, as well as of the Kabuki theatre and other forms of contemporary culture. By filling their *surimono* – both the verses and the images – with references to iconic models of the history, literature and legend, they not only demonstrated their scholarship, but also borrowed some of the authority and glamour of these other worlds.

The range of topics covered in *surimono* was extremely broad. A particularly popular source of imagery was the 'golden age' of refined courtly culture in the Heian period (794–1185) and the literature it generated, from imperial poetry anthologies to literary classics such as *The Tale of Genji*. Medieval folk tales and collections of didactic tales were also commonly featured. By the mid-Edo period most of the Japanese classics were available as woodblock-printed books, often with illustrations or commentaries to make them more accessible. Poets also looked to the indigenous Shinto religion and to the myths of Japan's origins as outlined in the eighth-century chronicle, the *Kojiki*.

The appearance of such nostalgic themes was influenced by the growth of the Kokugaku (National Learning) movement. Japan's ruling Tokugawa shogunate had adopted neo-Confucianism as the intellectual foundation of their government, and Confucian philosophy profoundly influenced the thought and behaviour of the educated classes. The Kokugaku movement attempted to shift the focus of Japanese scholarship away from the study of the Chinese Confucian texts that dominated intellectual life in Japan at the time, placing more emphasis on native Japanese sources instead. A number of *surimono* poets and designers were closely involved with this movement. At the same time, however, *surimono* made frequent references to Chinese literature and Confucian models of virtue and good government, sometimes transposed into a Japanese setting.

Surimono sometimes alluded to the classical past in a form of gentle parody known as '*mitate*'. In *mitate*, revered historical, religious or literary icons were depicted as contemporary figures such as courtesans or actors (for example cat.23, where the Chinese immortal Rogō is portrayed as a courtesan). The device of *mitate* was a way of demonstrating esoteric knowledge and imbuing an image with an air of elegance and refinement, as well as creating a connection between the poets and their illustrious forebears. For viewers, identifying the figures, poems or books alluded to within the *mitate* added a further enjoyable layer of puzzle to solve.

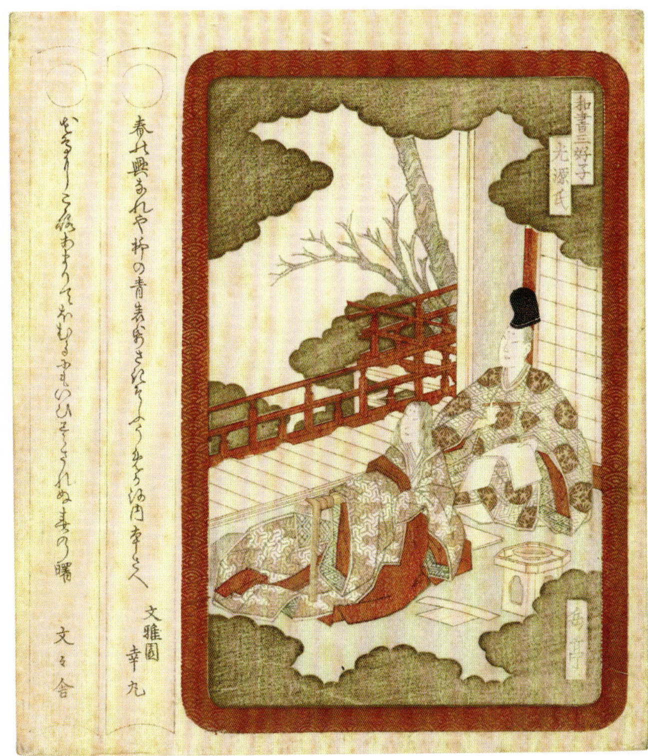

Fig.19 *The Shining Genji* (*Hikaru Genji* 光源氏). Series: Three Gentleman of Japanese Literature (*Washo sankōshi* 和書三好子). Commissioned by the Katsushika-ren circle. Yashima Gakutei (*c*.1786–*c*.1855) 八島岳亭. Artist's signature: *Gakutei* 岳亭. *c*.1819–20. Colour woodblock print with metallic pigments and embossing. 20.9 × 18.5 cm, *shikishiban* format. Presented by Mrs E. M. Allan and Mr and Mrs H. N. Spalding from the Herbert H. Jennings Collection, EAX.4564

17

Ono no Tōfū (小野道風)

Series: A Series for the Gathering of the Elders of Poetry
(*Shōshi-kai bantsuzuki* 尚齒會番續)
Commissioned by the Hanazono-ren circle
TOTOYA HOKKEI (1780–1850)
Artist's signature: *Hokkei* 北溪
*c.*1822
Colour woodblock print, with blind relief printing and metallic pigments
21.4 × 18.4 cm, *shikishiban* format
Purchased with the assistance of the Story Fund, EA2014.36

The title of the series to which this *surimono* belongs refers to a tradition of holding literary assemblies to honour the elderly (*shōshi-kai*). The custom is said to been started in China by the Tang poet Bai Juyi (772–846), who invited seven elderly poets to a party to enjoy composing poems and playing music. The custom was taken up by the court nobility in Japan during the Heian period (794–1185). In the Edo period (1603–1867) *shōshi-kai* poetry parties were often held in the New Year to celebrate the arrival of spring.

The figure illustrated in this *surimono* is Ono no Tōfū (894–966), a prominent Japanese statesman, poet and calligrapher at the Heian court. He is considered the founder of Japanese-style calligraphy, as distinct from Chinese-style calligraphy, and was regarded as one of the three best calligraphers of the period (known as the 'Three Brush Styles', or '*Sanseki*').

The *surimono* illustrates a famous anecdote about Ono no Tōfū in which, as a young man, he became dispirited by the inadequacy of his calligraphy. Setting out for a walk in the rain, he was contemplating giving up his art when he caught sight of a frog attempting to leap up on to the branch of a willow tree. After many futile efforts the frog eventually succeeded and, inspired by its perseverance, Ono no Tōfū decided to continue as a calligrapher. This well-known story has been retold in many different versions; in 1754 it was adapted for the Kabuki stage as the play *Ono no Tōfu aoyagi suzuri* (The green willow ink stone of Ono no Tōfū). In this play Ono no Tōfū wears his courtly robes and black court hat (*eboshi*), along with an umbrella and tall wooden clogs, when he encounters the frog. Hokkei's depiction of the poet striking a theatrical pose and wearing the appropriate accessories was probably based on this Kabuki scene.

The two poems here refer to calligrapher's brush and a frog respectively: for the literary-minded readers of this poem this would have immediately recalled the famous calligrapher Ono no Tōfū. In the first poem the Japanese word for a horsetail fern is *tsukushi*. Although the word is here written in phonetic *hiragana* script (つくし), contemporary readers would have known that the word could also be written with the characters 土筆, or 'earth brush', in reference to the brush-like shape of the plant. The imagery of a calligrapher's brush is continued later in the poem with the words '*fude no shiri*' (the end of a brush handle), referring to the profession of teaching and correcting poems. This use of associated words (here relating to brushes) within a semantic field is called *engo*.

The second poem makes a pun on '*utabukuro*', which means both a frog's vocal sac and a bag for holding manuscripts of *waka* poems. '*Aoyagi*' (green willow) is an example of a 'pillow word' (*makurakotoba*), a poetic epithet used in a set phrase with other fixed words to add resonance to a poem. *Aoyagi* was invariably used together with the word '*ito*' (thread) in the phrase 'threads of green willow' (*aoyagi no ito*) to enhance the spring-like feeling of an image. '*Aoyagi*' also refers to the title of the Kabuki play mentioned above (*Ono no Tōfu aoyagi suzuri*).

The emblem of the Hanazono-ren circle – three 'の' characters (the '*no*' of 'Hanazono') arranged like the petals of a plum blossom – appear at the top of the series title cartouche at the bottom right of the print.

春の野に
生ふるつくしを
つみためて
ふての尻とる
身とハなりけん

haru no no ni
ouru tsukushi o
tsumitamete
fude no shiri toru
mi towa nariken

In the spring fields I gathered horsetail ferns – now I am a teacher of poetry and writing.

SHUNKŌTEI MISAKO 春江亭美佐古

青柳の
糸に蛙のうた袋
ぬふ影水に
見えてうねゝゝ

aoyagi no
ito ni kawazu no
utabukuro
nuu kagemizu ni
miete une une

A thread of a green willow is sewing a pouch like a frog's throat sac or a bag for sheets of poetry; its reflection ripples on the surface of the water.

SHŌNOYA TOMOHIRO 笑の屋友廣

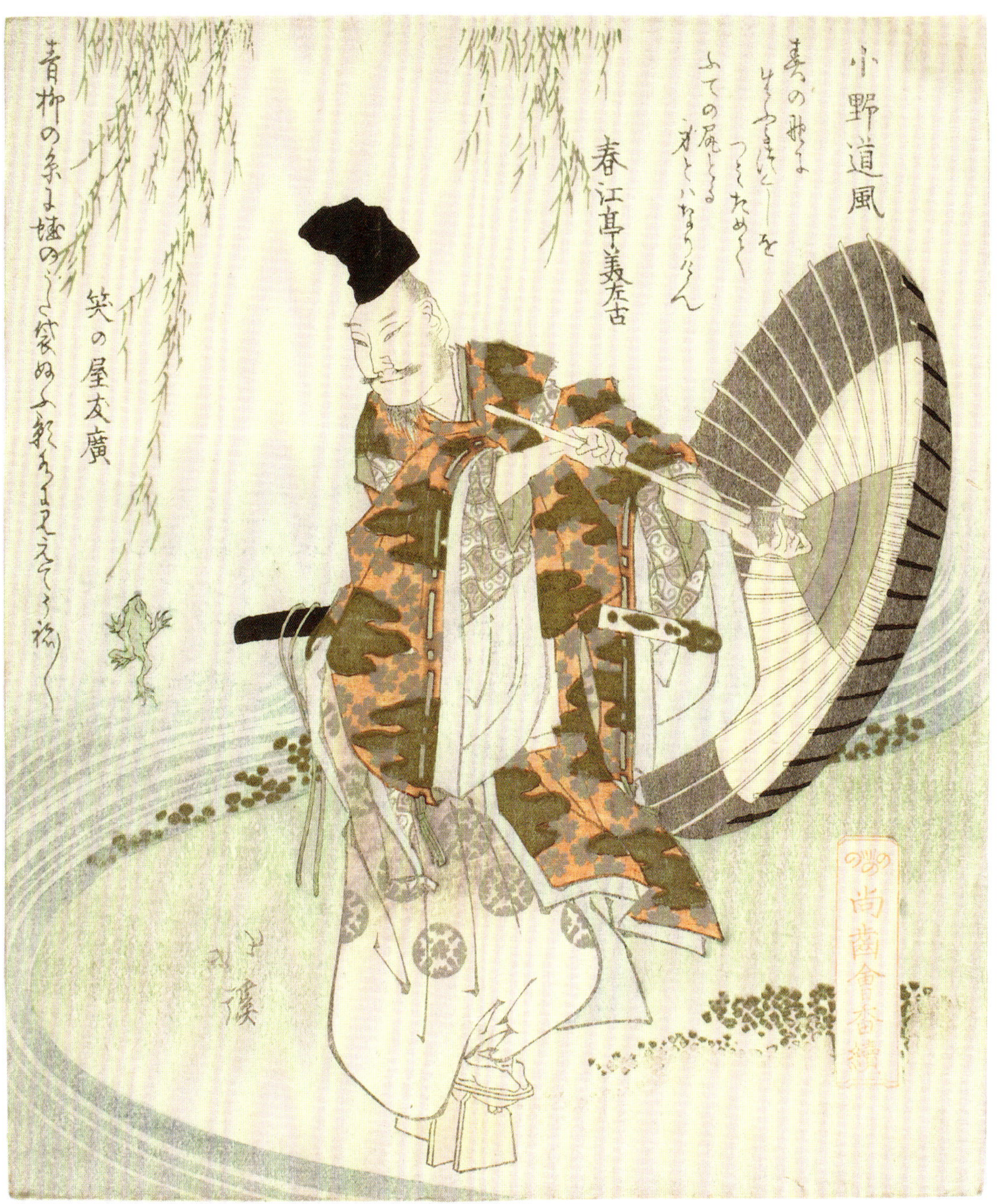

18

Henjō, who has fallen (*Henjō ware ochiniki to* 遍昭我落にきと)

Series: The Six Immortal Poets (*Rokkasen* 六歌仙)
Commissioned by the Sugawara-ren circle
UTAGAWA KUNIYASU (1794–1831) 歌川国安
Artist's signature: *Ippōsai Kuniyasu ga* 一鳳斎國安画
1820s
Colour woodblock print with metallic pigments and embossing
21.8 × 18 cm, *shikishiban* format
Presented by Mrs E. M. Allan and Mr and Mrs H. N. Spalding
from the Herbert H. Jennings Collection, EAX.4588

This *surimono* is from a series entitled 'The Six Immortal Poets' (*Rokkasen*), in which six great classical poets are represented by ordinary people engaged in various everyday activities. This is an example of *mitate*, where common people from the present were used to depict famous historical or literary figures. The group of Six Immortal Poets was selected by the tenth-century poet Ki no Tsurayuki in his preface to an imperial poetry anthology of 913, *Kokin wakashū* (A Collection of Ancient and Modern Poetry).

The young female tightrope walker in this *surimono* represents the *waka* poet and Buddhist priest Henjō (816–90). She balances precariously on the rope, holding a parasol and a fan to help her balance. She is appropriately dressed for such a demanding performance: her hair is tied back in a red hairband, she has tucked up the sleeves of her kimono and secured them with purple cords and she wears a pair of red gaiters on her legs.

The title of this *surimono* is '*Henjō, ware ochiniki to*' or 'Henjō, who has fallen'. This is a quote from one of Henjō's most famous *waka* poems, number 226 in the *Kokin wakashū*:

> 名にめてて　をれるはかりそ　をみなへし　我おちにきと人にかたるな
> *na ni medete　oreru bakari zo　ominaeshi　ware ochiniki to　hito ni kataru na*
>
> I plucked you because your name entranced me, maiden flower – please tell no-one that I have fallen.

Henjō's poem plays on the plant name *ominaeshi* or 'golden lace' (patrinia), which is written with characters that mean 'maiden flower' (女郎花). The phrase '*ware ochiniki to*' means 'I have fallen' in the sense of breaking the vows of chastity taken by the priest Henjō when he took Buddhist orders. Moreover the preface of the *Kokin wakashū* mentions that Henjō's poem was composed when he fell off his horse on catching sight of a field full of maiden flowers. The *surimono* title plays on these links between Henjō and the theme of falling, while Kuniyasu's illustration of an acrobat in real danger of falling creates another, more literal connection.

In the first poem the warbler crossing the valley is like the young woman crossing the tightrope. The second poem also includes a reference to the setting or 'falling' of the sun in the sky. The child playing with the kite in the poem is saddened as he sees it sink in the sky like the setting sun, bringing an end to his time of playtime. *Ōgidako* means a kite in the form of a fan, and in his illustration Kuniyasu portrays the acrobat carrying a fan decorated with the rays of the sun.

花かさハ
梅にさゝせて
身かるにぞ
たにわたりする
うくいすのころ

hanagasa wa
ume ni sasasete
migaruni zo
taniwatari suru
uguisu no koro

Leaving the flower umbrella at the plum tree, the warbler flies lightly across the valley in the springtime.

SAIRAIKYO 西来居

夕日をも
まねくかとミる
扇凧
にしにおつるを
をしむをさな子

yūhi omo
manekuka to miru
ōgidako
nishi ni otsuru o
oshimu osanago

A fan-shaped kite appears to invite the evening sun – it falls in the west and a small child laments.

SHAKUYAKUTEI 芍薬亭

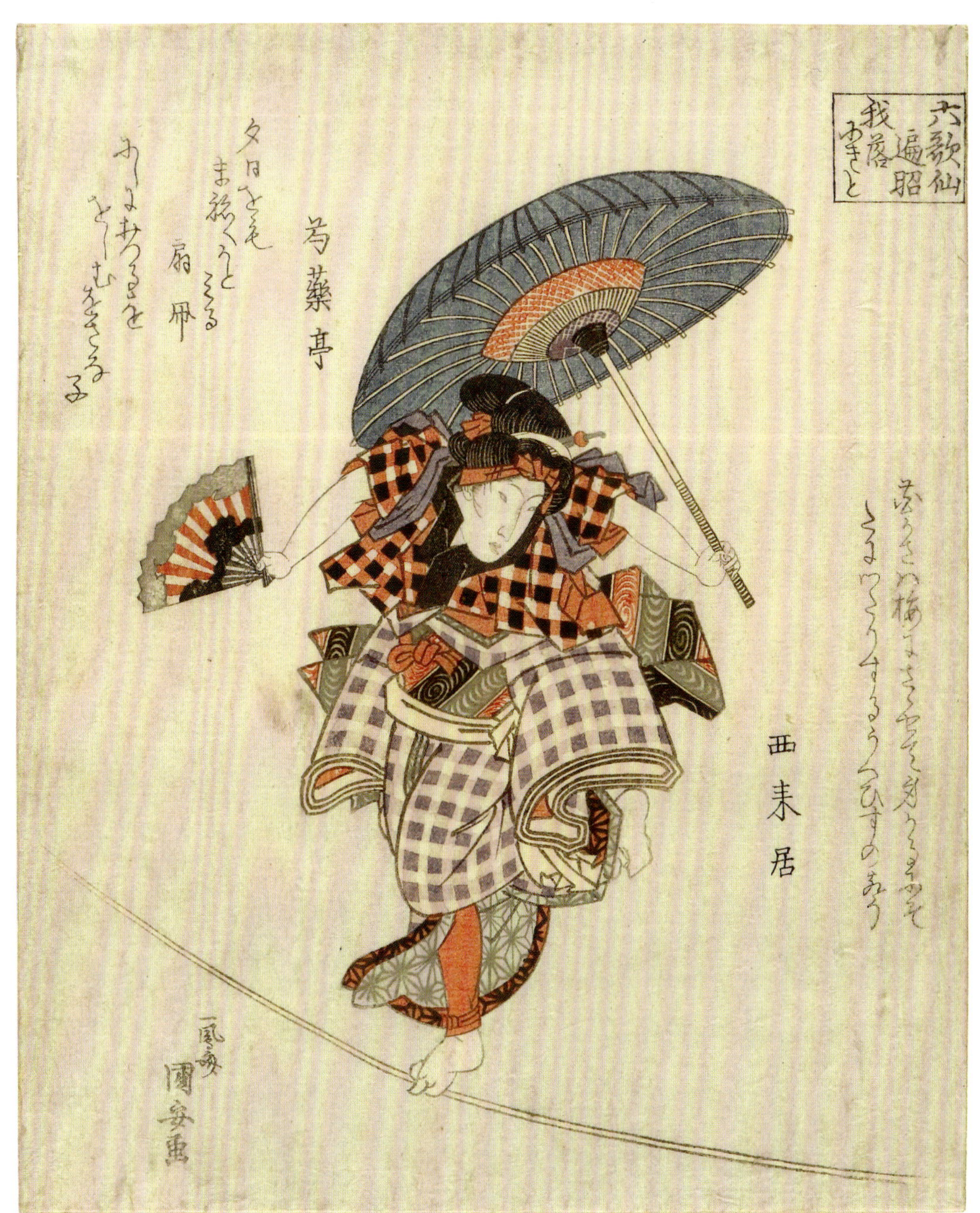

19

The Kuronushiyama festival float (黒主山)

RYŪRYŪKYO SHINSAI (active 1799–1823) 柳々居辰斎
Artist's signature: *Shinsai* 辰斎
1890s (after an original of 1820)
Colour woodblock print with metallic pigment and embossing
21.3 × 14.5 cm, *shikishiban* format
Presented by Mrs E. M. Allan and Mr and Mrs H. N. Spalding
from the Herbert H. Jennings Collection, EAX.4598

This *surimono* depicts one of the many festival floats (*yama*) paraded through the city of Kyoto every summer as part of the annual Gion Festival. The figure on the float is dressed as the ninth-century poet Ōtomo no Kuronushi, who is named as one of 'Six Immortal Poets' (*Rokkasen*) in the imperial poetry anthology *Kokin wakashū* (A Collection of Ancient and Modern Japanese Verse) of the early tenth century. In the preface to the anthology Ōtomo no Kuronushi is likened to a humble mountain woodcutter resting beneath a cherry tree; he is said to have come from Ōmi Province (modern Shiga Prefecture). Many of Kuronushi's poems demonstrate his close ties with Ōmi and nearby Shiga, and he is enshrined at Shiga. In Shinsai's image, Kuronushi is depicted as a silver-haired old man with a topknot. He holds a cane in the manner of an elegant courtier. In his left hand he holds a model of a bird, probably a type of gull known as a 'capital bird' (*miyakodori*), mentioned in the first poem. The float is decorated with cherry blossoms and pine branches, with short curtains hanging from the sides, and a pair of sacred white paper decorations called *gohei* at the front.

This *surimono* appears to have been slightly cropped. It is a reproduction of an original dating from the 1820s that bears two different poems by different poets. The two poems on this later *surimono* are obliquely linked to Kuronushi; both allude to a famous verse by Taira no Tadanori (1144–84) from the twelfth-century imperial anthology *Senzai wakashū* (Collection of a Thousand Years):

> ささなみや志賀の都は荒れにしを昔ながらの山桜かな
> *sasanami ya shiga no miyako wa arenishi o mukashinagara no yamazakura kana*
>
> The old capital at Shiga of the rippling waves has become a ruin, but the mountain cherry blossoms on Mount Nagara bloom as of old.
>
> —Taira no Tadanori Tadanori, *Senzai Wakashū,* poem no.66

The first poem on the *surimono* borrows the distinctive phrase '*sasanamiya shiga no*' from Tadanori's poem. This allusion to an older poem within a poem – instantly recognisable to educated readers – is a traditional poetic technique called '*honkadori*'. The word '*sasanami*' is an example of a 'pillow word' (*makurakotoba*), a fixed epithet used in combination with certain words as a poetic embellishment. '*Sasanami*' literally means 'rippling waves'; the term originally referred to the coastal area to the southwest of Lake Biwa in Ōmi Province, but later fell out of use. In poetry the word was always used in association with the neighbouring areas of Shiga, Ōtsu and Ōmi. '*Shiga no yamaji*' refers to mountain paths in the Shiga area that lead to the capital, Kyoto.

In the second poem the word for mountain cherry blossoms, '*yamazakura*', is also taken also from Tadanori's poem. To the poets for whom this *surimono* was made, the connection with Ōtomi no Kuronushi would have been clear just from the references to Shiga and to cherry blossom. A further witty comparison with Kuronushi is implied in the mention of a *miyakodori*, which means 'capital bird'. Although Kuronushi was raised in the rural Shiga area, he later became one of the Six Immortal Poets in the capital city of Kyoto, which was also referred to as '*miyako*'. In the same way a 'capital bird' raised in the remote mountain paths of Shiga is able to sing a song exquisite enough to be worthy of the name '*miyako*'.

さゝ波や
志賀の山路に
そたちても
歌に妙なる
都鳥

sasanami ya
shiga no yamaji ni
sodachi temo
uta ni taenaru miyakodori

Although brought up on the mountain paths at Shiga of the rippling waves – how exquisitely the capital bird sings!

KIKUNOYA NO MAGAKI 菊廼屋真垣

風高み
霞のきぬを
身におはて
寒くやあらん
山桜花

kaze takami
kasumi no kinu o
mi ni owade
samuku ya aran
yamazakurabana

In the high winds, clad not even in robes of mist, are you not cold, O mountain cherry blossom?

RYŪSAI CHIMATA 柳齋千萬多

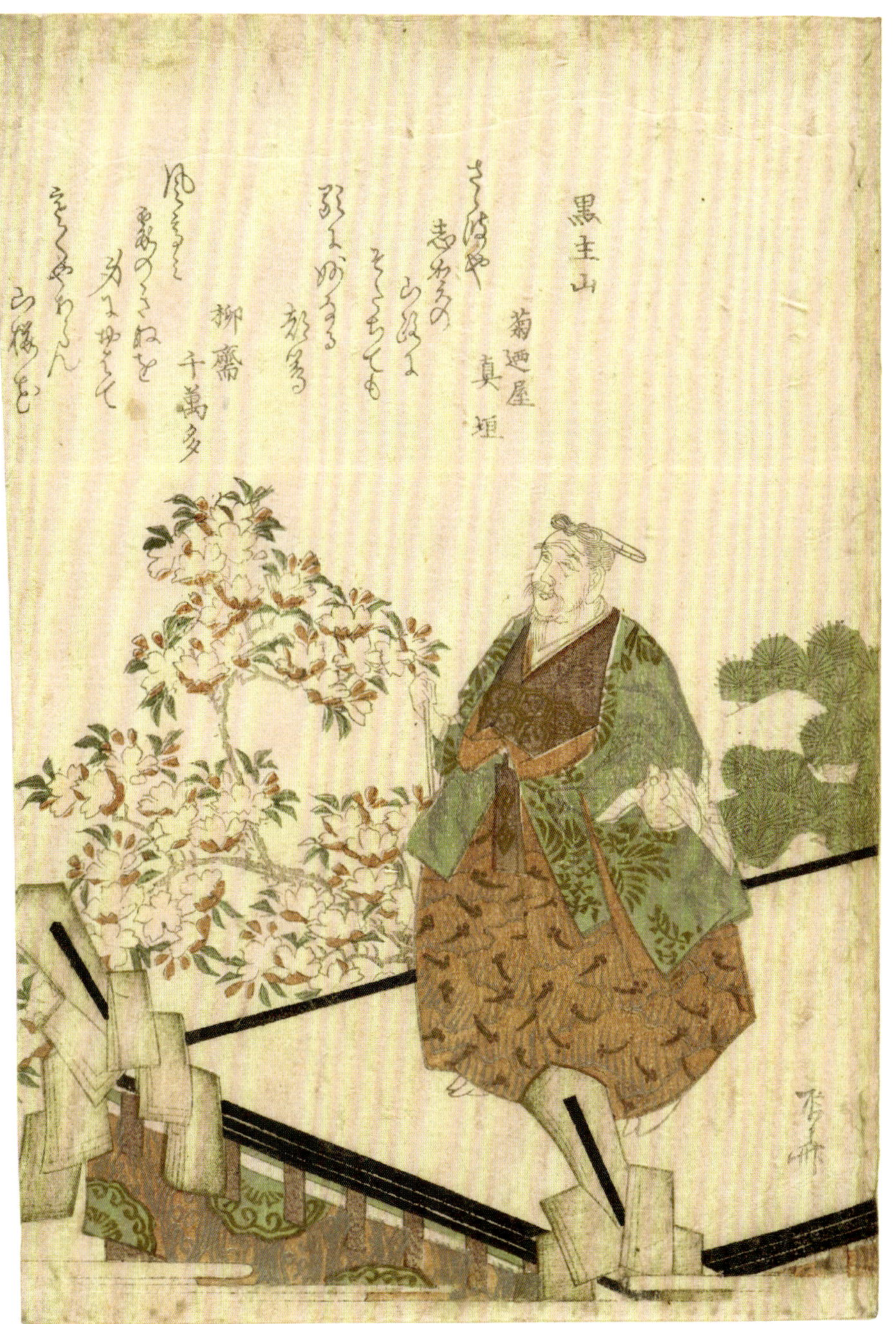

20

Genzanmi Yorimasa (源三位頼政)

Series: 'Six Immortal Warrior Poets' (*Buke Rokkasen* 武家六歌仙)
YASHIMA GAKUTEI 八島岳亭 (*c.*1786–*c.*1855)
Artist's signature: *Gakutei* 岳亭
Collector's seal: *Hayashi Tadamasa* (1853–1906) 林 忠正
Colour woodblock print with metallic pigments and embossing
*c.*1825
20.9 × 18.8 cm, *shikishiban* format
Purchased with the assistance of the Story Fund, EA2014.35

This *surimono* depicts the Heian period warrior Minamoto no Yorimasa (1104–80), of the aristocratic Genji clan. Renowned for his many feats of bravery, Yorimasa was also an accomplished *waka* poet, making him a suitable subject for a *surimono*. So highly regarded were Yorimasa's poetic accomplishments that at the age of 75 he was honoured with the court title Genzanmi or 'Minamoto of the Third Rank', and his work was collected into an anthology (*Genzanmi Yorimasa kashū*). Soon afterwards, in 1180, Yorimasa joined a rebellion to overthrow the ruling Heike clan. Although the plot was discovered and Yorimasa committed *seppuku* after defeat in the resulting Battle of Uji River, the revolt ultimately led to the fall of the Heike.

The *surimono* shows Yorimasa in his final years, with greying hair and moustache. He sits gazing into the distance, a distinguished and determined warrior. The figure is depicted on an unusually large scale, filling almost the entire picture space and so emphasising his power and strength. He wears courtly robes over his armour and a formal black headdress (*eboshi*) on his head, with a short sword at his side and arrows on his back. Lying behind him is a long sword in a protective fur bag. These accoutrements refer to episodes in Yorimasa's life, as do the two accompanying poems.

The most famous of all Yorimasa's exploits was his capture of a demon called a *nue*. This was described in *The Tale of the Heike*, the epic account of the struggle between the Heike and Genji clans for control of Japan in the late twelfth century. According to the tale, when the Emperor Konoe was troubled by a black cloud emitting eerie cries, Yorimasa shot down the demon with his bow and arrow. Overjoyed, the emperor bestowed on Yorimasa a sword named *Shishiō* or 'Lion King'. Ten years later another *nue* appeared at the palace, this time in the form of a giant bird. Again Yorimasa shot down the *nue*, this time with a whistling arrow. The delighted emperor awarded Yorimasa a robe; perhaps this is the robe Yorimasa wears over his armour in Gakutei's design. The first poem refers to a lion dance traditionally performed to celebrate the New Year, which can be linked with Yorimasa's auspicious Lion King sword. Yorimasa's name is incorporated wittily into this poem using a homonym, '*yori masa*[*n*]', meaning 'to increase'. Another pun is incorporated in the word '*naru* [*ru*]': one meaning is 'to sound' a drum; the other is 'to be accustomed to'.

The second poem alludes to Yorimasa being raised from the rank of warrior to that of courtier. 'Spring' (*haru*) is a metaphor for the granting of Yorimasa's official court rank, with the words 'on the clouds' (*kumo no ue*) referring metaphorically to the imperial court. '*Toshi no uchi ni haru*' ('spring within the year') also refers to a phenomenon of the lunar calendar in which the first day of spring falls before the year's official end.

The lavish use of gold and silver pigments in this *surimono* is typical of the work of the designer Gakutei. It has been stamped with the red circular seal of the Paris-based art dealer Hayashi Tadamasa (1853–1906).

豊さは
こそよりまさん
まふ獅子の
太鼓になるる
鳥のはつ春

yutakasa wa
kozo yori masan
mau shishi no taiko ni naruru
tori no hatsuharu

In this year, more bountiful than the last, birds become accustomed to the drumming of the New Year's lion dance.

WAHŌTEI ITONAGA 和凰亭糸長

年の内に
春ハ来にけ
ん雲の上ふみな
れしやうに見
ゆる日のあり

toshi no uchi ni
haru wa kiniken
kumo no ue
fuminareshi yōni
miyuru hi no ari

The spring will come before the year's end – it seems that the day is approaching when I may walk upon the clouds.

GORYŪEN 五柳園

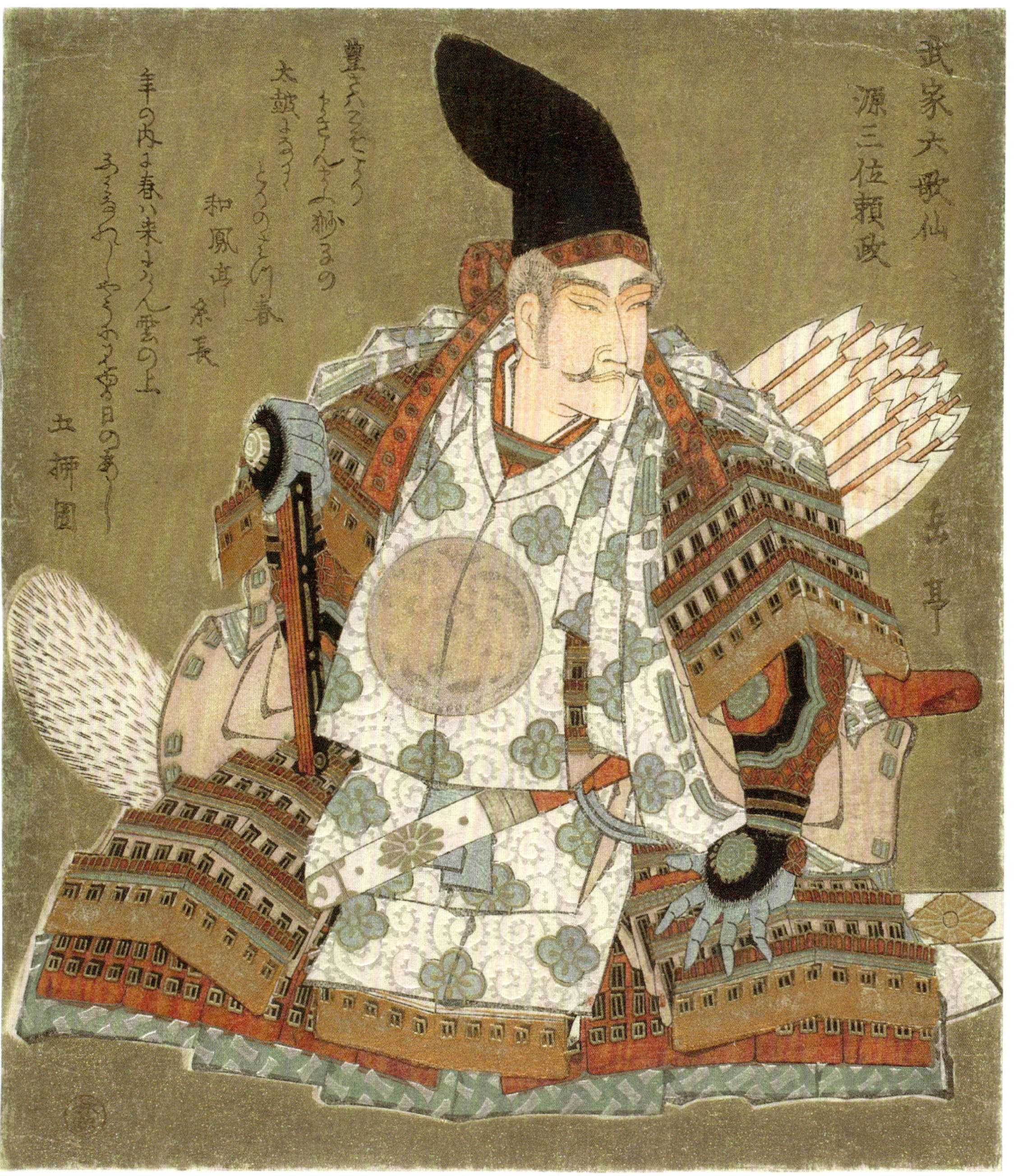

21

Dancing at Furuichi for the Hisakataya poetry circle, a pentaptych (*Hisakataya Furuichi odori* 1–5 久かた屋 古市をどり 一 ~ 五)

Commissioned by the Hisakataya-ren circle
YASHIMA GAKUTEI (*c.*1786–*c.*1855) 八島岳亭
Artist's signature: *Gakutei Sadaoka hitsu* 岳亭定岡筆
1890s (after an original of *c.*1822)
Colour, woodblock print with metallic pigment and embossing
21 × 18.6 cm (each sheet), *shikishiban* pentaptych
Presented by Mrs E. M Allan and Mr and Mrs H. N. Spalding
from the Herbert H. Jennings Collection, EA4757–4761

The entertainment district of Furuichi is located on the road to the Grand Shrine at Ise, a complex of Shinto shrines dedicated to the worship of the sun goddess Amaterasu, who is believed to dwell here. The Ise shrines became a popular pilgrimage spot in the Edo period and Furuichi developed during the early nineteenth century to cater to growing numbers of travellers *en route* to the shrine. This *surimono* shows a group of geisha from the Bizenya teahouse performing a series of dances called the Furuichi Dances (*Furuichi odori*). The geisha are dancing on one of the wooden side-stages that ran at right angles to the main stage. Blossoming cherries and pine trees are visible in the garden beyond. A man in a black *haori* overcoat dances among the geisha.

The emblem of the Bizenya was the wheel of the ox-drawn carriage traditionally used by court nobility. In Japanese this carriage is called '*gissha*' and so the tea house was also known as the Gissharō. The second poem on the second print compares Gissharō's wheel emblem to the wheels of the ox-drawn carriages often depicted in illustrations of the eleventh-century literary classic *The Tale of Genji*, thus imbuing the rollicking scene at the teahouse with elegant classical glamour. The lanterns hanging above the stage and the short curtains along the front are decorated with the same wheel emblem; so are the geishas' elegant kimonos.

The set of five prints was commissioned by the Hisakataya circle (opposite, from right to left). In the original version of this print the man's robe bears the Hisakataya emblem, and it has been suggested that this may be a humorous portrait of one of the Hisakataya poets. The figure's relaxed demeanour suggests that he has completed his pilgrimage and is now celebrating the end of a period of pious abstinence. The prints are numbered in sequence and each has two poems printed in gold onto the black background. The verses are full of allusions to spring, to dancing and to the sacred shrines nearby. The reference to Uzume in the first poem on the first print, for instance, alludes to an account in the eighth-century chronicle *Kojiki* (Records of Ancient Matters), in which the goddess Uzume danced to lure the sun goddess Amaterasu out of the cave in which she was hiding. While Amaterasu is enshrined at Ise, Uzume is enshrined at the Nagamine Shrine in Furuichi and is traditionally worshipped by dancers, singers and entertainers.

Gakutei was known for his series of multiple-sheet *surimono*.

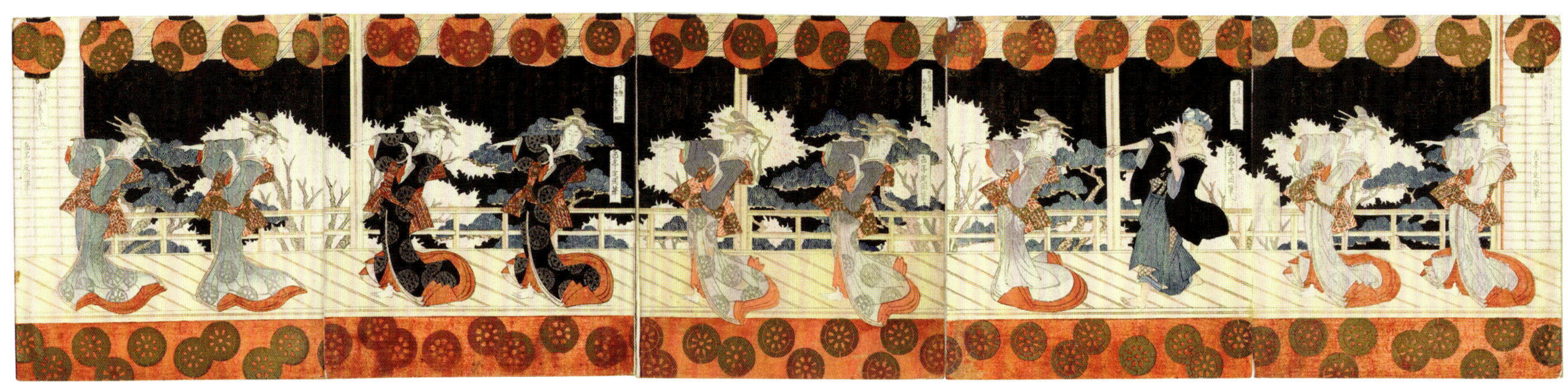

1

はる霞
ひくやうす女の
神をとり
世をふる市に
つたへとそ見る

harugasumi
hiku ya uzume no
kamiodori
yo o furuichi ni
tsutaete zo miru

The curtain of spring mist has lifted at Furuichi where the ancient dance of the goddess Uzume is still performed.

MINOGAME OSAMARU 蓑亀尾佐丸

氷きえて
みつはやみたる
宮川の
きしへにおとる
春のいろくす

kōri kiete
mizu hayamitaru
miyagawa no
kishibe ni odoru
haru no irokuzu

The ice melts; the water of the Miyagawa river flows swiftly; spring fish dance beside the bank.

HISAKATAYA 久かた屋

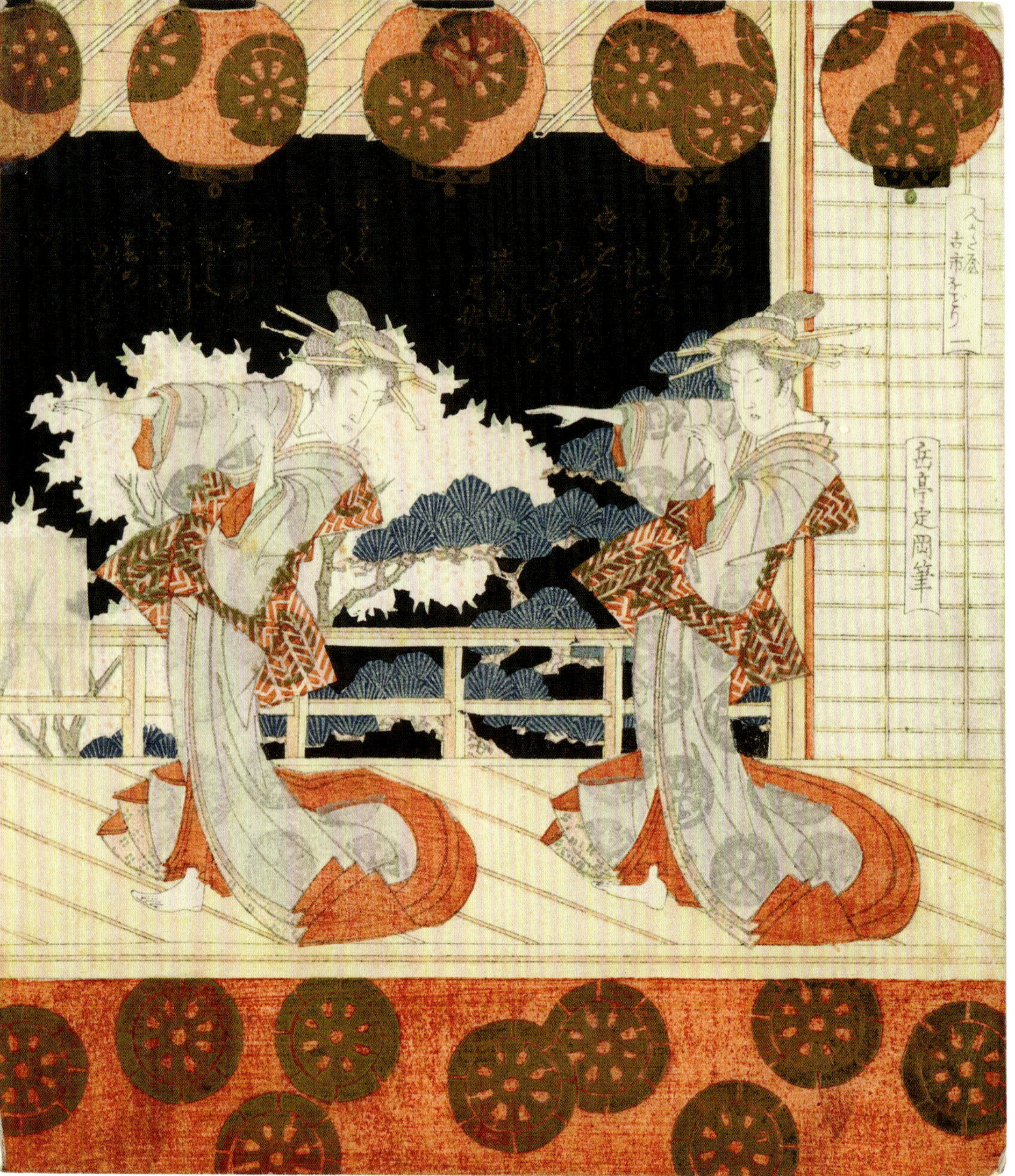

2

春風に
手ふりをみせつ
しめわらの
ふしをそろへて
調ふかと松

harukaze ni
teburi o misetsu
shimewara no
fushi o soroete
shirabu kadomatsu

The sacred rope ornament sways in the spring wind; the New Year pine decoration sings along in harmony.

AMANOYA WAKASHIBA
天の屋若芝

定紋の
幕の日の出の
かけ光る
源氏車の
春のあけほの

jōmon no
maku no hinode no
kage hikaru
genjiguruma no
haru no akebono

The emblem on the stage curtain shines like the rising sun, lighting up the ox-drawn carriage of the Shining Prince Genji at dawn in the spring.

HISAKATAYA 久かた屋

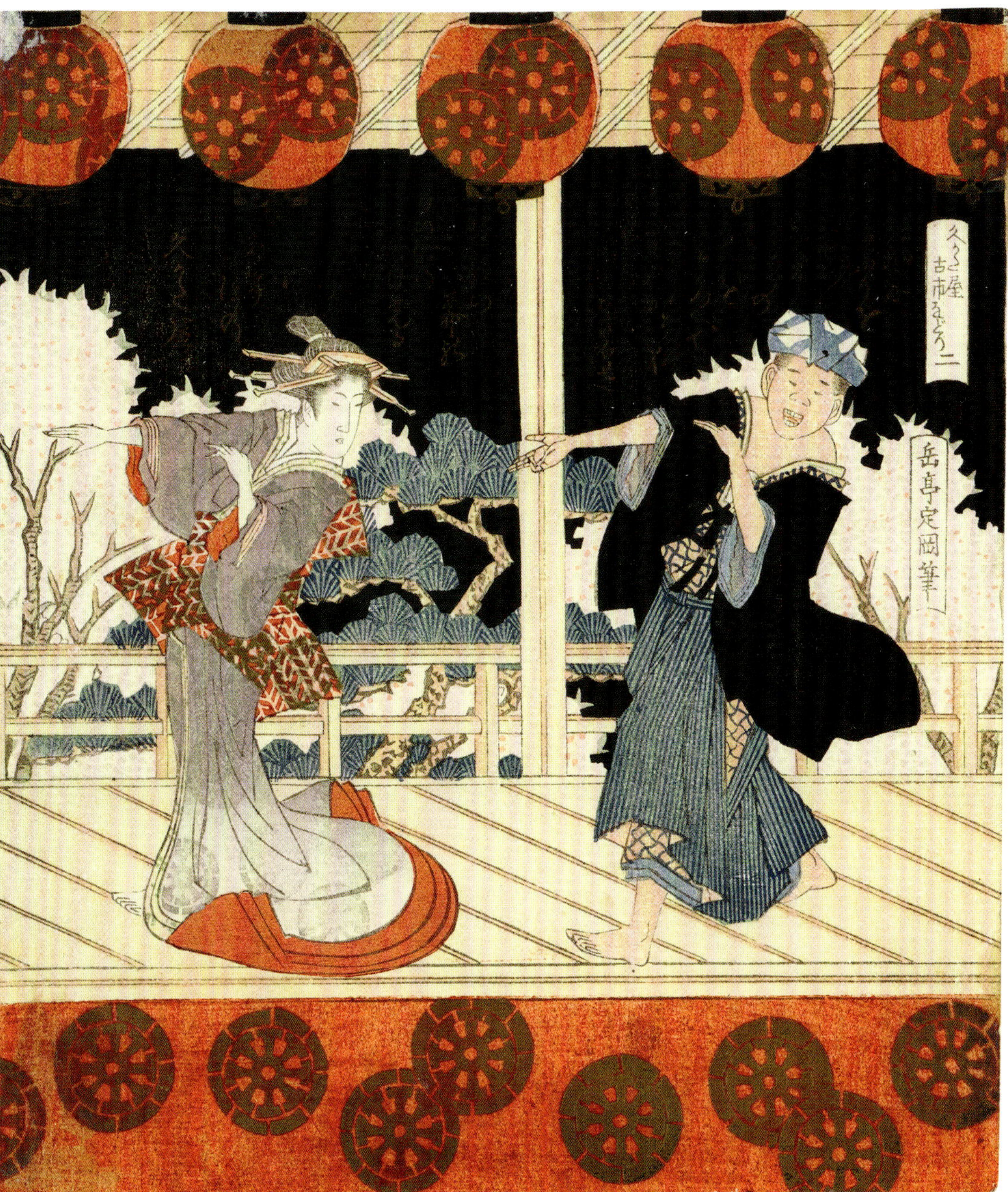

3

古市の
はるのゆうへハ
よしの山
花のすかたの
ひと目千金

furuichi no
haru no yūbe wa
yoshinoyama
hana no sugata no
hitome senkin

A spring evening at Furuichi is like Mount Yoshino – the sight of flowers in bloom is worth a thousand pieces of gold.

SUIHŌTEI KOMATSU
翠峯亭小松

手弱女ハ
をとりなからも
咲きいつる
花におとらぬ
風情ありけり

taoyame wa
odori nagara mo
sakiizuru
hana ni otoranu
fuzei arikeri

Graceful dancing maidens are as elegant as the blossoming cherry.

HISAKATAYA 久かた屋

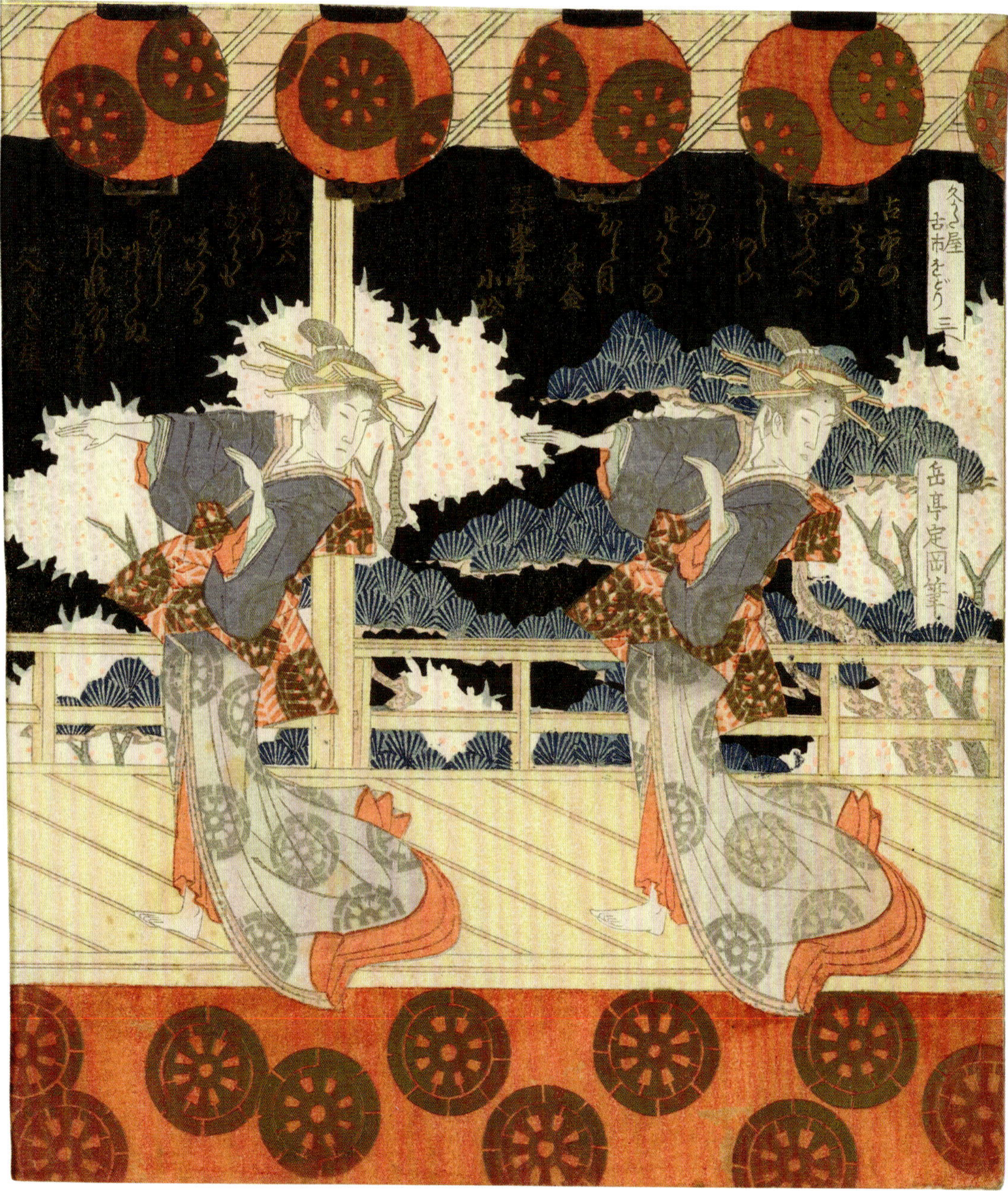

4

初日影
千はやの袖を
ふる市に
のこせし神の
おんとしるけき

hatsuhikage
chihaya no sode o
furuichi ni
nokoseshi kami no
ondo shirukeki

In the first sunrise of the New Year the white sleeves of shrine maidens wave with the ancient songs of gods passed down through the generations in Furuichi.

SAWANOYA KATSUMI
澤の屋 勝見

手弱女の
袖ふる市に
さく梅の
かわさき音頭
香におふなり

taoyame no
sode furuichi ni
sakuume no
kawasaki ondo
ka niounari

The elegant maidens wave their sleeves in the Kawasaki Dance with the scent of plum blossoms drifting in Furuichi.

HANAMITEI TOKIWA
花實亭常盤

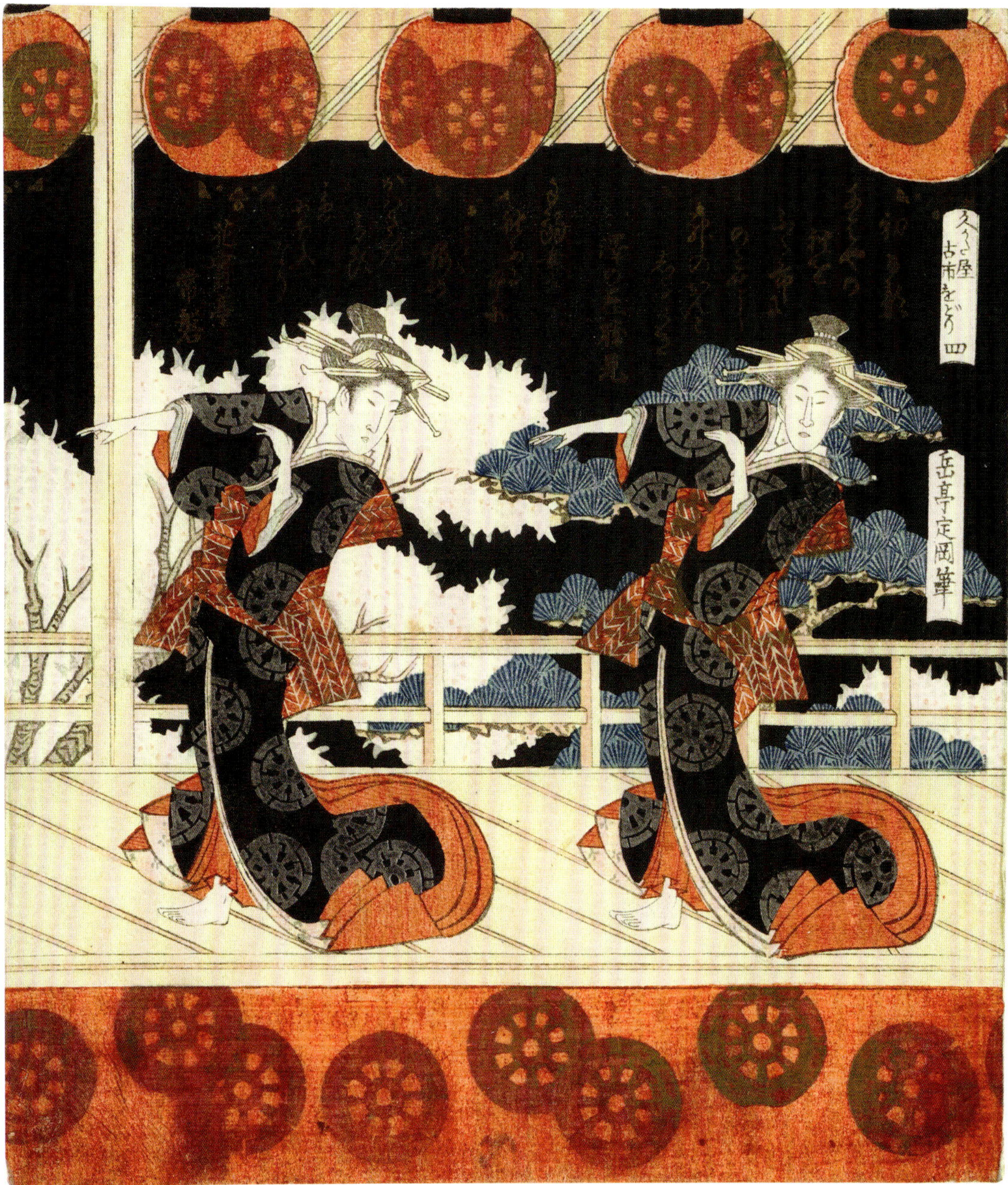

5

いとさくら
柳のいとに
雨のいと
おなし手ふりを
見する春風

itozakura
yanagi no ito ni
ame no ito
onaji teburi o
misuru harukaze

The tendrils of the weeping cherry and the weeping willow and the streaks of rain all dance in unison in the spring breeze.

SEIKAITEI KAMENDO 青海亭亀人

はる雨も
やゝふる市の
潦
ならんてをとる
軒の玉水

harusame mo
yaya furuichi no
niwatazumi
narande odoru
noki no tamamizu

The spring rain pools on the ground in Furuichi the drops of water like jewels dance along the eaves.

HISAKATAYA 久かた屋

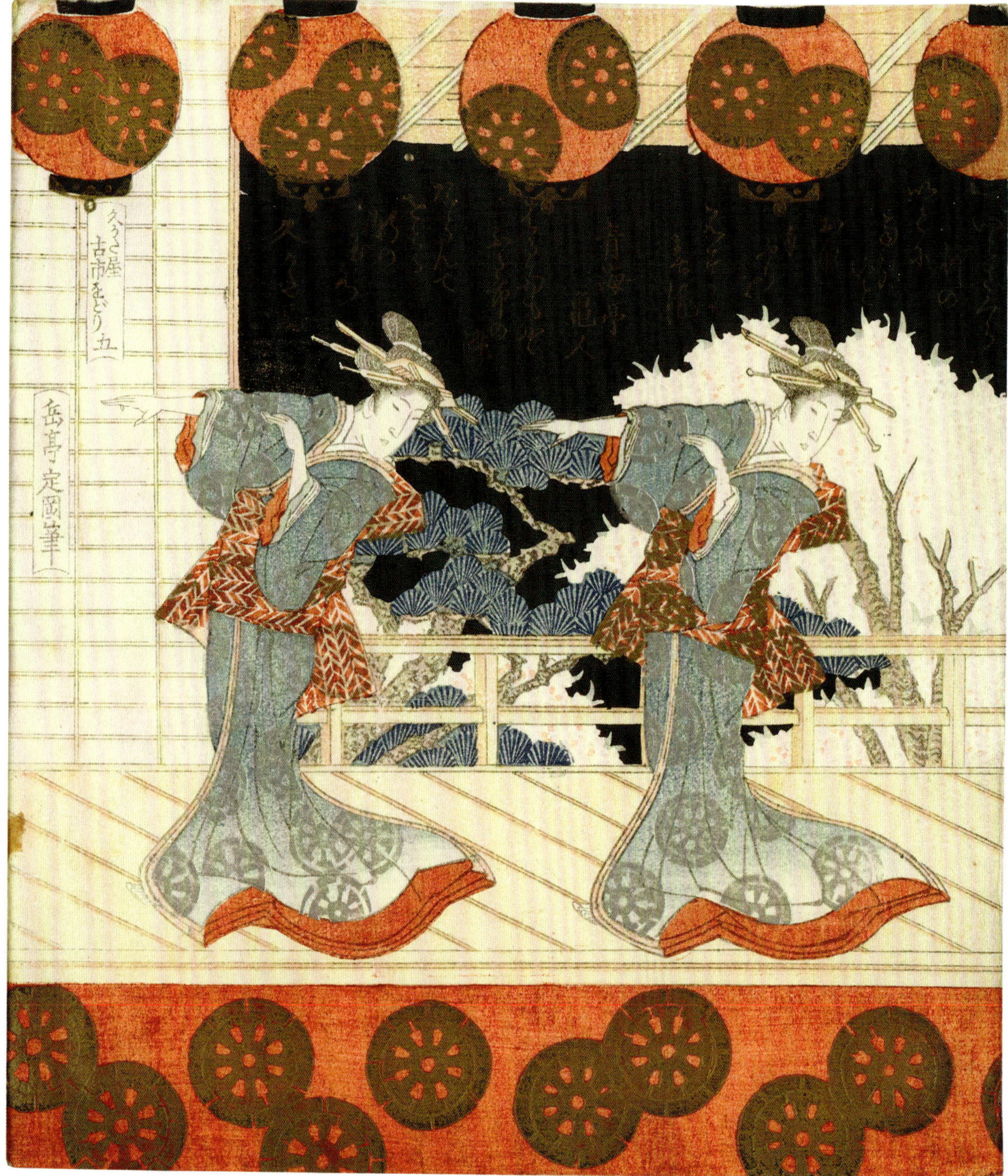

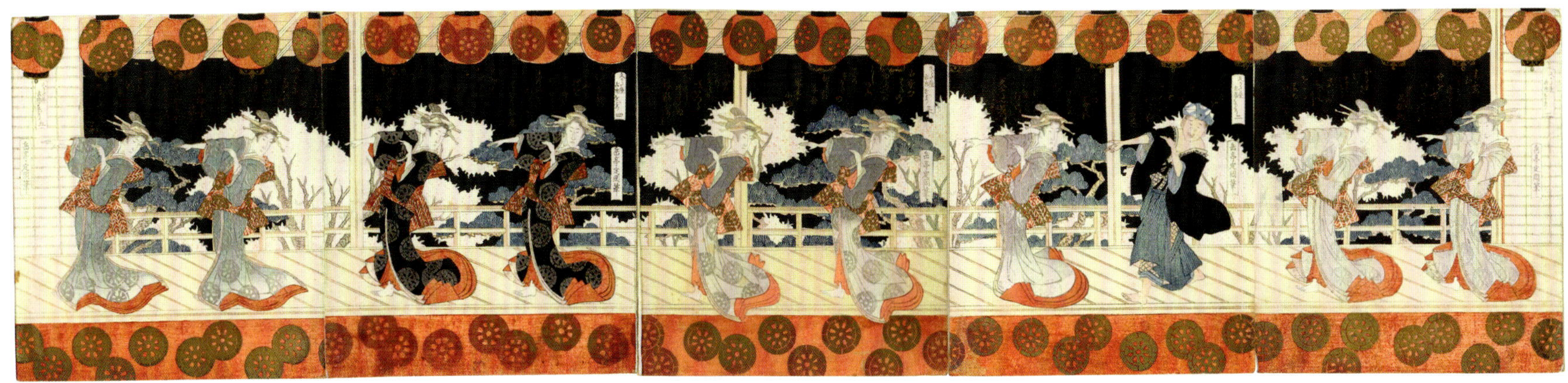

22

Two courtesans in front of a screen with Mount Fuji

Series title: All about dances (*Odori-zukushi* 踊盡)
Commissioned by the Kasumi-ren circle
KATSUSHIKA HOKUSAI (1760–1849) 葛飾北斎
Artist's signature: *Gakyōjin Hokusai ga* 画狂人北斎画
1805 or 1808
Colour woodblock print with metallic pigments
14 × 12.4 cm, originally *kokonotsugiri* format
Presented by Mrs E. M. Allan and Mr and Mrs H. N. Spalding
from the Herbert H. Jennings Collection, EAX.4580.a

This *surimono* shows two courtesans in front of a folding screen depicting Mount Fuji. The standing courtesan on the left wears a *yarō-bōshi* (rascal hat), worn by Kabuki female impersonators and a *haori* overcoat. She holds a rolled-up hanging scroll in her right sleeve and a bamboo pole in her left, for hanging up the scroll. The seated courtesan on the right wears an *age-bōshi* (hat fixed with hairpins). She holds a long pipe and picks up a portable tobacco tray containing a small brazier filled with charcoal.

The print appears to be a cropped version of an almost identical *surimono* now in the Bibliothèque Nationale in Paris. The Paris version of the print includes two *kyōka* poems on the left; it is one of seven prints in a series depicting beauties as characters in popular dances of the period. From the two *kyōka* poems on the print it is evident that the Kabuki dance represented is '*Sono omokage ninin Wankyū*' (The image of two Wankyūs). This dance tells the tragic love story of Wan'ya Kyūemon, known as Wankyū, the son of a rich Osaka merchant who became besotted with the beautiful Matsuyama, a high-ranking courtesan in the city's Shinmachi pleasure quarters. Wankyū's infatuation drew him into such a frivolous and dissipated life that his parents locked him up and he eventually went insane. In his delirium he had a vision of Matsuyama dancing before him wearing his *haori* as if she herself were Wankyū – hence the name 'two Wankyūs'. The two courtesans in the *surimono* presumably represent the lovers Wankyū and Matsuyama. Their intimate relationship is further suggested by the inclusion of a low screen, of a type typically used in the bedchamber, and by the complementary postures and costumes of the couple (one sitting, one standing; one wearing a short yellow overcoat, the other a long pinkish-brown overgarment; both holding items in each hand).

The Ashmolean version of the print has the same image, but been trimmed, removing the two *kyōka* poems and part of the pole held by the standing courtesan. Instead of the two *kyōka* poems, a single *haiku* poem has been handwritten in the remaining space on the left-hand side. This *haiku* poem includes a reference to Matsuyama, suggesting that the poet was familiar with the *kyōka* verses of the original.

The term '*hiki hajime*' in the poem relates to a tradition called '*koto hajime*' (literally 'something for the first time'). On the second day of the New Year it was customary for people to practise activities such as calligraphy, sewing and playing musical instruments for the first time. The term '*toshi no kure*' (spring before the end of the year) refers to a feature of the Japanese lunar calendar known as *nennai risshun*. *Risshun*, which falls in early February, is the first day of spring. Once every few years this day fell before the lunar New Year, when it was called *nennai risshun*. Hokusai has signed the *surimono* 'Gakyōjin Hokusai ga' (designed by the mad painter Hokusai), a signature which he only used between 1801 and 1808. It is thus possible to date this *surimono* to the *nennai risshun* year of either 1805 or 1808.

弾始
春松山や
としのくれ

hiki hajime
haru matsuyama ya
toshi no kure

A stringed instrument
first played by Matsuyama in the spring
before the ending of the old year.

KEIRAKU 恵洛

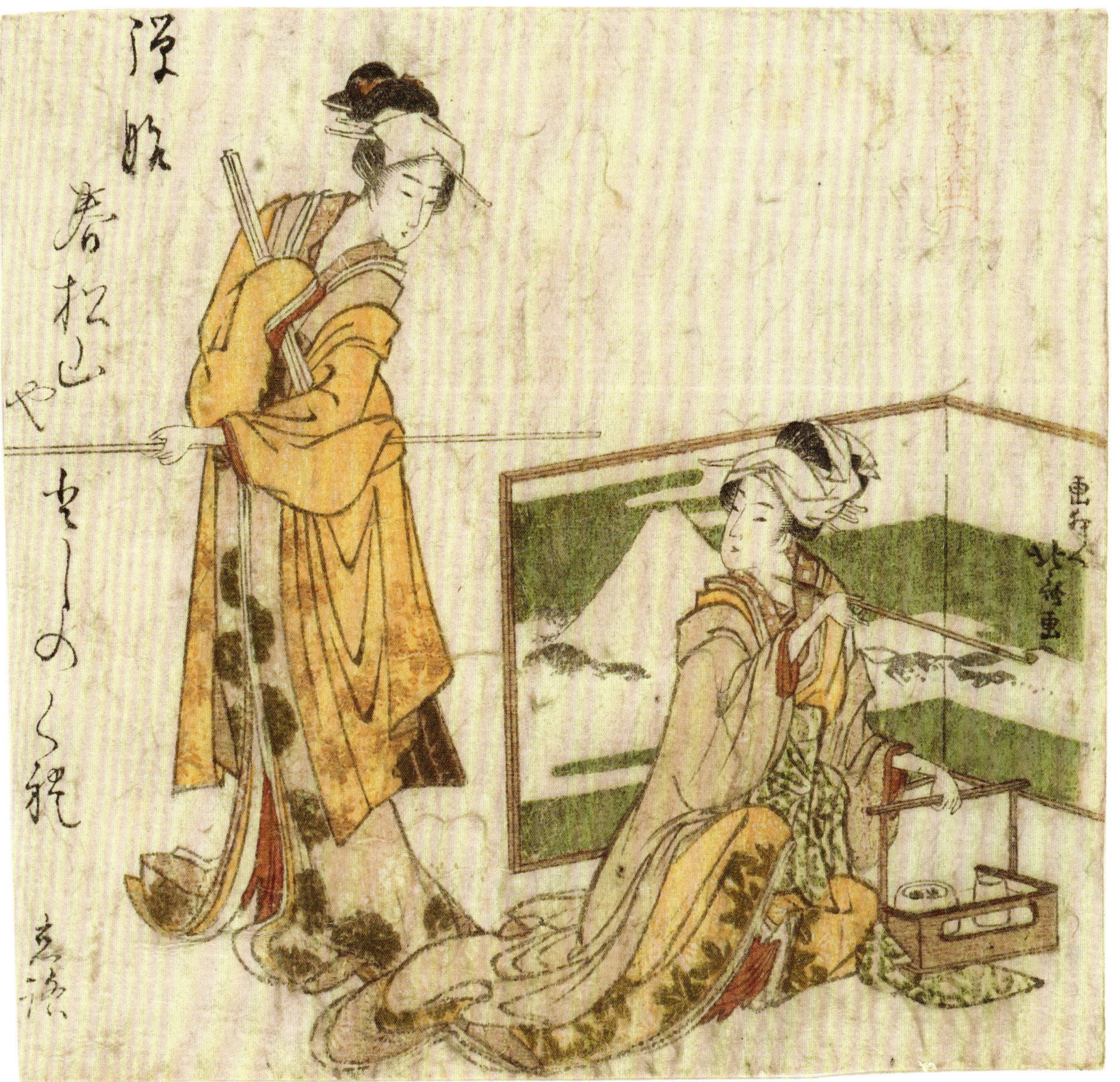

23

The Immortal Rogō (*Rogō* 盧敖)

Series: The biographies of immortals parodied by courtesans: a set of seven
(*Keisei mitate ressenden: nanaban no uchi* 傾城見立列仙伝 七番の内)
Possibly commissioned by the Tsurunoya group
YASHIMA GAKUTEI (*c.*1786-*c.*1855) 八島岳亭
Artist's signature: *Tōto Gakutei* 東都岳亭
Artist's seal: *Sadaoka* 定岡
1890s (after an original of the 1820s)
Colour woodblock print with metallic pigments
20.8 cm × 18.5 cm, *shikishiban* format
Presented by Mrs E. M. Allan and Mr and Mrs H. N. Spalding
from the Herbert H. Jennings Collection, EAX.4561

This *surimono* is one of seven prints in a series designed by Yashima Gakutei, possibly for the Tsurunoya poetry group. The series likens famous courtesans to venerated immortals of the Chinese Daoist tradition. Here the allusion is to the immortal Rogō (Lu Ao in Chinese), who is often depicted riding on the back of a turtle. Appropriately, the courtesan depicted here has a design of a long-tailed turtle on the bottom of her splendid kimono, as if she were seated on its back. From her elaborate hairstyle and the way in which her broad sash is tied at the front in a long draping style, the courtesan depicted is evidently an *oiran* (the highest-rank of courtesan) from the Yoshiwara pleasure quarters in Edo.

The long-tailed turtle is an auspicious symbol of longevity in both Japan and China. In Japan it is called a *minogame* or 'straw-raincoat turtle', referring to the tail of seaweed said to grow on the back of a turtle when it reached the age of 10,000, as if it were wearing a straw raincoat. The turtle imagery is continued in this print in the distinctive tortoiseshell pattern on the courtesan's *obi* sash and on the upper part of her kimono. This motif was typically found on the armour of the deity Bishamonten, one of the Seven Gods of Good Fortune and Buddhist guardian of the north – the direction represented by a turtle.

The sleeve of Rogō's kimono is also decorated with a stylised bird emblem. This emblem corresponds to the bird-shaped cartouche around the series title and may refer to the Tsurunoya poetry group that is thought to have commissioned the print; the '*tsuru*' in the group's name means crane. Many of the poetry groups had identifying emblems which were used as decorative motifs on the *surimono* they commissioned. Thus the decorative crane medallions on the pale blue background of the print also represent the group. The series was reprinted several times.

The turtle is associated with an ancient East Asian practice of divination (*uranai*) in which a turtle shell was heated until cracks appeared on the surface. These cracks would foretell future events. In this poem the practice is linked with personal fortune-telling techniques, by which courtesans would predict whether clients would keep their appointments. The predicted fortune was known as *urakata*; if the fortune happened as predicted it was called *uramasa*. In the poem the word *uramasa* conveys a courtesan's delight at a visitor arriving swiftly, 'just as foretold'. *Kinanshita* means 'he has arrived' in *kuruwa kotoba*, the special dialect used exclusively among courtesans of the Yoshiwara pleasure quarters in the Edo period.

The Edo artist Gakutei first studied painting under Tsutsumi Shūei (d.1814) and began designing commercial *ukiyo-e* prints around 1815. He also became a pupil of the notable *surimono* designers Hokusai and Hokkei and was an accomplished *kyōka* poet himself, studying with leading poets such as Rokujuen. In the 1820s Gakutei became one of the most prolific illustrators of *kyōka surimono*, particularly noted for his innovative use of silver and gold pigments on *shikishi* square-format *surimono*. Around 1827 he moved to the Kamigata region (Kyoto and Osaka), returning to Edo in 1834–5. On this *surimono* he uses the signature 'Toto Gakutei' or 'Gakutei of the Eastern Capital (i.e. Edo)', suggesting that he may have produced the print while he was living in Kamigata.

うちかけの
亀のうらかた
うらまさに
はやきなんした
春のまらうと

uchikake no
kame no urakata
uramasa ni
haya kinanshita
haru no marōdo

She wears a trailing robe decorated with a turtle; just as foretold, the spring visitor has arrived swiftly.

SAIKAEN CHŌCHŌSHI 菜花園蝶々子

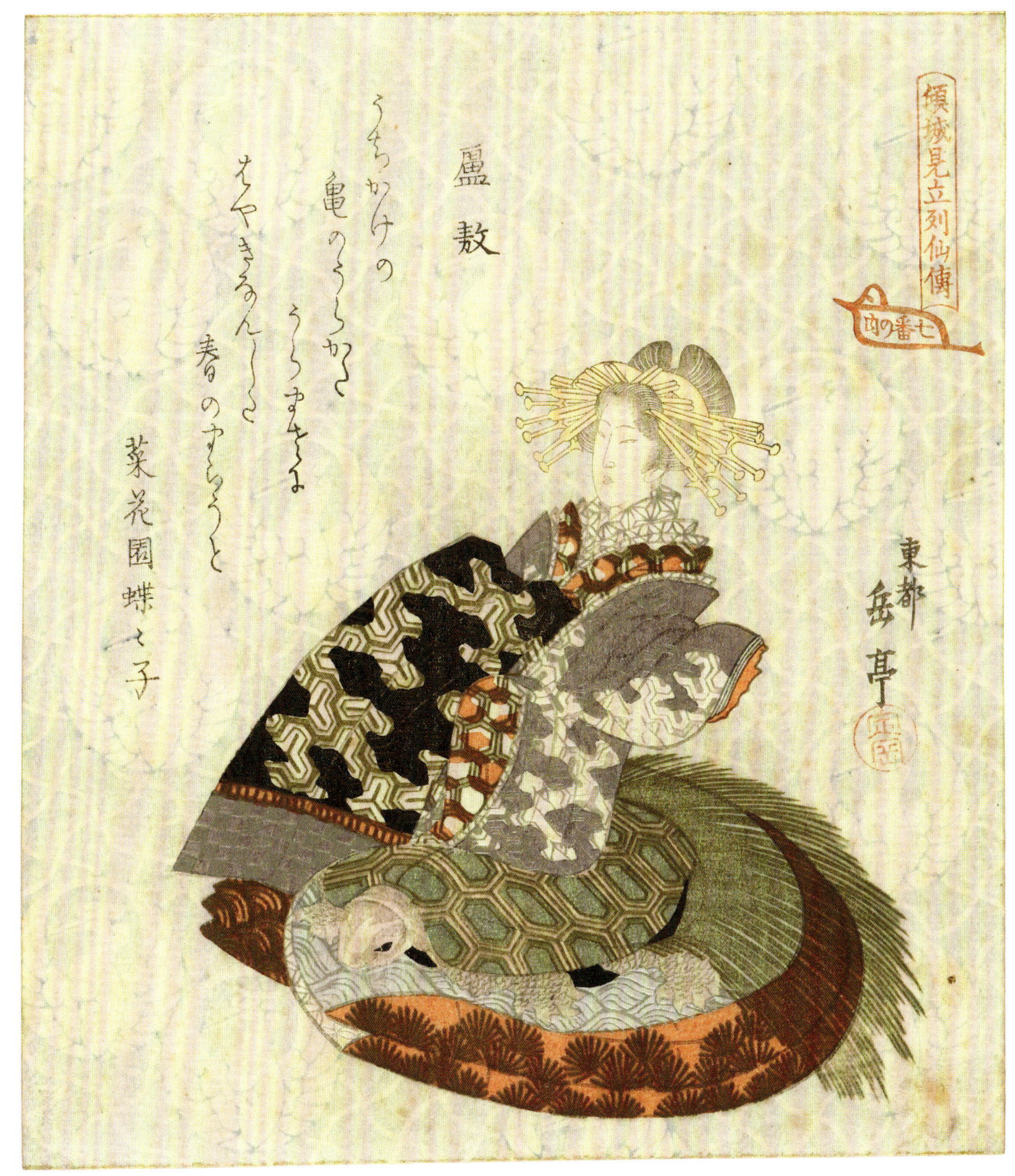

24

A courtesan dressed as the Chinese monk Kanzan

From a series depicting the costume parade of the Shinmachi Quarter in Osaka
YANAGAWA SHIGENOBU I (1787–1832) 柳川重信
Artist's seal: Yanagawa 柳川
*c.*1823
Colour woodblock print with metallic pigments and embossing
21.6 × 18.6 cm, *shikishiban* format
Presented by Mrs E. M. Allan and Mr and Mrs H. N. Spalding
from the Herbert H. Jennings Collection, EAX.4660

This untitled series of *surimono* depicts courtesans dressed up for the Nerimono Costume Parade – a festive summer event held in Shinmachi, Osaka's licensed pleasure district. In the festival, geisha and courtesans paraded in the streets, dressed as famous literary, historical or legendary figures and accompanied by musicians and dancers. The organisers of the event produced a programme listing which courtesans were playing which famous characters and set up a gallery for the entertainment of viewers.

The courtesan shown here is dressed as the legendary Chinese Zen poet Kanzan (Hanshan in Chinese). Kanzan, together with another eccentric monk called Jittoku (Shide), was a popular subject of Japanese painting, typically shown holding a scroll and with unkempt hair. The courtesan here wears a multi-layered kimono in black and white, along with a bright red undergarment. She holds an unrolled scroll and has dressed her hair to imitate Kanzan. She is portrayed turning to her left, as if looking towards her fellow eccentric Jittoku. A depiction of Jittoku from the same series is in the Chiba Art Museum. The two *surimono* may have been intended to be viewed together.

The Edo artist Yanagawa Shigenobu – the pupil and adopted son of the renowned print designer Katsushika Hokusai – started working on *surimono* and *kyōka* books in the late 1810s. He moved to Osaka for a year from 1822 to 1823, where he introduced the *shikishiban* square *surimono* format to *kyōka* circles. During his visit he produced a series of commercial *ukiyo-e* on the subject of the Nerimono Parade (entitled '*Osaka Shinmachi Nerimono*' or 'Costume Parade of the Shinmachi Pleasure Quarters'). The depictions of courtesans posing as Kanzan and Jittoku in the *ukiyo-e* series bear strong resemblance to those in the *surimono* series. Indeed Shigenobu may have based his *surimono* series on his *ukiyo-e* designs.

うつくしき
すかたにもてる
文よりも
見るもろ人に
したをまかしつ

utsukushiki
sugata ni moteru
fumi yori mo
miru morobito ni
shita o makashitsu

How gracefully the woman holds the writing scroll – much more breathtaking to see her than the scroll itself.

KINOSHITA HANAHIKO 棋下鼻彦

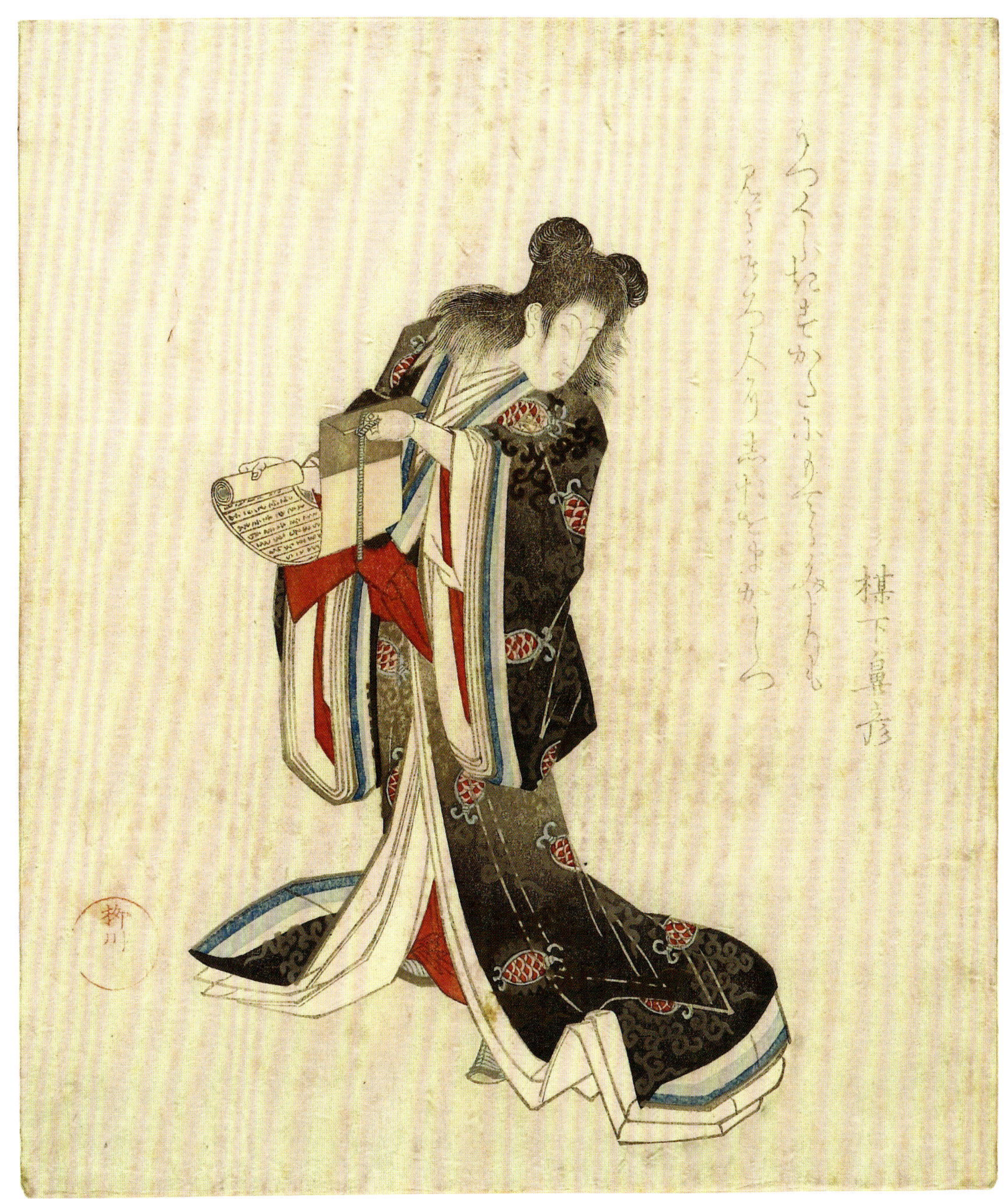

25

At the Yōrō Waterfall

KEISAI EISEN (1790–1848) 渓斎英泉
Artist's signature: *Keisai* 渓斎
1890s (after an 1820s original)
Colour woodblock print with metallic pigment
20.8 × 18.5 cm, *shikishiban* format
Presented by Mrs E. M. Allan and Mr and Mrs H. N. Spalding from the Herbert H. Jennings Collection, EAX.4611

This *surimono* illustrates the story of the Yōrō Waterfall, a tale of filial piety related in the *Jikkinshō* (Stories selected to illustrate the Ten Maxims), a mid-thirteenth century anthology of over 280 didactic tales based on Buddhist and Confucian principles. According to this tale, a poor woodcutter called Gen Jōnai from the province of Mino (modern Gifu Prefecture) worked hard every day, cutting and selling firewood so that he could buy *sake* (rice wine) to make his aged father happy. One day, when working in the mountains as usual, he discovered a waterfall that flowed not with water but with *sake*, provided by the gods who were touched by his filial devotion. Gen Jōnai filled his gourd to take back to his father. This story was reported to the capital, Nara, and an imperial envoy was sent to observe the miraculous waterfall. In the fifteenth century the story was dramatised as a Nō play entitled *Yōrō*.

In the *surimono* the waterfall, shrouded in drifting mists, provides a spectacular backdrop. The woodcutter kneels before the imperial envoy, his axe and bundle of wood, decorated with a sprig of plum blossom, placed respectfully behind him. He holds out his gourd, filled with *sake* taken from the waterfall. The courtier, dressed in full formal court costume with a voluminous black outer robe, a special court cap with a decorative band, a long train and colourful *hakama* loose trousers, listens intently to the woodcutter's tale. His attendant, however, looks incredulous.

養老の
めでたき瀧の
しら玉を
千とせの春の
数とりにせむ

yōrō no
medetaki taki no
shiratama o
chitose no haru no
kazutori ni sen

At Yōrō, the auspicious waterfall,
white gems of spray are counted in
the spring of a thousand years.

AKINOYA HISAKO, formerly KYŌJO
秋廼屋 狂女改 久子

梅の末枝に
小蝶も露を
吸筒の
ひさごにうける
養老の酒

ume no suhae ni
kochō mo tsuyu o
suizutsu no
hisago ni ukeru
yōrō no sake

At the top of a plum tree, a small
butterfly collects dew drops in a
gourd bottle – Yōrō *sake.*

SHŪCHŌDŌ MONOYANA
秋長堂物簗

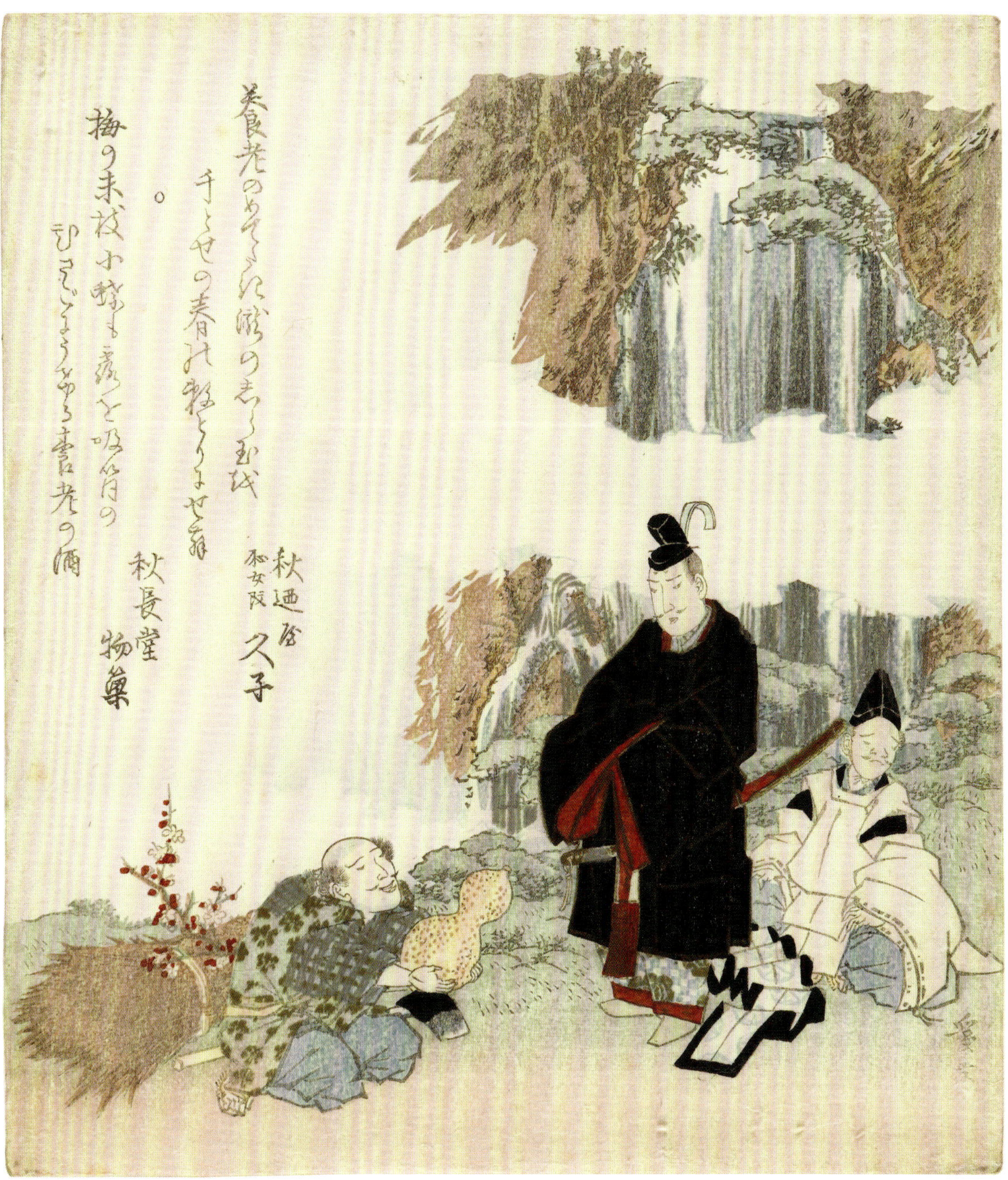

26

Rochishin (*Lu Zhishen* 魯知深)

Series: Five Elements of the Water Margin: Wood (*Suiko gogyō moku* 水滸五行木)
Commissioned by the Hanazono-ren circle
TOTOYA HOKKEI (1780–1850) 魚屋北渓
Artist's signature: *Go Hokkei* 呉北渓
*c.*1890s (after an original of the early 1830s)
Colour woodblock print with metallic pigments and embossing
21.1 × 17.9 cm, *shikishiban* format
Presented by Mrs E. M. Allan and Mr and Mrs H. N. Spalding
from the Herbert H. Jennings Collection, EAX.4722

This *surimono* is one of a set of five prints from a series entitled 'Five Elements of *The Water Margin*' (*Suiko gogyō*). The series links the five elements of Chinese philosophy (wood, fire, earth, metal and water) with characters from the fourteenth-century Chinese novel *The Water Margin* (*Shuihu zhuan*, or *Suikoden* in Japanese). The novel, considered one of the four great classical novels of Chinese literature, relates the exploits of a group of Robin Hood-like outlaws on Mount Liang in eastern China. It was first translated into Japanese in the mid-eighteenth century and a hugely successful Japanese version of 1805, written by Takizawa Bakin (1767–1848) with illustrations by Hokusai, spurred a *Suikoden* craze in the early nineteenth century.

The five elements played a major role in Chinese astrology, medicine and philosophy. The hero Rochishin (Lu Zhishen in Chinese) is associated with wood from an episode in which he uproots a willow tree with his bare hands in order to drive away some noisy nesting crows. The artist Hokkei, a student of Hokusai's and a prolific *surimono* designer, recreates the scene here. Rochishin was nicknamed *'Kaoshō'* or the 'Flowery Monk' because of the flower tattoos on his body, and Hokkei has covered the hero's back and upper arms with magnificent blue cherry blossom tattoos. Behind Rochishin an orange cloth bag containing his personal belongings is attached to his thick wooden monk's staff. He carries a short sword at his waist, decorated with red cross-shaped straps. These straps echo the cross formed by the trunk of the willow tree and the wooden staff. The strong diagonals within the composition serve to emphasise Rochishin's strength and vigour.

This *surimono* design is thought to have originated in the 1830s. It was commissioned by the poet Garyūen Umemaro (1793–1859) of the Hanazono-ren (Flower Garden circle), a sub-division of the Yomo-gawa group. Several later versions also exist, of which the Ashmolean's print is one. As *surimono* texts and images were usually carved onto separate blocks, it was relatively simple to replace either poem or image. The Ashmolean's *surimono* was produced from completely re-cut blocks around 1890, and details of both text and image differ from the original.

春風の
ちからためしや
いさましく
柳をゆする
梅の花和尚

harukaze no
chikara dameshi ya
isamashiku
yanagi o yusuru
ume no kaoshō

How powerful the Flowery Monk as he shakes the willow tree – as strong as the spring wind!

KACHŌYA NORIYASU of Shigaraki in Gōshū
江州信楽 花鳥屋乗康

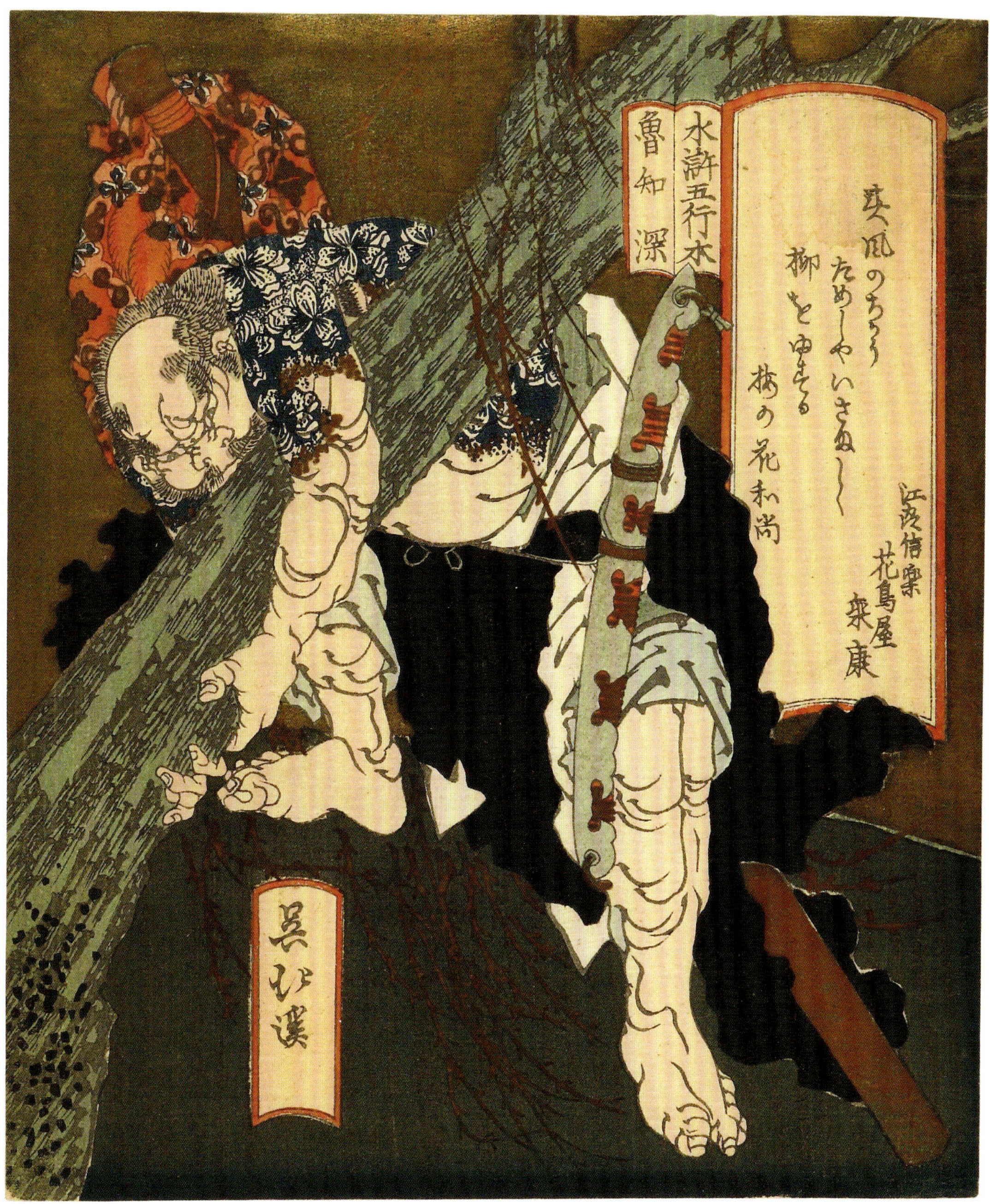

27

The Palace of the Moon

Commissioned by the Shippō-ren circle
TOTOYA HOKKEI (1780-1850) 魚屋北渓
Artist's signature: *Hokkei* 北渓
1831
Colour woodblock print with metallic pigments and embossing on paper
42.6 × 18 cm, *shikishiban* vertical diptych
Presented by Mrs E. M. Allan and Mr and Mrs H. N. Spalding
from the Herbert H. Jennings Collection, EAX.4571

This lavishly printed, double-sized *surimono* shows two Chinese figures standing amidst clouds outside the Palace of the Moon. References in the two poems to an elixir of longevity and a loving couple confirm that the subject of the *surimono* is a scene from the tragic Chinese love story of the Tang Emperor Xuanzong (Gensō in Japanese) and his favourite consort Yang Guifei (Yōkihi). The tale relates how the emperor's negligence of state affairs because of his infatuation with Yōkihi sparks a rebellion, during which Yōkihi is put to death. The grief-stricken emperor sends a Daoist magician to search for her soul in the land of immortals and to pass on a message of his undying love for her. When the magician finds Yōkihi she promises to meet the emperor in the afterlife, when she will play music and dance for him as she had done on earth.

This story was perhaps most famously told in 806 by the great Tang poet Bai Juyi (772–846) in his classic narrative poem 'The Song of Everlasting Sorrow' (*Chang hen ge,* or *Chōgonka* in Japanese). It also became the subject of numerous poems, novels and plays. The legend was enormously popular in Japan after it was first introduced in the ninth century. It was famously mentioned in the early eleventh-century *The Tale of Genji* and subsequently retold many times in paintings and woodblock-printed books, as well as in Nō, Kabuki and puppet plays. The work would certainly have been familiar to the cultivated members of *kyōka* poetry groups.

The *surimono* depicts the Daoist magician meeting Yōkihi at the Palace of the Moon, where the couple will be reunited after the emperor's death. The magician points towards the entrance of the palace and the celestial staircase he has conjured up for the emperor to use. Yōkihi bears a bag on her back in which she carries a zither, with which she entertained the emperor during her lifetime. In her left hand she holds a silver cup, presumably filled with the elixir of long life referred to in the first poem. The word '*chōsei*' means 'longevity'; it also formed the name of the Chōseiden Palace in which Emperor Gensō lived with Yōkihi (literally 'Palace of Longevity'). The first poem links the 'elixir of immortality' with a type of spicy *sake* called *toso,* made from various medicinal herbs and traditionally served in Japan at the New Year to toast the good health and happiness of family and friends.

This *surimono* was commissioned by the Shippō-ren poetry circle, affiliated to the Go-gawa group. The Shippō-ren poets' emblem of four interlocking circles is used as a motif on Yōkihi's red overgarment. The *surimono* was commissioned in 1831, the Year of the Rabbit. In Japanese folklore the rabbit is closely associated with the moon, where the moon rabbit is said to abide; in this image the young woman at the gate of the palace holds a moon rabbit in her arms. In the second poem the word '*mutsumaji*', which means 'harmonious' or 'friendly', is also associated with a poetic name for the first month of the year (*mutsuki*). Traditionally the contents of the first dream of the New Year (*hatsuyume*) would foretell the luck of the dreamer in the year to come.

長生の
薬にとその
さかつきを
我にも値
千金の春

chōsei no
kusuri ni toso no
sakazuki o
ware nimo atai
senkin no haru

Give me a cup of New Year's *sake* as an elixir of longevity – this spring is worth a thousand pieces of gold.

KAGENDŌ TSUGIHO 花源洞継穗

夫婦中
むつまし月の
はつ夢に
みるもめてたき
宮殿楼閣

meoto naka
mutsumajizuki no
hatsuyume ni
miru mo medetaki
kyūden rōkaku

A loving couple is fortunate to see the auspicious towers of the Moon Palace, in their first dream of the first month of the year.

SEIYŌKAN UMEYO 青陽館梅世

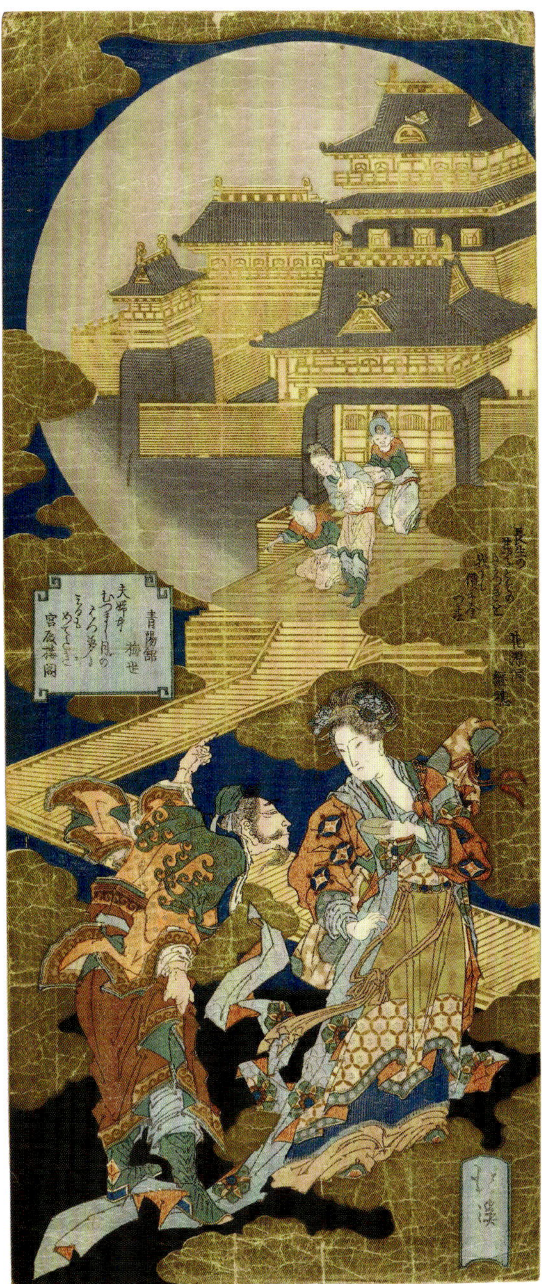

28

Left: A Daoist sage with a tiger
Right: Benten with a dragon, playing the *koto*

Series title: Two Prints: Dragon and Tiger (*Ryūko niban* 竜虎二番)
Commissioned by the Go-gawa group
YASHIMA GAKUTEI (*c.*1786–*c.*1855) 八島岳亭
Artist's signature: *Yashima Gakutei* 八島岳亭
*c.*1820
Colour woodblock print with metallic pigments and embossing
21 × 18.8 cm (left) and 20.7 × 18 cm (right), *shikishiban* format
Presented by Mrs E. M. Allan and Mr and Mrs H. N. Spalding
from the Herbert H. Jennings Collection, EAX.4781, EAX.4780

This pair of *surimono* shows two figures from Chinese mythology with their associated animals. On the right Benten, goddess of music and the arts, sits beneath a pine tree encircled by an enormous dragon. On the left, next to two bamboos, stands a Daoist sage with a tiger. The prints were commissioned by the Go-gawa group and the print title is framed within a cartouche in the form of the Go-gawa group's emblem – a stylised character five (五, pronounced '*go*'). The group was headed by the poet Rokujuen, who composed the second poem in each *surimono*.

A well-known scholar of Japanese classics and Chinese popular novels, Rokujuen was the poetry teacher of the artist Yashima Gakutei, who designed the prints. Gakutei cleverly created the two prints to stand as independent designs, but also to work as a pair when viewed together, visually united by the way in which the landscape elements (the rocks, bamboo leaves and the band of mist in the foreground) continue across the two prints. The two compositions are beautifully balanced. The sage and goddess face towards each other, their gazes lowered, one standing, one sitting; the dragon and tiger, their heads at the same level, stare intensely into each other's eyes; and the bamboo on the left counterbalances the pine tree on the right.

The visual pairing of tigers and dragons has a long history in East Asia, with both creatures said to represent power. Each direction of the compass is traditionally believed to be ruled by a celestial animal: the tiger is associated with the West, the dragon with the East. The pairing of a tiger and a dragon was considered well balanced, with tigers existing in the real world and dragons in the imaginary. In the Chinese *yin–yang* (negative–positive) principle found in Daoist belief, the tiger represents the male element and the dragon the female. Both creatures also have strong Buddhist associations.

The goddess Benten, or Benzaiten, who originated from the Hindu goddess Saraswati, was revered as the goddess of knowledge, music, arts and wisdom, as well as of water. The worship of Benten was brought to Japan from China in the sixth century, along with Buddhism. In Japan she became one of the Seven Gods of Good Fortune (*Shichifukujin*), emphasising her role in bestowing wealth, and was one of the most popular deities of the Edo period. Associated with snakes and dragons (often conflated in Japan), Benten is usually depicted holding a *biwa*, a musical instrument resembling a lute. Here she plays a type of one-stringed zither known as an *ichigenkin*. The goddess is seated on a mossy rock, her feet resting on a stool carved out of rock.

The Daoist sage on the left has a Chinese hairstyle and wears a voluminous robe. Probably intended to be a Chinese garment, in fact it includes a number of Japanese features, such as the tassels and all-over pattern of a stylised lion's mane. In his left hand the sage holds a military leader's fan, a symbol of power and dignity; his right hand rests on the tiger he has tamed. The tiger is depicted humorously, with stylised stripes and a wry expression that echoes that of the sage. It is likely that the artist Gakutei had never seen a real tiger, instead borrowing an image from an illustrated book or painting to create his own imaginary

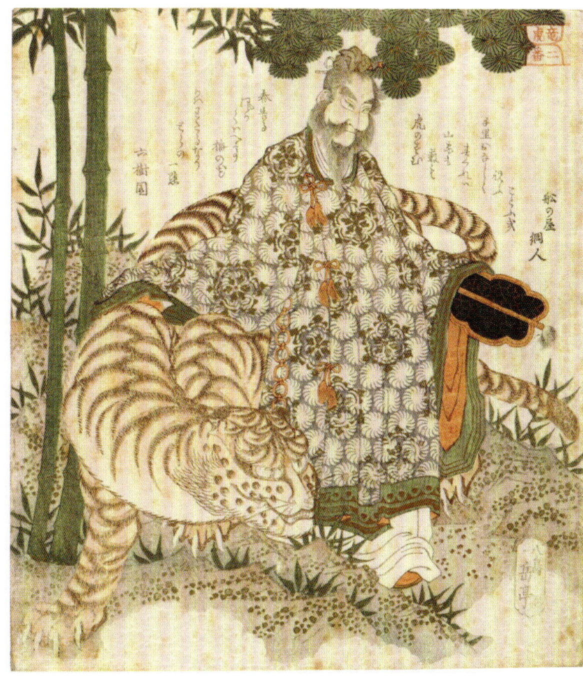

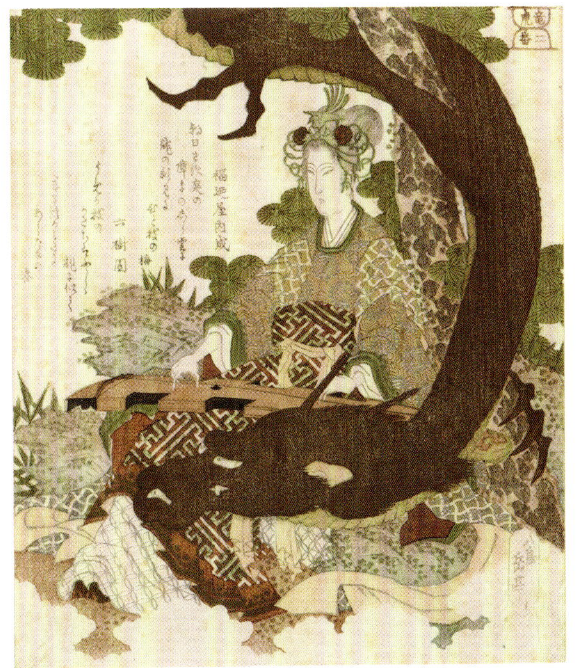

version. In Japan the tiger is usually depicted against a background of bamboo, whereas in China and Korea it is often shown with pine trees.

The poems link typical spring themes with dragon and tiger imagery. The second poem of the Benten print puns on the word '*tama*' or jewel. This refers not only to the wish-fulfilling jewel that is the traditional attribute of the dragon (and therefore associated too with Benten), but also the term '*aratama*' – a conventional poetic epithet or 'pillow word' (*makurakotoba*) used to refer to the spring. The expression '*tora no itten*' in the second poem in the Daoist sage print is an expression of time. In Japan time was traditionally measured by water clock, with a day being divided into twelve two-hour sections, each represented by a zodiac animal. Each section was then subdivided into four periods of 30 minutes, the first of which was called *itten*. The hour of the tiger (*tora*) is at 4 am and so '*tora no itten*' was around 4.30 am.

Pine and bamboo are two of the trio of plants traditionally known in East Asia as the 'three friends of winter', because they flourish in the cold weather. The third 'friend' is the plum, not depicted in the print but present in three of the four poems.

虎のすむ
藪も山家も
春くれハ
千里おなしく
祝うことふき

tora no sumu
yabu mo yamaga mo
haru kureba
senri onajiku
iwau kotobuki

The bamboo forests where tigers stalk and the mountain villages where people reside are a thousand leagues apart, but when spring comes all begin the celebration of long life.

FUNANOYA TUNAHITO
船の屋 綱人

春告る
風かくハえて
梅の花
かハわたるなり
とらの一點

haru tsugeru
kaze ga kuwaete
ume no hana
ka wa watarunari
tora no itten

The wind announces the arrival of spring, carrying the plum blossom – fragrance spreads at the break of dawn.

ROKUJUEN 六樹園

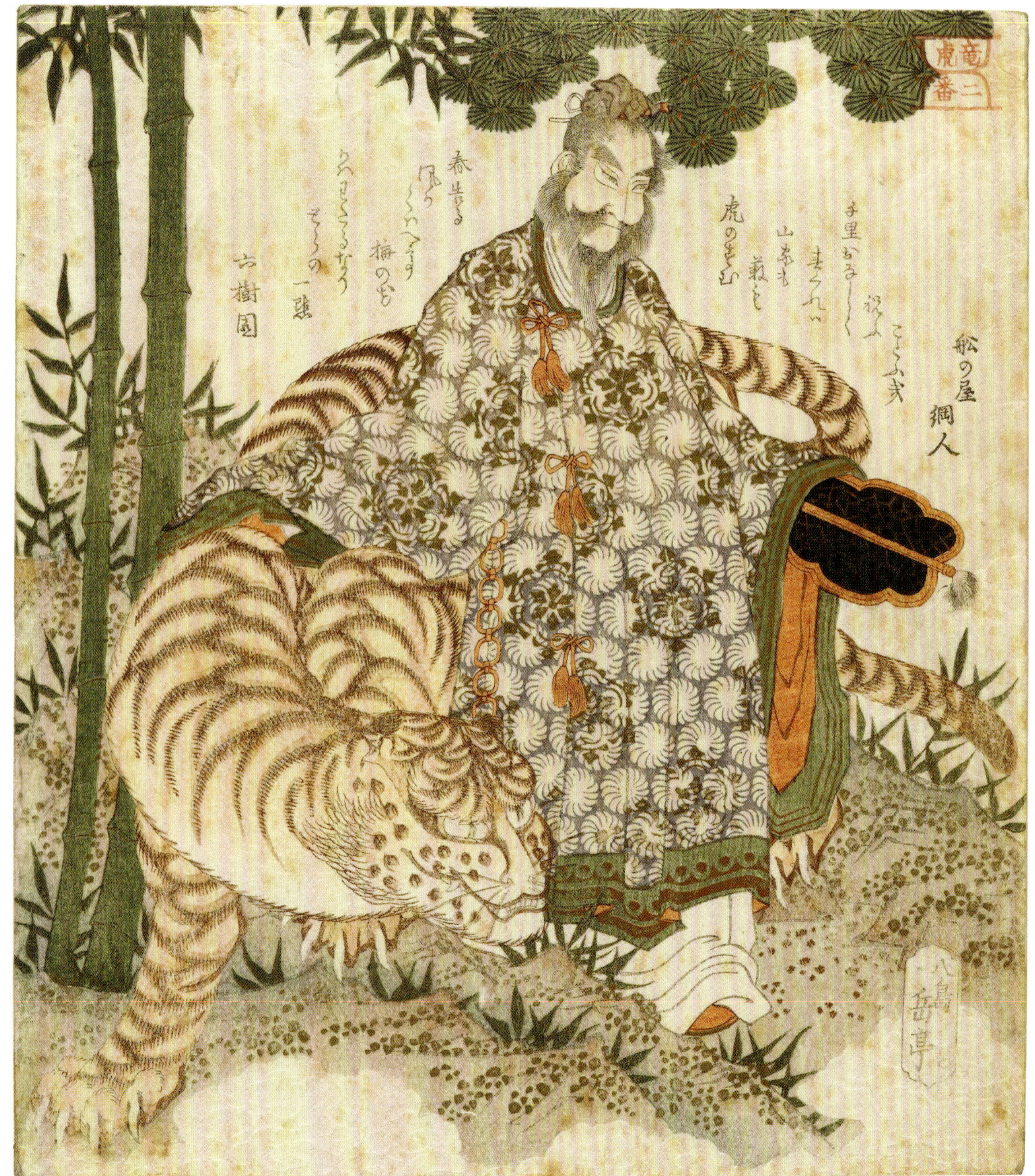

朝日さす
庭の障子の
しら雲に
龍の影見る
ひと枝の梅

asahi sasu
niwa no shōji no
shirakumo ni
ryū no kage miru
hitoeda no ume

The branch of a plum tree in the garden, illuminated by the morning sun, creates the silhouette of a dragon in clouds on the white paper of a sliding door.

FUKUNOYA UCHINARI 福廼屋内成

うめか枝の
かたちけふしる
龍に似て
手につかみたる
あらたまの春

umegae no
katachi kyō shiru
ryū ni nite
te ni tsukamitaru
aratama no haru

Today I saw the branch of a plum tree in the shape of a dragon holding a wish-fulfilling jewel in its claws; I too wish to grasp a lucky jewel for the New Year.

ROKUJUEN 六樹園

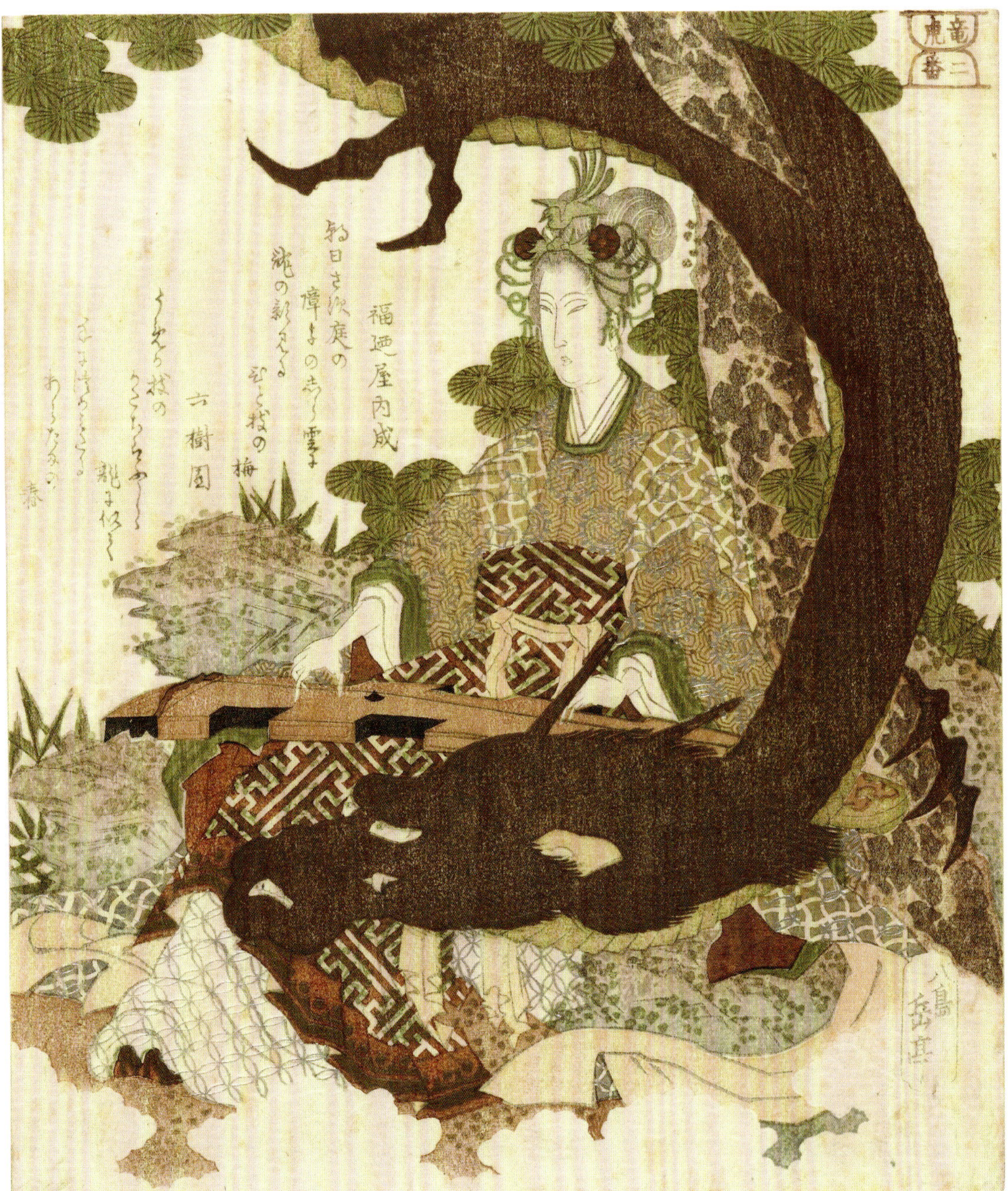

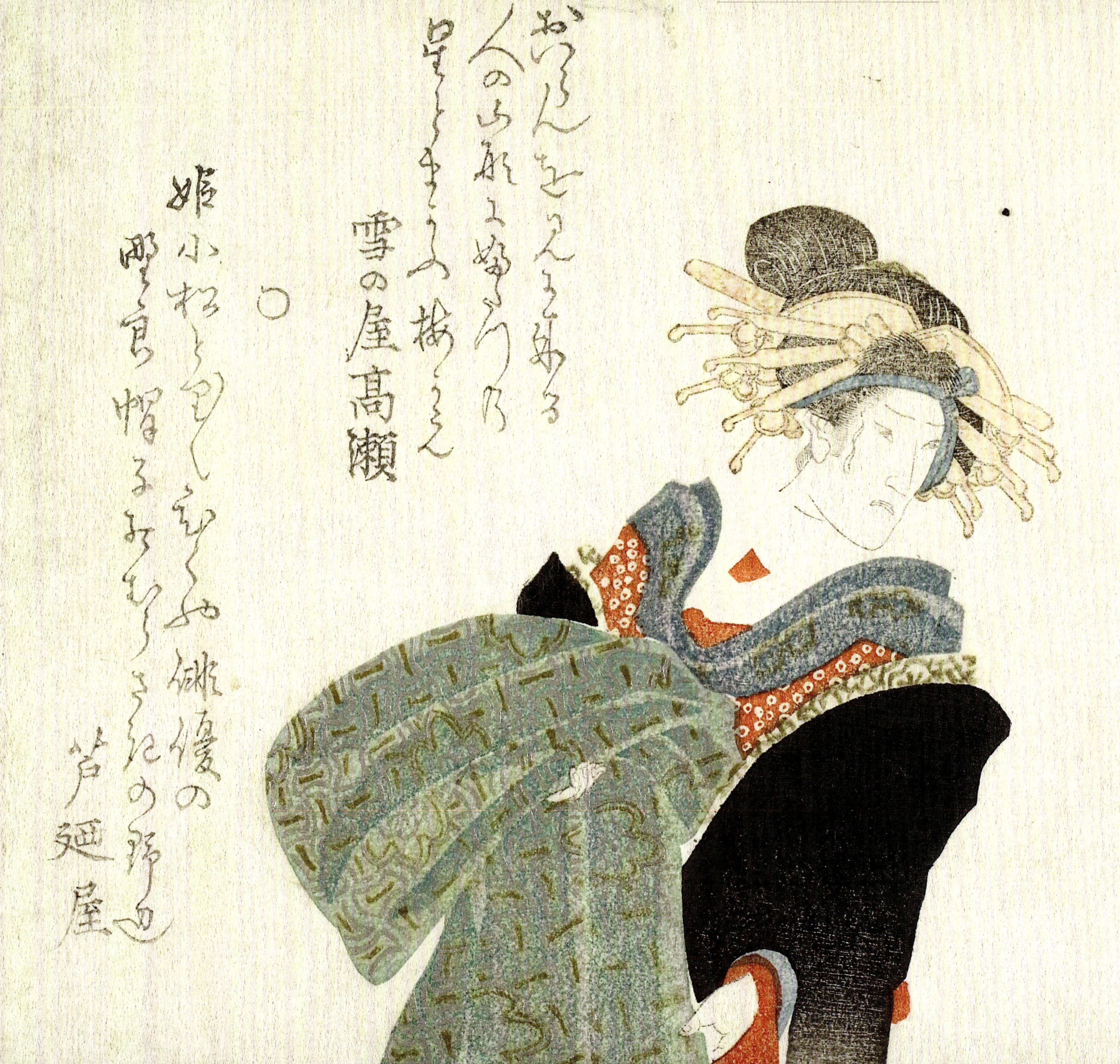
雪の屋高瀬
芦廼屋

V

Kabuki

The Kabuki theatre emerged in the early seventeenth century as a fusion of music, dance and drama. In contrast to the aristocratic Nō theatre, which was supported by the ruling warrior class, Kabuki rapidly became an enormously popular form of entertainment for all sectors of the urban population. Kabuki plays entertained viewers with complex plots based on traditional legends and historical events, with elaborate stage sets, lavish costumes and dramatic make-up.

When it began, Kabuki was performed solely by women, but in 1629 the Tokugawa shogunate banned female performers because of widespread prostitution. After this Kabuki was performed by young men, who took on both male and female roles. In 1652 this form of Kabuki was also prohibited, again because of concern for morals, and older male actors took over. It is this form of all-male Kabuki that has continued to the present day. Actors performing female roles were known as *onnagata*.

Leading Kabuki actors became popular celebrities and there was a huge demand for commercially published prints of actors in their most famous roles. Large print runs kept prices down and an *ukiyo-e* print could be bought for the price of a large bowl of noodles – less than the price of a theatre ticket. It is hardly surprising that Kabuki actors were also a popular subject of *surimono*. Some *kyōka* poetry clubs served as Kabuki fan clubs, with members commissioning *surimono* to commemorate special performances of their favourite actors or to honour important name changes (occasions when a prestigious stage name was passed down from one generation of actors to the next to mark progress in an actor's career). Many Kabuki actors were *kyōka* poets themselves and personally commissioned artists to design *surimono* for them. The calligraphy used for poems on this kind of *surimono* tends to be large and flamboyant, reflecting the dynamic stage personalities of the actors.

Kabuki *surimono*, like *ukiyo-e*, depicted actors in important scenes from recent performances or behind the scenes within a domestic setting. Unlike *ukiyo-e*, however, the actors' names, roles and the titles of their plays are never included in *surimono*, although sometimes these facts may be deduced from the accompanying poems.

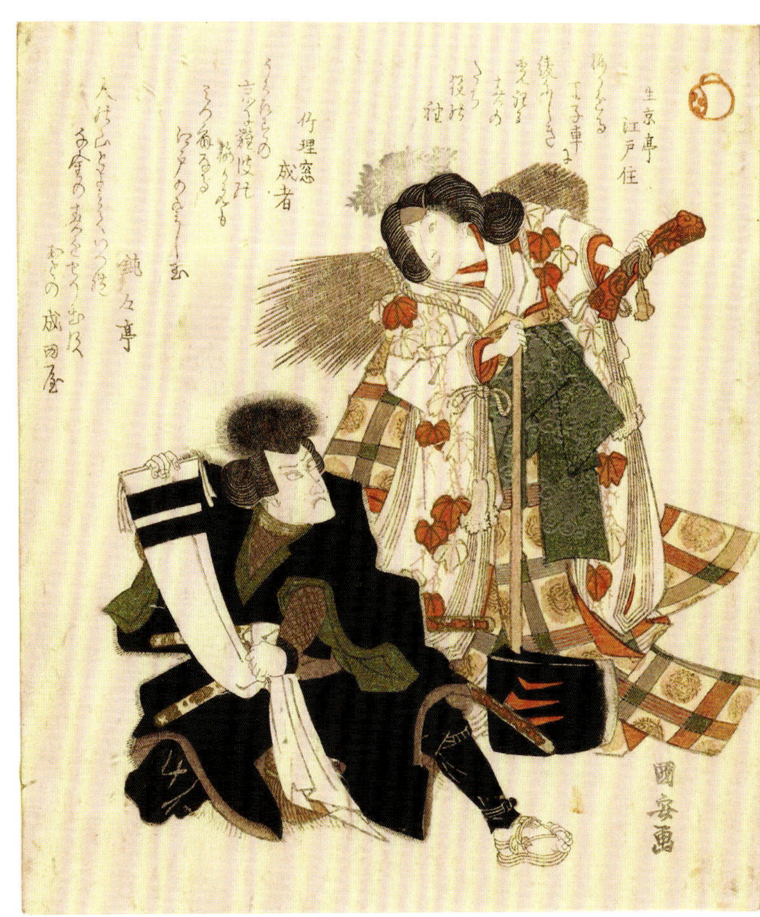

Fig.20 *The Kabuki actors Ichikawa Danjūrō VII and Iwai Hanshirō V*. Commissioned by the Taiko-gawa group. Utagawa Kuniyasu (1794–1834) 歌川国安. Artist's signature: *Kuniyasu ga* 国安画. 1820s. Colour woodblock print with metallic pigments and embossing, 20.1 × 18.7 cm, *shikishiban* format. Presented by Mrs E. M. Allan and Mr and Mrs H. N. Spalding from the Herbert H. Jennings Collection, EAX.4655

29

A Kabuki actor in the role of Umeōmaru

Commissioned by the Go-gawa group
UTAGAWA KUNISADA (1786-1864) 歌川国貞
Artist's signature: *Kōchōrō Kunisada ga* 香蝶楼國貞画
Artist's seal: double red '*toshidama*' circular seal
*c.*1826 (later than 1825, when Kunisada first used his 'Kōchōrō' signature)
Colour woodblock print with metallic pigments on paper
21 × 28.5 cm, *shikishiban* format
Presented by Mrs E. M. Allan and Mrs H. N. Spalding from the
Herbert H. Jennings Collection, EAX.4657

This *surimono* depicts a Kabuki actor in the role of Umeōmaru in the hugely popular Kabuki play *Sugawara Denju Teranai Kagami* ('Sugawara and the Secrets of Calligraphy'). The play is based on the life of the ninth-century courtier and calligrapher Sugawara no Michizane, who is falsely accused of treason and banished from the court. Umeōmaru, loyal retainer to Michizane, is one of three brothers, each serving one of the main characters. Each of the brothers is represented by a different plant: Umeōmaru by plum blossom (*ume*), Sakuramaru by cherry blossom (*sakura*) and Matsuōmaru by pine (*matsu*). The plum blossom pattern on Umeōmaru's under-robe identifies him in this print.

Here Umeōmaru strikes an intense pose known as a '*mie*', his eyes crossed and arms outstretched. This pose is intended to draw the audience's attention to a particularly important and emotional part of a performance. Umeōmaru wears the striking stage make-up called '*kumadori*', worn by Kabuki actors when performing in the dynamic 'rough' style of acting known as *aragoto*. Umeōmaru's winglike sidelocks and topknot add to his dramatic presence as a bold young samurai.

The *surimono* was commissioned by the Go-gawa poetry group. The background of the print is decorated with the Go-gawa's emblem, an hourglass motif that is a stylised rendering of the character for five 五 (the '*Go*' of 'Go-gawa'). Both of the poems refer to plum blossom at New Year. In Japan the warbler is said to start singing when the plum begins to blossom, just as the cuckoo's call is associated with the arrival of spring in Europe.

人ミなハ
なんときいたか
梅かえに
初音を告る
鶯の夢

hito mina wa
nan to kiita ka
umegae ni
hatsune o tsugeru uguisu no yume

In the first song of the year the warbler on the plum branch sings of his dream – I wonder what people think he is saying.

CHŪUEN SUITEI 仲雨園水亭

雪霜を
しのくミさをの
梅の花
兄の松にも
おとらさりけり

yukishimo o
shinogu misao no
ume no hana
ani no matsu nimo
otorazari keri

The plum blossom is more honourable than the snow and frost, and no less honourable than its elder, the steadfast pine.

ROKUJUEN 緑樹園

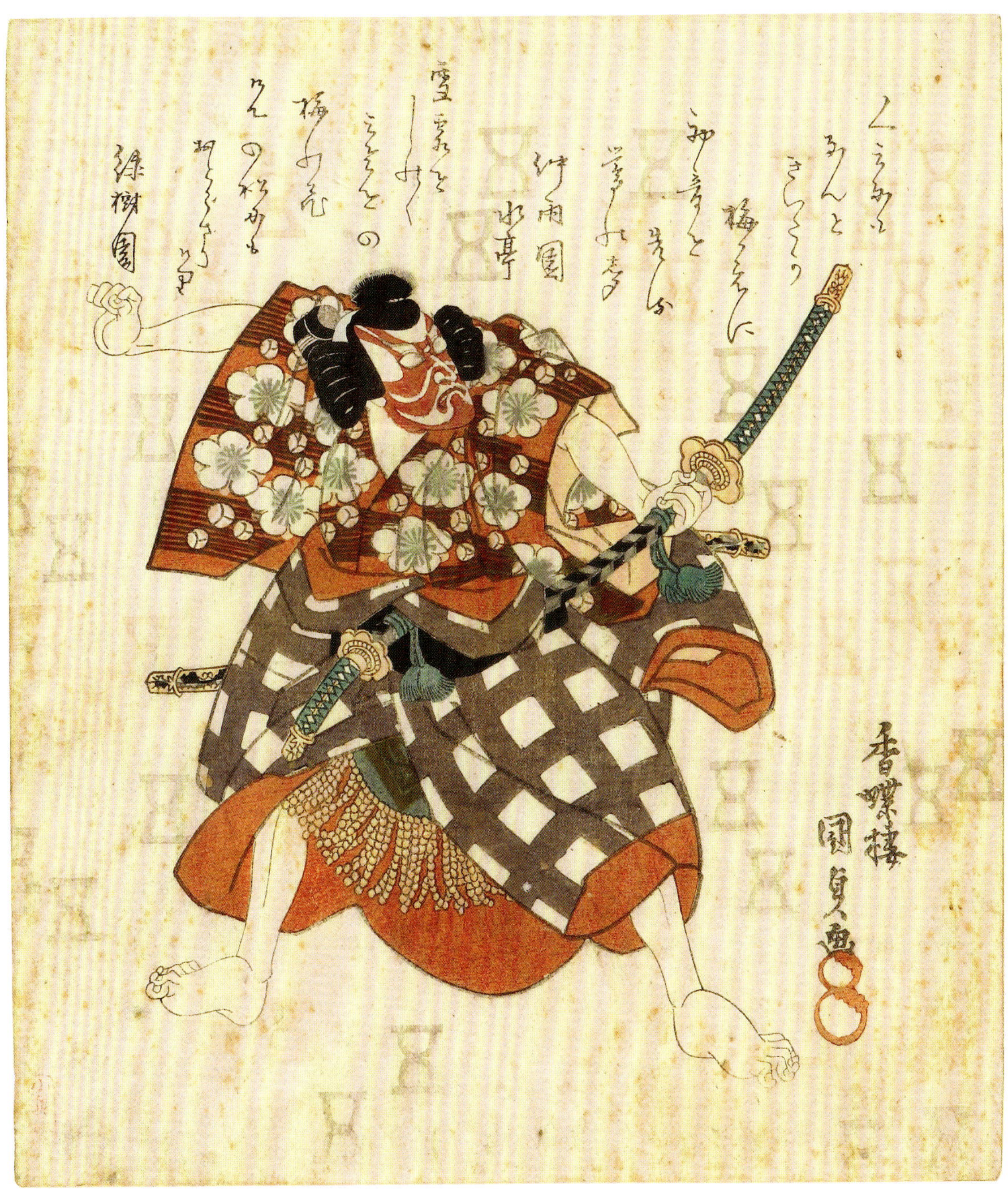

30

Kabuki actors in the 'armour-tugging' scene

UTAGAWA KUNISADA (1786–1864) 歌川国貞
Artist's signature: *ōju Gototei Kunisada ga* 應需五渡亭国貞画
1827
Colour woodblock print with gold pigment and embossing
21.2 × 18.4 cm, *shikishiban* format
Presented by Mrs E. M. Allan and Mr and Mrs H. N. Spalding from the Herbert H. Jennings Collection, EAX.4659

This *surimono* depicts a scene from a Kabuki play based on the epic *Tale of the Soga Brothers*. The story, which tells of warrior siblings Soga no Jūrō and Soga no Gorō, who avenged their father's wrongful death in 1175, became the subject of numerous Nō and Kabuki plays, and of Jōruri sung narrative performances. Depicted here is the 'armour-tugging' scene (*kusazuri-biki*), in which the brothers' supporter Asahina grabs the skirt of Gorō's armour to prevent him from rashly confronting his enemy. Gorō resists his efforts, and the struggle between two legendary strongmen forms one of the highlights of the play.

In Kunisada's image, Gorō wears an outer robe decorated with butterfly crests, a costume traditionally associated with this role. The side locks of his wig are arranged in dramatically protruding strands in a style known as *kuruma-bin*. Gorō wears the distinctive red and white *kumadori* stage make-up worn by *aragoto* 'rough style' Kabuki actors to emphasise their masculinity. He towers over the bare-chested Asahina, who wears his robe turned down over his belt. Asahina's robe is decorated with the crests associated with this role: the *maru ni mitsubiki-mon* (three horizontal lines in a circle) and the *tsurumaru-mon* (crane in a circle). The 'circular crane crest' mentioned in the first poem thus refers to Asahina. A further allusion to the famous armour-tugging scene in this poem is a pun on the verb '*hikeru*', which can mean to 'tug' as well as to 'trail' like the spring mist.

The style of Kunisada's signature dates the *surimono* to the mid-1820s. The actors depicted are recognisable as Ichikawa Danjūrō VII (1791–1859) and Bandō Mitsugorō III (1773–1831), who performed the roles of Soga no Gorō and Asahina respectively at the Ichimura Theatre in Edo in 1827. It was a custom for all the Edo theatres to produce a drama or dance based on the tale of the Soga brothers (known as *Sogamono*) as part of their New Year programme; the armour-tugging scene was particularly popular because it was associated with the idea of 'tugging in good fortune' for the New Year. This association made the subject highly suitable for *surimono*.

千代のはる
ひける霞の
ころもてに
めたつ日向の
鶴の丸紋

chiyo no haru
hikeru kasumi no
koromode ni
medatsu hinata no
tsuru no marumon

The trailing mists of eternal spring lift to reveal the striking circular crane crest on the magnificent robe of the one who tugs.

YUKINOYA TAKANE 雪廼屋高根

さわらひの
にきり拳も
はねのけて
いさみたちたる
はるの若駒

sawarabi no
nigiri kobushi mo
hanenokete
isami tachitaru
haru no wakakoma

Pushing aside the clenched fists of fresh bracken ferns, the young pony prances along in the springtime.

HŌSHITEI MASUNARI 宝市亭升成

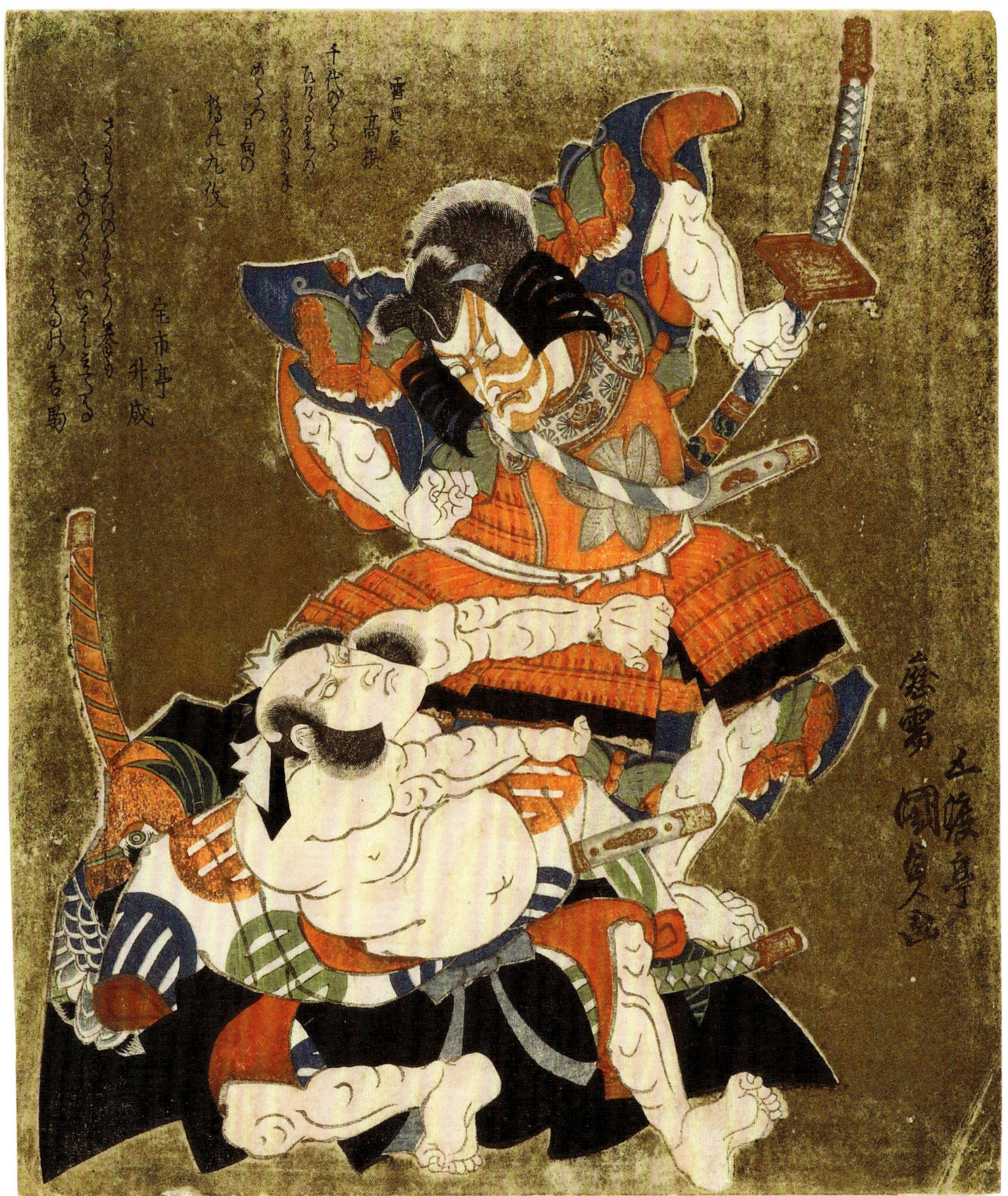

31

The courtesan Komurasaki

HANNICHIAN NAN’A (active early nineteenth century) 半日菴南蛙
Artist’s signature: *Hannichian Nan’a* 半日菴南蛙
Artist’s seal (left): unidentified
*c.*1823
Colour woodblock print, with metallic pigments and embossing
21.6 × 18.6 cm, *shikishiban* format
Presented by Mr Philip Harris, EA.2014.33

This *surimono* depicts a Kabuki actor in the role of a high-ranking courtesan (*oiran*) from the Yoshiwara pleasure quarters in Edo. The courtesan wears an overgarment in subdued tones of grey and black, beautifully printed with *bokashi* shading; beneath is worn a kimono and a red undergarment, its collar partially turned to show a scarlet lining. The colour scarlet, traditionally worn by high-ranking officials at the imperial court in Kyoto, was adopted by the top courtesans in Kyoto as a symbol of their high status and cultural refinement; it was later adopted by courtesans in Osaka and Edo. Her blue hairband indicates illness, probably lovesickness, and her expression is downcast; strands of hair escape on one side of her face. Known as ‘*shike*’ in Kabuki terminology, these strands enhance the figure’s melancholy beauty.

The courtesan depicted is Komurasaki of the Miuraya House in the Yoshiwara, noted for her role in a tragic real-life love story. When her lover Shirai Gonpachi was executed in 1679 for a murder he had committed for her sake, Komurasaki killed herself on his tomb. The story was adapted for the Kabuki theatre under various titles, one of which is *Ukiyozuka hiyoku no inazuma* (The Fleeting Life of Lovers, a Double Grave Mound and the Lightening Sword Hilt). This play was performed in the third month of 1823 at the Ichimura Theatre in Edo, with the famous Kabuki actor Onoe Kikugorō III (1784–1849) in the female role of Komurasaki. Later that year the actor travelled from Edo to Osaka to play at the Kado-za Theatre. Onoe Kikugorō’s *haiku* poetry name (*haimei*) was Baikō 梅幸, a word that includes the character for plum (梅). References to plum blossom in the poems are deliberate allusions to this actor.

The first poem refers to Naniwa-e, the bay area of what is now Osaka city, famous for its reed beds (*ashi*). The poem suggests that the Osaka theatre where the Edo actor Onoe Kikugorō performed was so packed that there was barely even standing room for the audience. In the second poem the use of the word ‘*komurasaki*’, meaning ‘deep purple’, suggests the name of the courtesan in the picture. Deep purple was associated with the city of Edo (the colour was even sometimes known as *Edo murasaki*) and so ‘*komurasaki*’ also alluded to the actor Baikō, who came from Edo to Osaka.

The third poem refers to the *Yoshiwara saiken*, a special guidebook used by customers visiting the Yoshiwara to help them ascertain courtesans’ rank. *Oiran*, the highest-ranking courtesans, were indicated by the symbol of two interlocking chevrons and dots ( ). By comparing the dots to plum blossoms, the poem creates a link to the *oiran* played by Baikō. The *yarō-bōshi* mentioned in the fourth poem was a scarf of purple silk, worn by a Kabuki actor playing a female role (*onnagata*). The garment was also called ‘*murasakibōshi*’ or ‘purple hat’. The reference to uprooting pine saplings refers to an ancient aristocratic custom of gathering wild pine saplings early in the New Year, to bring happiness for the year ahead.

Nothing is known about Hannichian Nan’a, the designer of this *surimono*, but he is thought to have been an Osaka artist.

梅みんと
むれくる人に
芦の錐
たつる所も
なにはえの春

ume min to
murekuru hito ni
ashi no kiri
tatsuru tokoro mo
naniwa-e no haru

Crowds of people coming to view the plum blossoms stand at Naniwa Bay in the springtime – there is no space between them, not even for a single young reed.

KESŌ FUMITO 懸想不美人

梅か香を
霞の袖に
にほはせて
濃紫なる
あけほのの空

umegaka o
kasumino sode ni
niowasete
komurasaki naru
akebono no sora

The sky at dawn is deep purple, and the sleeves of spring mist are perfumed with the fragrance of plum blossoms.

MEITEI HAYANE 酩亭早祢

おいらんを
見に来る人の
山形に
ふたつの星と
まかう梅かこん

oiran o
mi ni kuru hito no
yamanari ni
futatsu no hoshi to
magau ume ga kon

The high-ranking courtesan is marked out for her many customers with the sign of chevrons and two plum blossom dots.

YUKINOYA TAKASE 雪の屋高瀬

姫小松
とりゝゝひくや
俳優の
野郎帽子の
むらさきの野辺

himekomatsu
toritori hiku ya
wazaogi no
yarōbōshi no
murasaki no nobe

A Kabuki actor wearing a *yarō-bōshi* on his head uproots pine saplings from the field of purple grasses.

ASHINOYA 芦廼屋

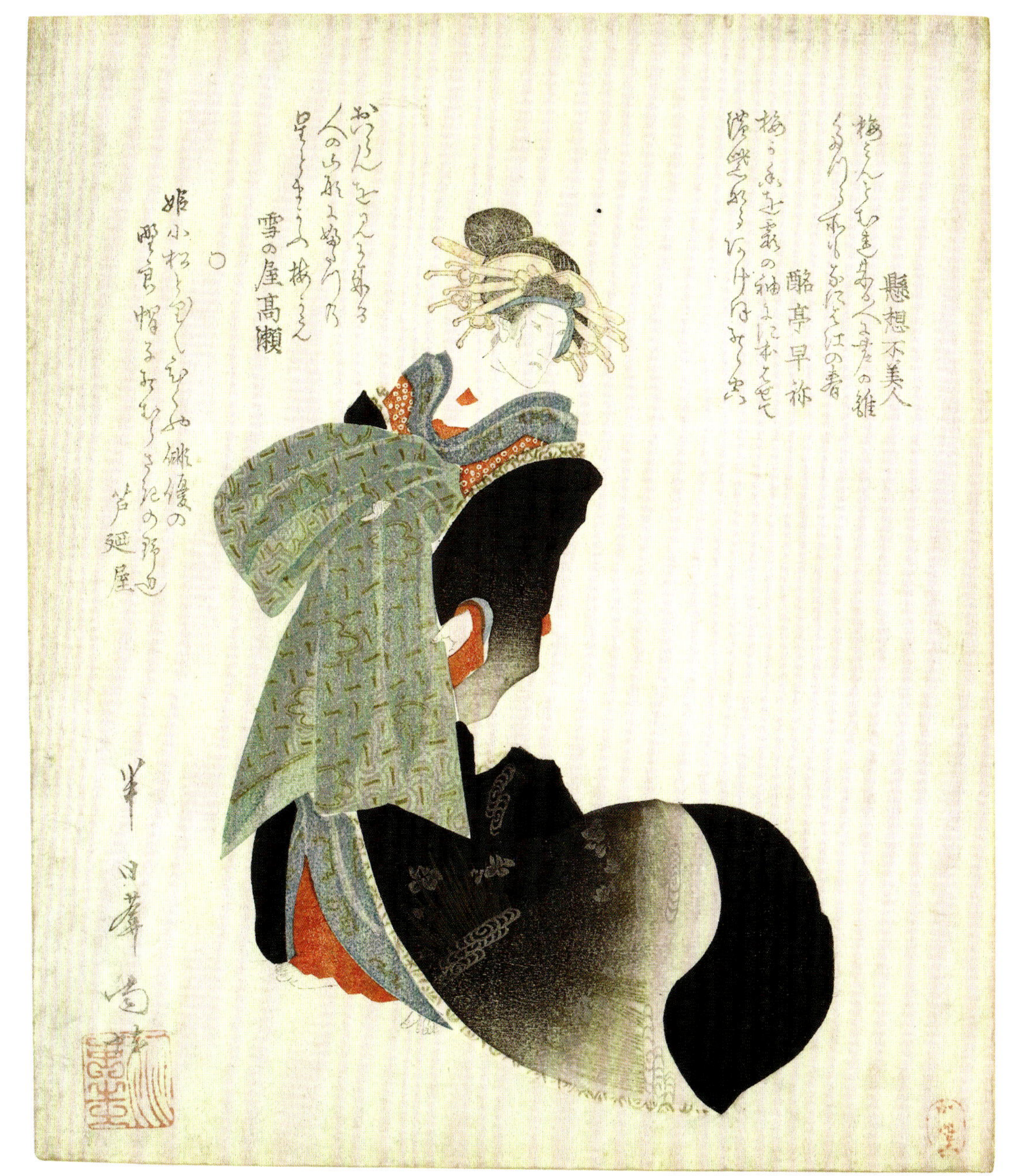

32

Portrait of Ichikawa Danjūrō VII with his two sons and an *onnagata* actor

UTAGAWA KUNINAO (1793-1854) 歌川国直
Artist's seal: *Kuninao* 国直
Late 1820s
Colour woodblock print with metallic pigments
20.2 cm × 18.1 cm, *shikishiban* format
Purchased with the assistance of the Story Fund, EA2014.37

The standing figure is the Kabuki actor Ichikawa Danjūrō VII (1791–1859), identifiable from the square white motif on his sleeve. This is the Ichikawa family crest, known as *mimasu*, a stylised depiction of three small, nested wooden boxes traditionally used in Japan for measuring rice and *sake*. Danjūrō is shown at home, wearing a formal black *haori* overcoat rather than a Kabuki costume, with his two sons and an *onnagata* (a Kabuki actor who plays female roles). The latter can be identified as an *onnagata* by his purple headdress (*yarō-bōshi*) and may be Iwai Hanshirō V (1776–1847). Both actors were working in Edo during the early nineteenth century, a time of prosperity for the merchant class and a golden age for the Kabuki theatre, one of the favourite pastimes of the urban population.

The *surimono* illustrates the traditional New Year's custom of drinking spiced *sake*, or *toso*, to drive away evil and to pray for longevity. On a black and red lacquered stand in the foreground is a small red cupholder, designed to contain a set of three stacked *sake* cups of assorted sizes. On the floor behind the stand is a *sake* ewer containing *toso*, with a New Year's decoration attached to its handle. The mood of the image is humorous, as if some mischief is afoot. Danjūrō holds his younger son who brandishes a small *sake* cup, apparently happily tipsy. The older boy, holding a medium-sized *sake* cup, sprawls drunkenly on the floor. His father looks disapprovingly down at the *onnagata*, who bears the largest *sake* cup. Perhaps Danjūrō is rebuking his fellow actor for allowing such small children to get at the *toso*.

The poem contains no direct reference to the Kabuki theatre, but the last line of the poem, '*kabuku ono ebi*', cryptically encompasses several Kabuki references. '*Kabuku*', from which the word 'Kabuki' is derived, means 'to lean' or 'bend', both literally and in the sense of 'being out of the ordinary'. Indeed, the term 'Kabuki' itself suggests the bizarre or shocking qualities of this flamboyant theatrical form. The word '*ebi*' (lobster) was part of Danjūrō's *haiku* poetry name '*Jukai Rōjin*' 壽海老人. Lobster was considered an auspicious food to eat at New Year, partly because of its red colour, but also because its back is bent like an old person's, making it a symbol of longevity. The poem thus links the celebrated Kabuki actor to the lobster – the symbol of happiness, longevity and the New Year.

The *ukiyo-e* artist Utagawa Kuninao was a pupil of Utagawa Toyokuni I; he was also influenced by Hokusai. Kunisada was noted for his depictions of actors and beauties, and for his landscapes influenced by Western painting styles; he also designed a number of *surimono*. Artists of the Utagawa School had particularly close connections with poetry groups that served as Kabuki fan clubs.

千金の
春たちそめて
めでたさは
日の出の色の
かふくおの海老

senkin no
haru tachisomete
medetasa wa
hinode no iro no
kabuku ono ebi

Spring, worth a thousand gold coins, has begun – the rising sun is the auspicious colour of a lobster with a bent tail.

YAGAIRŌ NAKASUMI 野外楼中澄

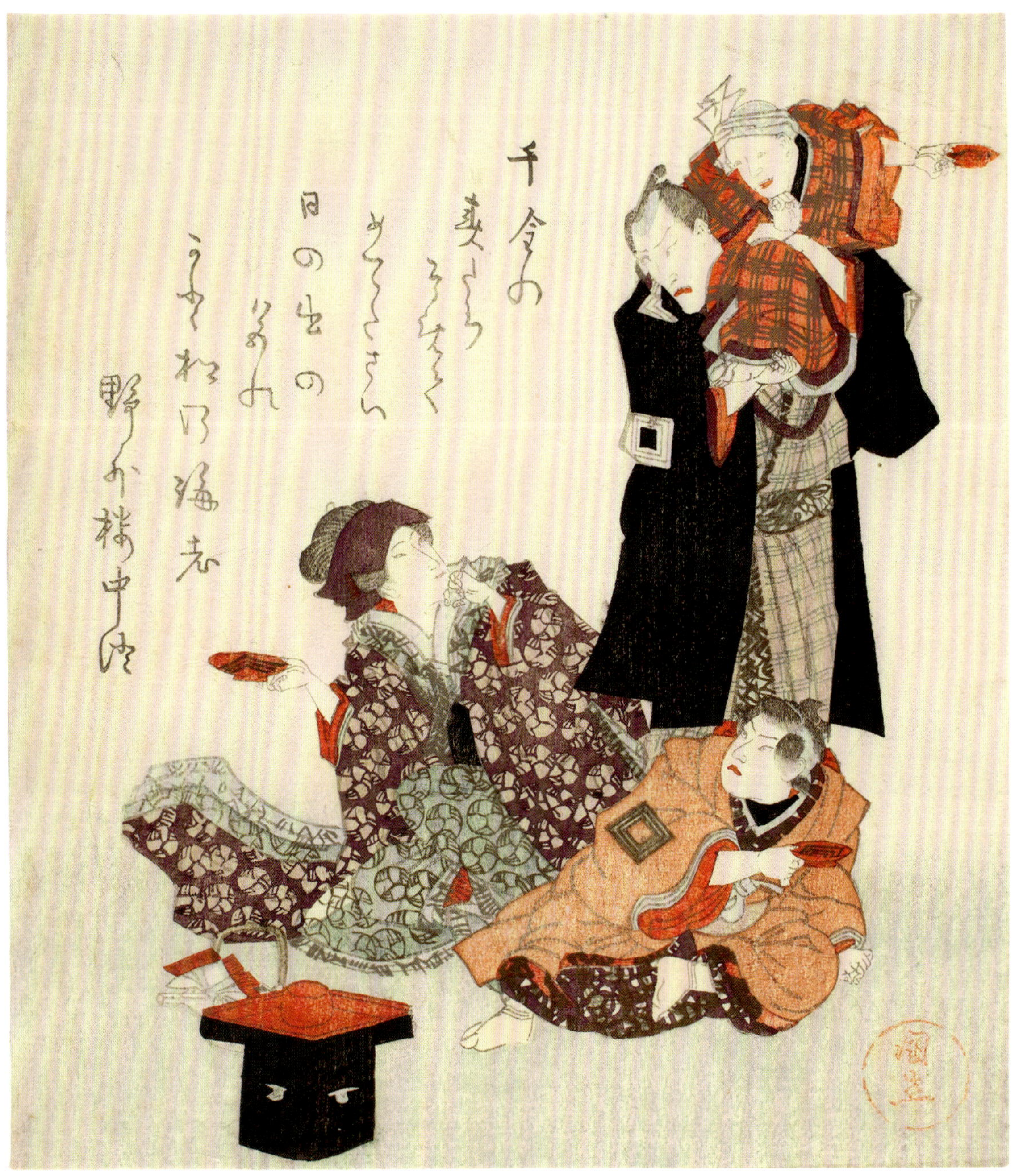

33

A young couple on a balcony

Attributed to KATSUSHIKA HOKUSAI (1760–1849) 葛飾北斎
Probably 1800 or 1812
Colour wooblock print on paper
13.6 × 8.6 cm, *koban* format
Presented by Mrs E. M. Allan and Mr and Mrs H. N. Spalding
from the Herbert H. Jennings Collection, EAX.4672

This tiny *surimono*, perhaps cut down from its original size, shows a young couple on a first-floor balcony. While both figures are depicted with delicate features and feminine clothes, the figure on the left is in fact a *wakashu* – an adolescent boy yet to go through the traditional Japanese coming-of-age ceremony. *Wakashu*, sometimes described as belonging to a 'third gender', were considered to be objects of desire for both men and women; their ambiguous style was often emulated by courtesans and young women of the Edo period. As an art motif the *wakashu* represented youth and vitality in much the same way as the figure of a young woman. It was therefore natural for *surimono* artists to employ these two evocative symbols in prints commissioned to celebrate special occasions.

The term *hanakatsuo* mentioned in the poem means 'flower bonito' and refers to shavings from a chunk of dried bonito, a Japanese cooking ingredient. These fish shavings are translucent and pale rose in colour, with the appearance of delicate flower petals. The poem, a *haikai* (also known as *haiku*) uses the metaphor of *hanakatsuo* to describe a young couple's tender love for one another. The poem was added later, by hand.

Here the beautiful young woman on the right leans against the wooden rail of the balcony, one sleeve of her kimono trailing over the rail and her other hand tugging at the collar of her partner's kimono. Her hair is arranged in the *shimadamage* style, a typical hair arrangement for young unmarried women in the Edo period (1603–1868). Her equally beautiful partner stands close behind her, his head propped on his hand. Although he wears a woman's kimono, he may be identified as a *wakashu* by his distinctive hairstyle. While adult males were required to shave the entire crown of the head, *wakashu* shaved only a small section of the crown, keeping side locks, and often forelocks, intact. The *wakashu* depicted here has tied his hair into a topknot and sports a special head cloth called a *yarō-bōshi* (literally 'rascal hat'). This may indicate that this *wakashu* is a Kabuki actor specialising in female roles (*onnagata*). Women were not allowed to become Kabuki actors, and so all female parts were taken by men. Actors playing female parts concealed the unfeminine shaven area of the head with a cloth made of purple silk crêpe.

The lovers are on the second floor of a famous Edo toothpick shop called Saruya (literally 'monkey shop'), as indicated by the characters on the fabric of the shop curtain (*noren*) in the lower right corner of the print. Hanging above the *noren* is a row of short curtains printed with the shop's trademark, a *kukuri-zaru* (literally 'tied-up monkey'), referring to a type of fabric charm traditionally hung beneath the eaves of a house to keep evil spirits away. The monkey imagery suggests that this *surimono* may have been commissioned in a Year of the Monkey, perhaps 1800 or 1812. Around this time toothpick shops in Edo such as Saruya were popular for the beautiful young women they employed to sell their products and were regarded as fashionable meeting places, perfect for romantic assignations. This may explain why the artist selected this particular setting for the young couple. Saruya, founded in 1704, still survives in Tokyo as Japan's only specialist toothpick shop.

娘若衆
恋の莟や
はな松魚

musume wakashu
koi no tsubomi ya
hana katsuo

A young woman and a *wakashu*
their love budding
like flowers of shaved bonito.

MATSUSHIZUKU 松雫

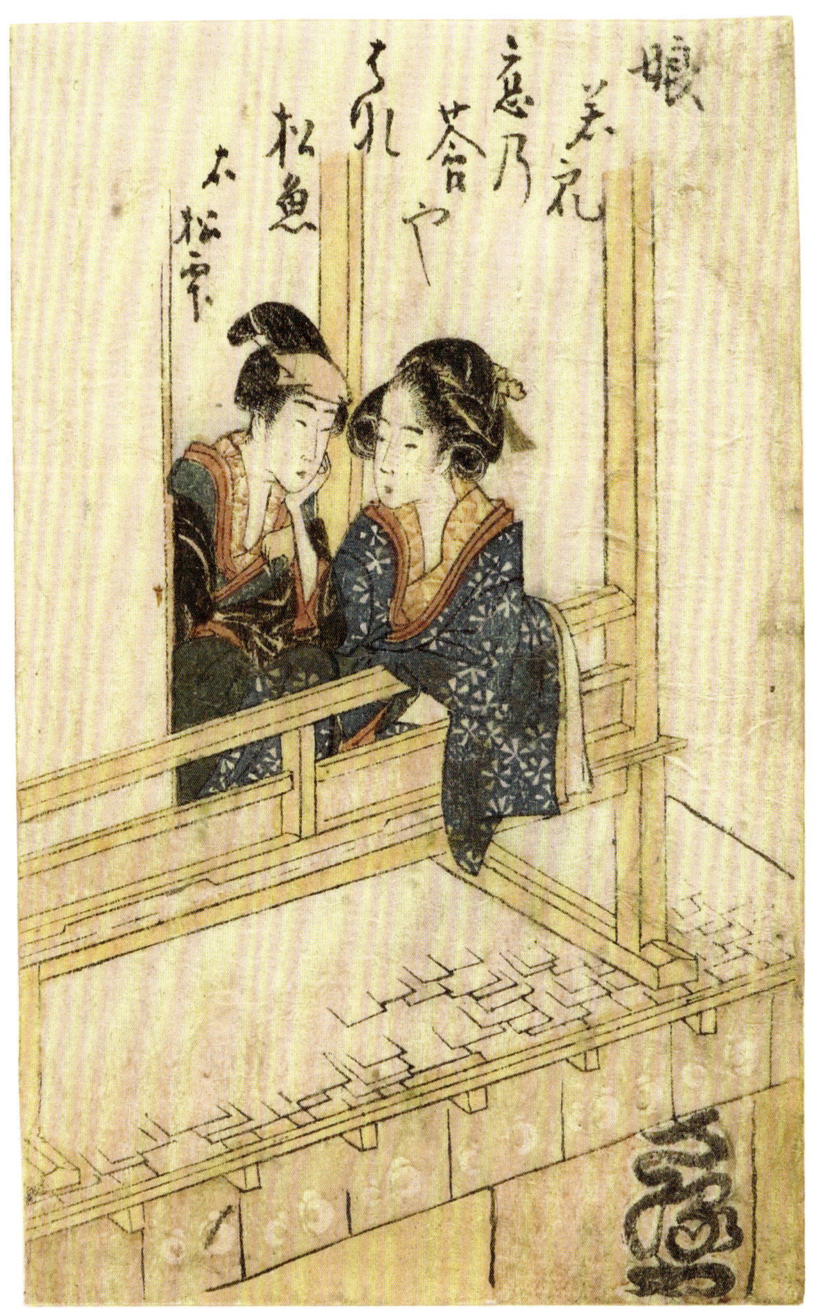

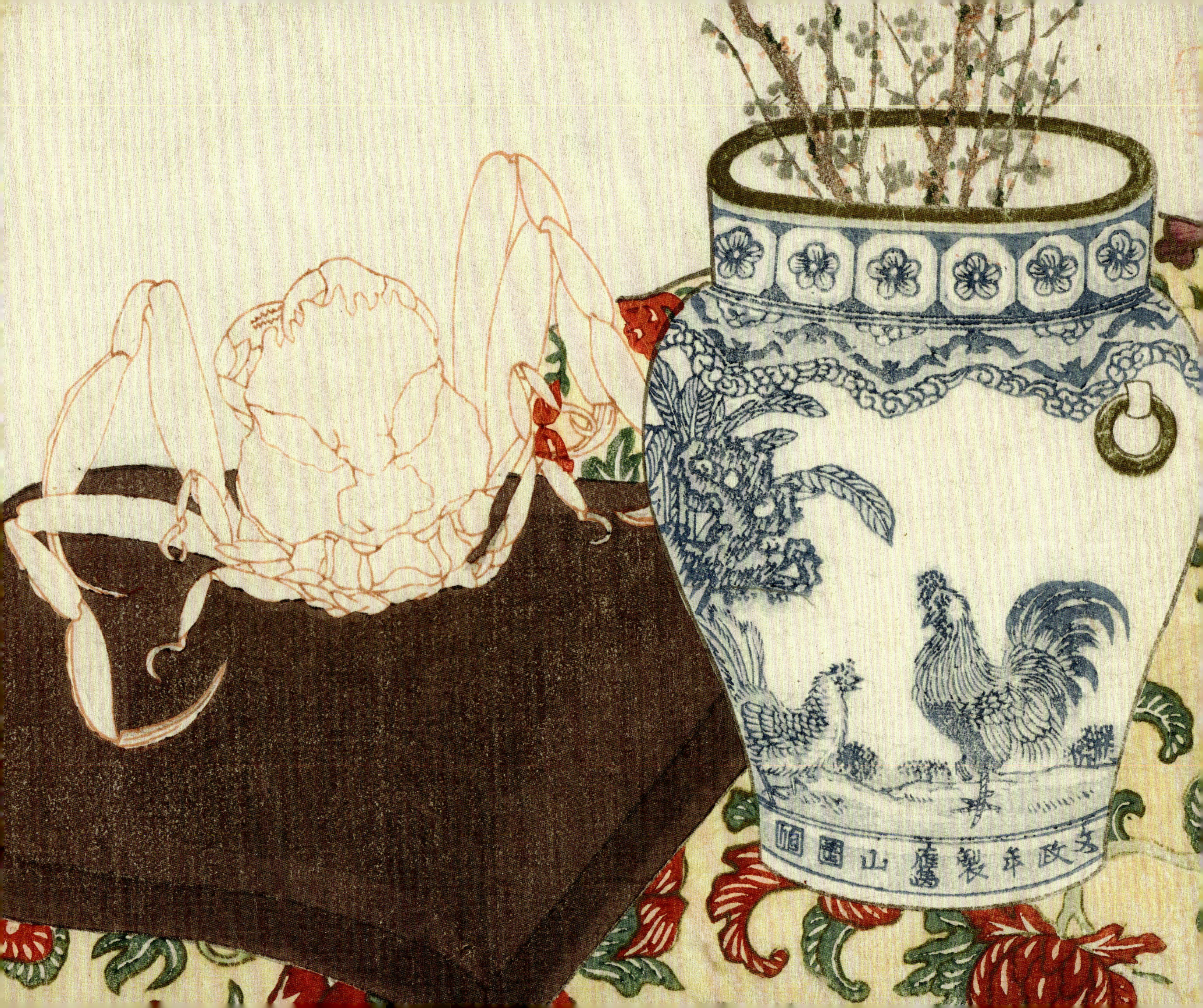
文政年製 鷹山

VI

Still Life

'Still-life' groups of objects were a popular subject for *surimono* although they were rarely seen in commercial *ukiyo-e*, which mostly depicted the living stars of the pleasure quarters and Kabuki theatres. The objects in still-life *surimono* were often chosen to represent New Year's activities or to evoke characters or events in classical tales well-known to the cultured audiences for whom the prints were intended. Occasionally the items represented a particular region or town – perhaps the place that the commissioning poet came from. Invariably celebratory and auspicious, their very 'stillness' made them particularly appropriate for the beginning of spring, which was associated with qualities of peacefulness and tranquillity.

There were a number of precedents for still-life *surimono*. It is likely that *kyōka surimono* designers were influenced by a type of early nineteenth-century *haikai* (*haiku*) *surimono* created by Osaka artists that included simple illustrations of flowers, plants or everyday objects. It has also been suggested that the artists designing still-life compositions for *surimono* may have looked to Chinese models – whether to the decorated letter papers of the late Ming dynasty (1368–1644), printed with images of flowers or bowls of fruit, or to early Qing dynasty (1644–1912) woodcuts that showed vases of flowers accompanied by couplets of Chinese verse. Imported European books, etchings and engravings were another possible source of inspiration.

Still-life *surimono* were also related to a custom that emerged among Edo *kyōka* poets of the late eighteenth century: that of holding 'treasure-matching' parties (*takara-awase*). In these meetings poets enjoyed showing off 'treasures' (usually ordinary, everyday items) selected for their special historical, literary or legendary associations. These were then used as inspiration for poetry composition.

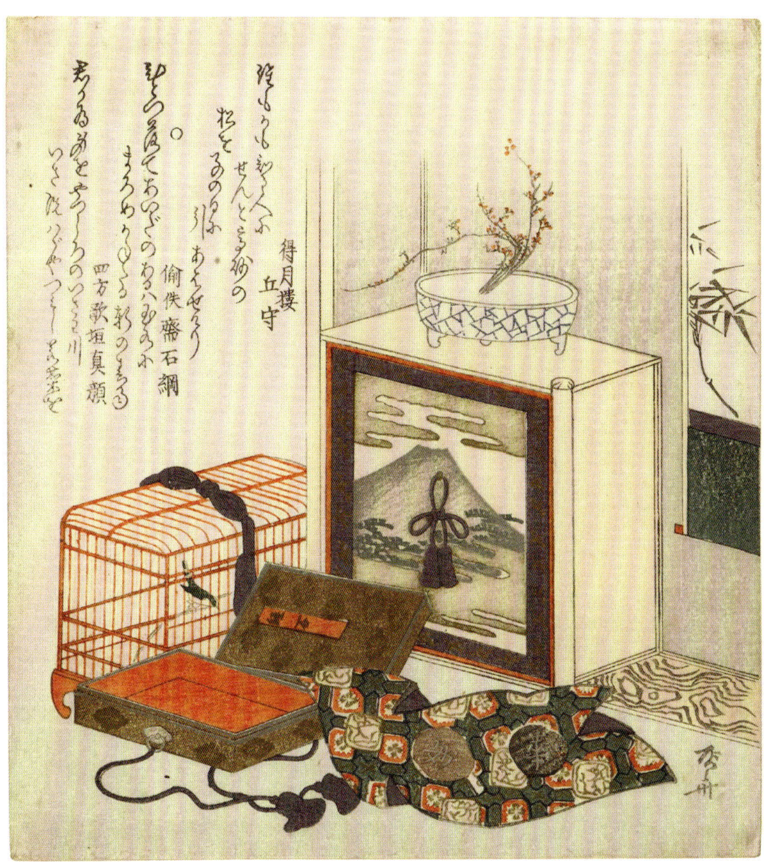

Fig.21 *Seasonal objects by a display alcove at the New Year*. After Ryūryūkyo Shinsai (active 1799–1823). Artist's signature: *Shinsai* 辰斎. 1890s (after an original of c.1800). Colour woodblock print with metallic pigments, 20.1 × 18.7 cm, *shikishiban* format. Presented by Mrs E. M. Allan and Mr and Mrs H. N. Spalding from the Herbert H. Jennings Collection, EAX.4665

34

Two folding fans decorated with emblems of longevity

TEISAI HOKUBA (1770–1844) 蹄斎北馬
Artist's signature: *Teisai* 蹄斎
Artist's seal: *Teisai* 蹄斎
Colour woodblock print with metallic pigments and embossing
1820s
20.1 × 28.3 cm, *chūban* format
Presented by Mrs E. M. Allan and Mr and Mrs H. N. Spalding from the Herbert H. Jennings Collection, EAX.4653

The two fans in this *surimono* are decorated with emblems of longevity, echoing a series of allusions in the six accompanying poems. The folding paper fan in the foreground shows a crane, said to live for a thousand years, flying over crashing waves on a ground of gold. The slatted *hiōgi* ceremonial court fan behind depicts a long-tailed turtle, believed to live to the age of ten thousand years. The turtle stands by a pond, against a backdrop of pine, bamboo and plum – a trio of plants traditionally known in China as the 'Three Friends of Winter' because they all flourish in the midst of winter. The ribs of the *hiōgi* fan are threaded together with red silk ribbon and the upper corners of the fan are adorned with sprays of artificial flowers fashioned from silk thread.

Mount Hōrai, mentioned in the fifth poem, was known as the dwelling place of the Daoist immortals, hence the references to long-lived cranes and turtles. *Toso* is a spiced *sake* (rice wine) that represents the elixir of life and is traditionally drunk at New Year. The poems are also full of allusions to springtime – willow, plum blossom and Mount Fuji; it was believed to be auspicious to dream of Mount Fuji during the first three days of the New Year's Day. '*Hatachi no yama*' in the final poem is a literary name for Mount Fuji, used in the tenth-century classic *The Tales of Ise*.

The print designer Hokuba was originally trained in the Kano style of painting and became an early pupil of the great *ukiyo-e* artist Katsushika Hokusai (1760–1849). He was best known as a painter, but also produced illustrations for *kyōka* poetry anthologies and for single-sheet *surimono*.

とある家に
よき井の有て
ききすなく

toaru ya ni
yoki i no arite
kigisu naku

In a certain person's house there is a good well and so the pheasant sings.

KŌZENRŌ ŌI 紅髯楼大井

紅粉うりに
傘かす
柳かけ

benikouri ni
kasa kasu
yanagi kage

To a seller of powdered rouge a parasol is offered by the shade of the willow.

EBIRA えびら

はつかしと
霞の袖を
口にあて
わらひそめけり
梅の初春

hazukashi to
kasumi no sode o
kuchi ni ate
waraisome keri
ume no hatsuharu

Blushing, she covers her mouth with sleeves of mist as she gives the first laugh of the new spring of the plum blossom.

AINARE あいなれ

春をしたゝか
うりつけつ
懸想文

haru o shitataka
uritsuketsu
kesōbumi

'Make the most of the springtime' – he peddles his lucky love charms.

MIYAMA 美山

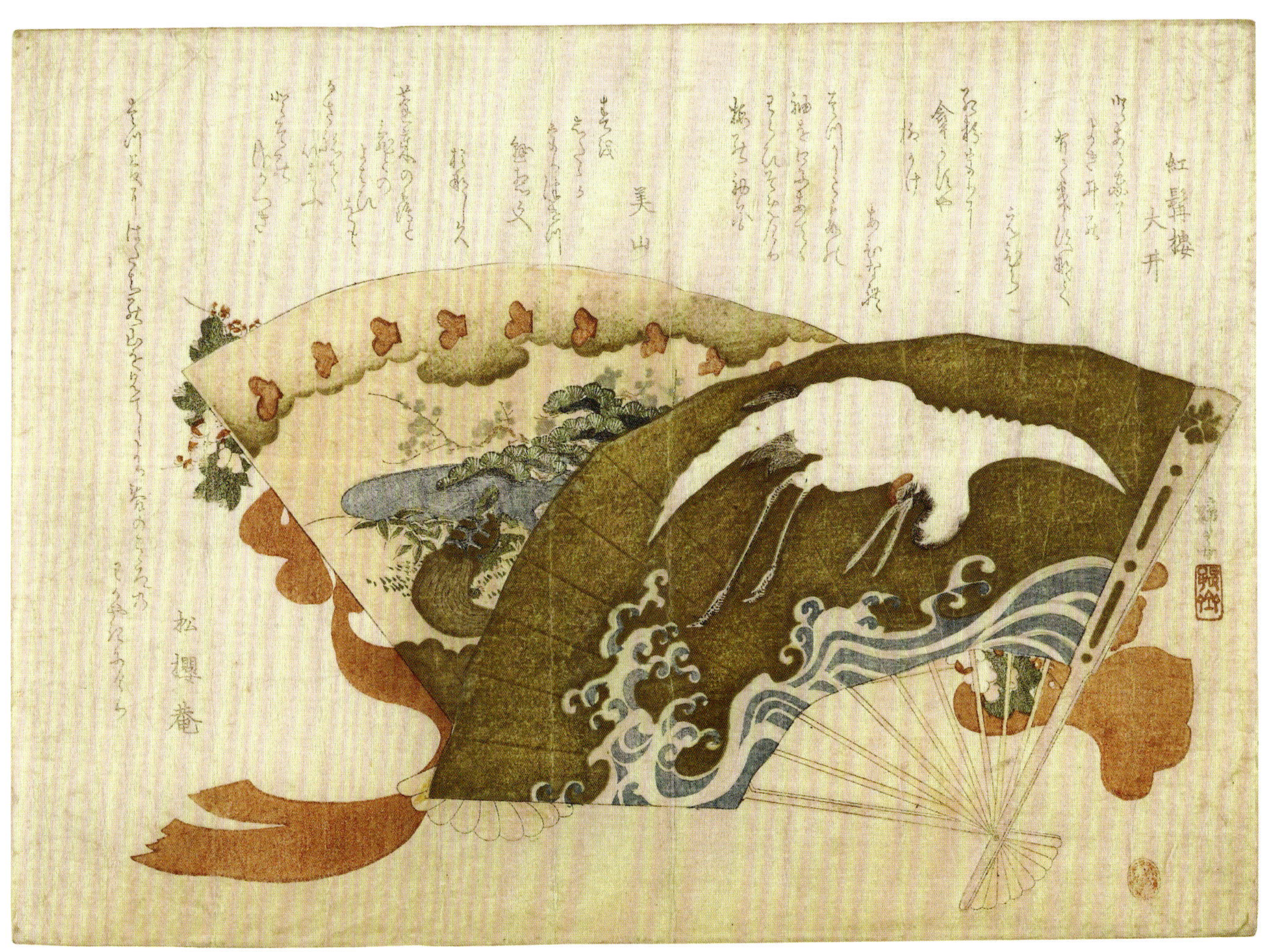

蓬莱の
鶴と亀との
よはひをも
重ねていはふ
とそのさかつき

hōrai no
tsuru to kame tono
yowai omo
kasanete iwau
toso no sakatsuki

On Mount Hōrai the crane and the turtle enjoy longevity; together we celebrate with a cup of *toso*.

—the same poet [MIYAMA]

はつ夢に
はたちの山を
見てしより
春のこころの
わかやきにけり

hatsuyume ni
hatachi no yama o
miteshiyori
haru no kokoro no
wakayagi ni keri

In the first dream of the New Year Mount Fuji appeared; after seeing it my heart feels fresh and new, like spring.

SHŌRŌAN 松櫻庵

35

The Divine Horse Grass (*Jinmesō* 神馬草)

Series: All about Horses (*Uma-zukushi* 馬盡)
Commissioned by the Yomo-gawa group
KATSUSHIKA HOKUSAI (1760–1849) 葛飾北斎
Artist's signature: *Fusenkyo I-itsu hitsu* 不染居爲一筆
1890s (after an 1822 original, Year of the Horse)
Colour woodblock print, with metallic pigment and blind printing
19.8 × 17.2 cm, *shikishiban* format
Presented by Mrs E. M. Allan and Mr and Mrs H. N. Spalding
from the Herbert H. Jennings Collection, EAX.4578

This still life is from a series of 30 *surimono* on the theme of horses, commissioned by the Yomo-gawa group, one of Edo's leading poetry groups, for the Year of the Horse in 1822. The image was provided by the well-known print designer Katsushika Hokusai. Better known today as a designer of commercial landscape prints, from the late 1790s Hokusai regularly contributed designs for both single-sheet *surimono* and albums of *kyōka* poetry. This *surimono* can be accurately dated to 1822 – the only Year of the Horse during the period when Hokusai was using the art name 'Fusenkyo I-itsu'. The red, hand-stamped title cartouche in the upper-right corner of each print is in the shape of a gourd. This makes a reference to the Daoist Immortal Chōkarō (Zhang Guolao in Chinese), who was known for his ability to conjure a horse from a gourd.

In this series 26 of the prints are still-life arrangements, here composed of a group of New Year's decorations. The golden, straw-like ornament at the centre of this print is composed of dried seaweed, the *jinmesō* or 'divine horse-grass' of the title. Also known as *hondawara* (sargassum), this type of seaweed was used in New Year celebrations as a symbol of abundant harvest. The name *jinmesō* is said to derive from a legend first recorded in the eighth-century chronicle *Kojiki* (Records of Ancient Matters), in which a sacred horse led by the Empress Jingū was fed with *hondawara* seaweed. Here the dried seaweed is wrapped around a straw core to form a decorative bundle. It is shown together with other auspicious New Year ornaments: sacred silver papers (*gohei*), a spiny lobster and a pine sapling wrapped in white paper and tied with a red cord (both white and red being celebratory colours). The lobster is a symbol of longevity, its shape said to resemble the bent back of an aged person; the evergreen pine symbolises both longevity and youth. Together these objects form a sacred display to greet the *Toshitokujin*, the god of the New Year, and to pray for wealth and a rich harvest. The seaweed bundle in the centre is the offering to the sacred horse on which the god of the New Year arrives.

Each of the poems plays with horse imagery in connection to divine seaweed and the arrival of spring. The first poem puns on the literal meaning of *jinmesō*, imagining the seaweed offerings made to the gods at a household shrine at the New Year. The words *jinmesō* (divine horse-grass) and the '*tazuna*', rope or reins, are both associated with horses. This use of semantically related words within poetry is called *engo*. Another poetic device used here is the 'pivot word' (*kakekotoba*): '*hiku*' means 'to pull' and can be read not only with '*jinmesō*' to mean 'pull out grass', but also with '*tazuna*', to mean 'pull the reins'. The image of strands of purple mist is conventionally used to indicate springtime.

神棚の
神にさゝくる
神馬草
ひくや霞の
紫手つな

kamidana no
kami ni sasaguru
jinmesō hiku ya
kasumi no
murasaki tazuna

On the holy altar an offering to the gods, the divine horse-grass is pulled by purple ropes made of strands of mist.

MANMANSAI MANAGA 萬々斎 真長

神馬草を
ほんとはねける
聲につれ
いさむる午の
春ハきにけり

jinmesō o
pon to hanekeru
koe ni tsure
isamuru uma no
haru wa kinikeri

The divine horse-grass rears up, and with this sound the high-spirited spring of the Horse Year arrives.

WASEIKEN IMARU 和清軒 伊丸

あら玉の
としの恵みも
あつ房の
かさり立派な
神馬草かな

aratama no
toshi no megumi mo
atsubusa no
kazari rippa na
jinmesō kana

The blessings of this new jewel of a year, rich like a thick-tasselled ornament – the splendid divine horse-grass.

SHITCHINSHA MANPŌ 七珍社万宝

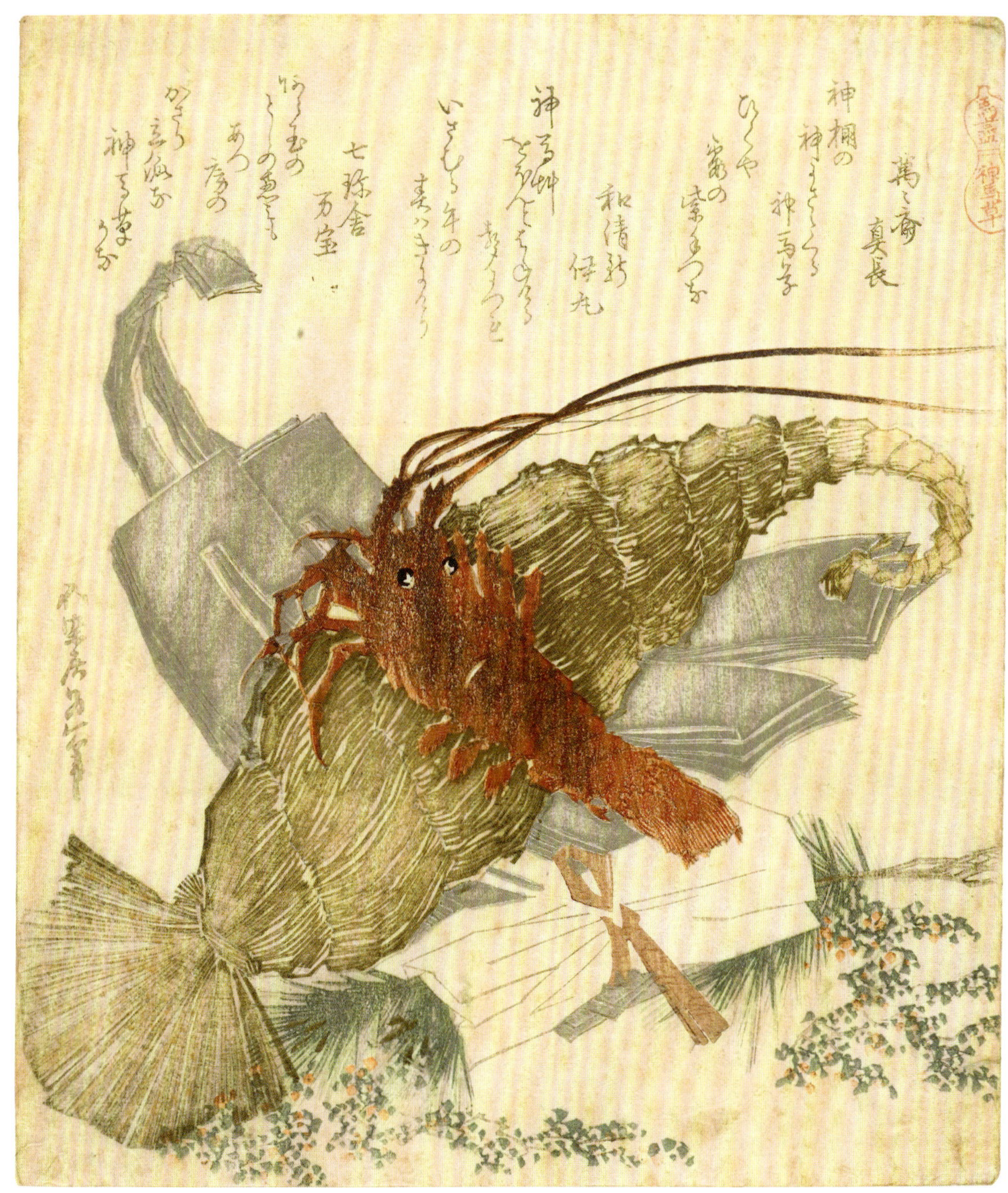

36

Yōkan jelly from Funabashiya in Saga-chō, Fukagawa (*Fukagawa Saga-chō Funabashiya yōkan* 深川佐賀丁舟ハし屋羊かん)

Series: Famous Products of Edo, produced by Shunman
(*Edo Meibutsu Shunman sei* 江戸名物俊満制)
Commissioned by the Go-gawa group
HOKUTEI (active 1810s–1830s) 北鼎
Artist's signature (lower left): *Hokutei Joren* 北鼎如連
Collector's signature (lower right): *Kyōsai aruji* 狂齊主, with seal *Kyōsai* 狂齊
1890s (after an original of 1817)
Colour woodblock print with metallic pigment and embossing
18.9 × 17 cm, *shikishiban* format
Presented by Mrs E. M. Allan and Mr and Mrs H. N. Spalding
from the Herbert H. Jennings Collection, EAX.4623

The title of each *surimono* in this series consists of the name of a well-known shop in Edo and its most famous product – in this case the sweet shop Funabashiya with its speciality of *yōkan* bean jelly. The print illustrates a block of *yōkan* in a bamboo-sheath wrapper, the fine lines of the sheath meticulously embossed for realistic effect. The *yōkan* sits in a yellow lacquered bowl decorated with a pair of mandarin ducks, symbols of conjugal happiness. Next to the bowl is a knife for cutting the *yōkan* and leaning against the bowl is a blue *noshi*, a folded paper decoration traditionally attached to gifts as a token of good wishes. Tucked into the *noshi* is a spray of plum blossoms, the stamens highlighted in gold. According to a document produced in the mid-1860s by a famous sweet shop in the city of Edo (*Kanazawa Tango monjo* 金沢丹後文書), it was customary for shops to send out *yōkan* as a New Year gift to important customers such as temples, shrines or samurai clans. This *surimono* may depict the joyful moment of unwrapping just such a gift.

A slip of paper resting on the sweet wrapper in this design bears the characters 難波 'Naniwa', together with what appears to be the upper part of the character 羹 *kan*, or jelly. The Funabashiya store, located at Saga-chō in the Fukagawa district of Edo, was famous for a type of *yōkan* called 'Naniwakan'. This means '*yōkan* from Naniwa', Naniwa being a name for ancient Osaka. Although Edo had become the capital of Japan in 1603 and had developed a thriving and distinctive cultural life, products from the cultured Kamigata region around Osaka and Kyoto, where the emperor still resided, were traditionally regarded as superior by the people of Edo. Ironically it seems that Naniwakan was in fact produced only in Edo.

The renowned *surimono* artist Kubo Shunman (1757–1820) was unusual in that he not only provided designs for *surimono*, but also ran his own *surimono* workshop, employing block cutters and printers. He was also a *kyōka* poet in his own right, active under the name Shōsadō, and was closely connected with many leading poets of the time. This *surimono* was produced by Shunman as a commission from the Go-gawa group and the design was provided by the artist Hokutei Joren, a pupil of Hokusai's who used the art names Joren and Teppitsu. The Go-gawa group's hourglass-shaped emblem and the series title, visible in the top right-hand corner of the print, were stamped in red on to the completed *surimono*.

In the first poem the phrase '*umashi to homen*' is a *kakekotoba* or 'pivot word' with two meanings: the first 'praising the delicious taste' [of *yōkan*] and the second 'praising good skill' [at playing the *shamisen*, the three-stringed Japanese instrument]. The word '*sao*' also has a double meaning, referring both to the neck of the *shamisen* and also to the Japanese unit of counting blocks of *yokan* jelly.

味ひを
うましとほめん
鶯か
哥三弦の
棹ととなへて

ajiwai o
umashi to homen
uguisu ga
utasangen no
sao to tonaete

Enjoying the sweet taste of the *yōkan*, the warbler sings admiringly along with the song of the *shamisen.*

SHINSHINTEI HATAMOCHI
森々亭畑持

難波かん
其名にめてて
大江戸の
梅か香そふる
風ののとけさ

naniwakan
sono na ni medete
ō-edo no
ume ga ka souru
kaze no nodokesa

The name of Naniwa *yōkan* is admired even in Great Edo, where the fragrance of plum blossom drifts peacefully on the breeze.

KŌSUITEI TOKUGYO
好水亭得魚

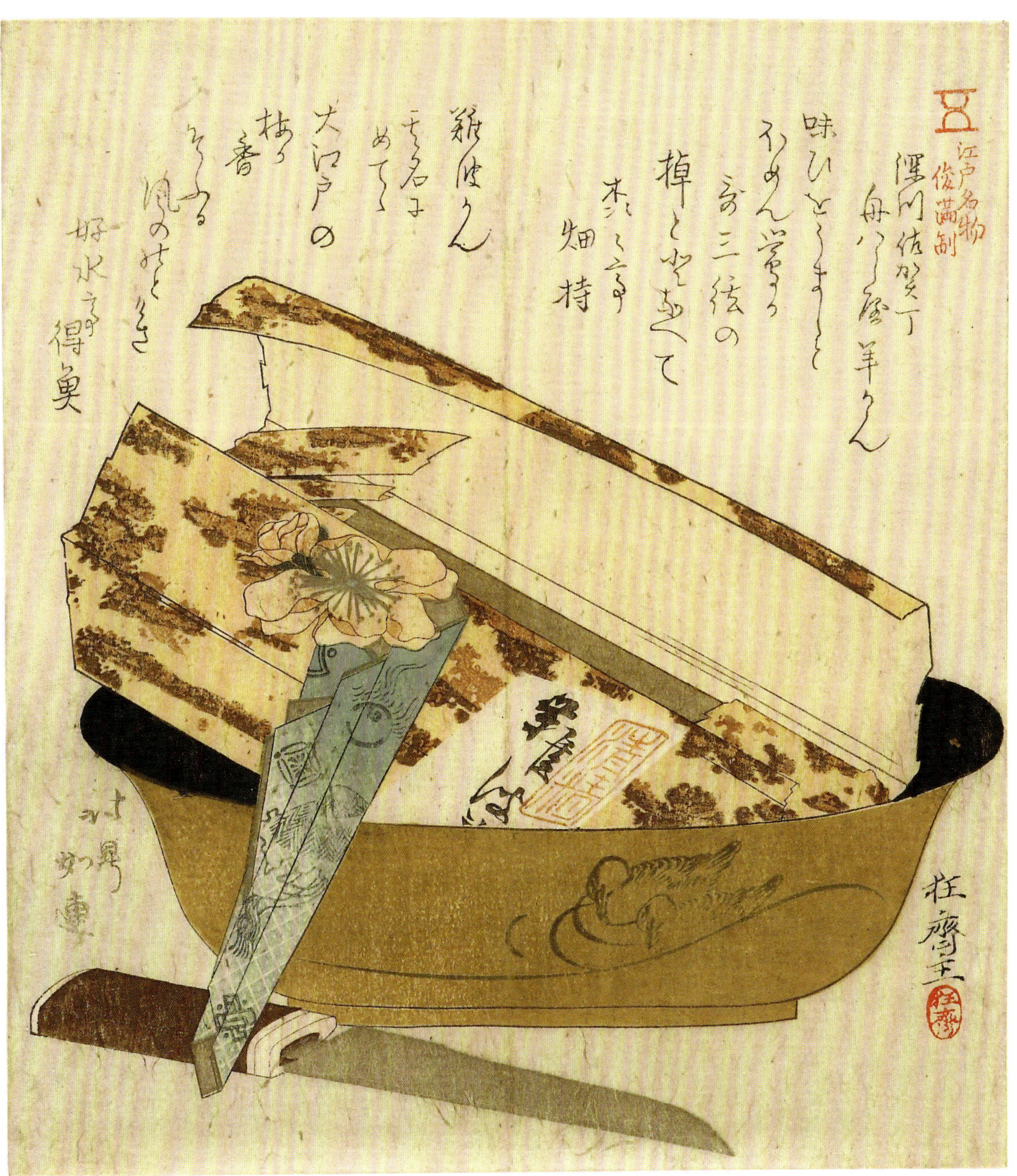

37

Pipe case and tobacco pouch with a *netsuke* and chain

After KIKUKAWA EISHIN (active *c.*1804–30) 菊川英信
Artist's signature: *Hōrai Eishin ga* 蓬莱英信画
Artist's seal: *Ei* 英
Early 1890s (after an 1820s original)
Colour woodblock print with metallic pigments and embossing
12.6 × 17.3 cm, *kokonotsugiriban* format
Presented by Mrs E. M. Allan and Mr and Mrs H. N. Spalding
from the Herbert H. Jennings Collection, EAX.4615

The picture shows fashionable smoking equipment: a colourful tobacco pouch and a long green pipe case with brown stitching. The tobacco pouch is fashioned from chintz-patterned fabric, known in Japan as *sarasa*. During the Edo period printed cotton textiles from India and Southeast Asia were highly prized in Japan for their bright colours and exotic designs, and they were often imitated. This appears to be Japanese chintz (*wasarasa*). The tobacco pouch is attached to a metal chain and a strap of *hyogo-gusari* (braided metal wire), ending in an ivory *netsuke* and a decorative fur pompom. *Netsuke* were hooked over the kimono sash to act as a counterweight to an attached *sagemono* ('hanging things', such as pipe cases, purses or *inrō* medicine containers). The *netsuke* in this *surimono*, probably made from a boar's tusk, is ingeniously depicted through blind printing, although this is hard to make out in photographic reproduction.

Tobacco was first brought to Japan by the Portuguese in the late sixteenth century. Smoking became popular among the dilettante in Kyoto at the beginning of the seventeenth century, and from there spread throughout Japan. After the government issued permits to grow tobacco on reclaimed land in the late seventeenth century, shops sprang up selling locally produced tobacco in a variety of cuts, catering to the tastes of individual customers. Both men and women of the Edo period enjoyed smoking, but this set probably belonged to a man. For women, smoking was almost exclusively confined to courtesans of the pleasure quarters, who tucked pipes and tobacco pouches into the front of their kimonos rather than hanging them from the sash. Elegant courtesans smoking long pipes was a popular motif in *ukiyo-e* paintings and prints.

The 'spring pouch' (*harubukuro*) in the poem was the first pouch made in the New Year by a young girl wishing for good luck. The word *haru* is a pun, meaning both 'spring' and also 'being full', as a spring pouch was intended to become full of happiness. The laughter referred to may be at the clumsy stitching of a young girl. In his illustration the artist Eishin has deliberately depicted irregular stitches on the pipe case. The case itself is empty, perhaps implying that someone is smoking the tobacco from the pouch.

Eishin was a pupil of the *ukiyo-e* designer Kikukawa Eizan (1787–1867) and was on friendly terms with Hokkei (1780–1850), the renowned *surimono* designer. Eishin was active in the early 1830s, but this print is a late nineteenth-century copy of his original design.

一杯に
つめる多葉粉の
はる袋
ぬひめを笑ふ
御代そめてたき

ippai ni
tsumeru tabako no
harubukuro
nuime o warau
miyo zo medetaki

Laughing at the stitches of a spring pouch fully packed with tobacco – what a joyful time!

URAMICHI CHIKAKI
裏道近喜

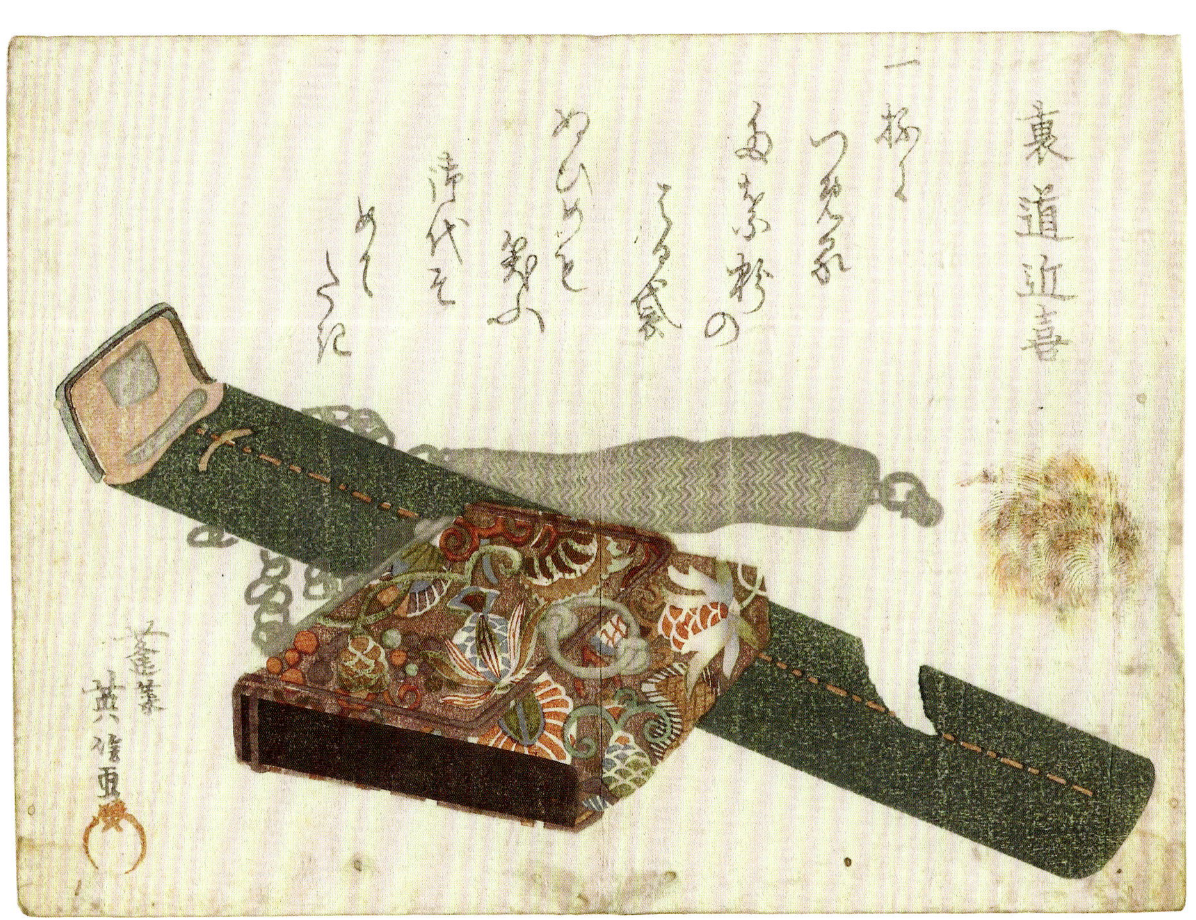

38

A vase with plum twigs and a crab on a court hat

RINTEI YŪSHIN (active 1780s–1820s) 林亭雄辰
Artist's signature: *Rintei* 林亭
Probably 1825 (Year of the Rooster)
Colour woodblock print
16.5 × 20.4 cm, *kokonotsugiriban* format
Purchased with the assistance of the Story Fund, EA2017.35

This still-life shows a length of *chintz* fabric, a porcelain jar containing branches of plum blossom and a crab on an *eboshi*, a type of lacquered black hat traditionally worn by high-ranking court nobles. The jar, a typical product of the porcelain town of Arita in Japan's southern island of Kyūshū, is decorated in underglaze blue with a pair of chickens by a banana tree and a Chinese scholar's rock. The inscription around the base of the jar refers to its date of production, the Bunsei era (1818–30). We can surmise that the *surimono* was commissioned in 1825, the only Year of the Rooster of the Bunsei era.

Placed on the *eboshi* next to the jar is a type of crab called a *Heike-gani* or Heike crab. The shell of the Heike crab has a pattern resembling a fierce human face. According to legend, these crabs are reincarnations of dead warriors of the Heike clan. The struggle of the Heike with the rival Genji clan to take control of the imperial throne in the late twelfth century was famously told in the epic *The Tale of the Heike* – a work that would have been well known by all members of *kyōka* poetry clubs. The *eboshi* court hat represents the Heike family, who had matrimonial links to the imperial court.

After a long military campaign the Heike warriors were finally defeated in the Battle of Dan-no-ura in the Shimonoseki Straits off the southern tip of Honshū, Japan's main island. Several of the poems allude to the site of this famous battle. In the first poem Anado is an archaic name for the Shimonoseki Straits, where the battle took place. The second poem refers to Akama inkstones, which were produced in Akamagaseki, an archaic name for the town of Shimonoseki. The colour purple (*murasaki*) was symbolic of Edo, hence the conceit that water from Edo would turn an Akama inkstone purple. Inkstones are still produced in this area today. In the fifth poem Akama features both as a place name and also as a reference to the red Heike crabs that gather there, as the name contains the character '*aka*' or 'red'. The crabs are believed to embody the fierce spirit of the Heike warriors.

The artist Rintei Yūshin studied under the painter Watanabe Gentai (1749–1822) of the Nanga (Chinese literati-style) painting school. He also contributed *kyōka* poems to several publications. Among these was the *Hajinshū* of 1823, compiled by the poet and literatus Ōta Nanpo, one of the pioneers of the Edo *kyōka* movement (also known by the *kyōka* poetry name Yomo no Akara).

和布刈せし
あとにかまめの
ふたつみつ
かすむ穴戸の
曙の海

mekari seshi
ato ni kamame no
futatsu mitsu
kasumu anado no
akebono no umi

After gathering seaweed, two or three seagulls above the misty dawn seas at Anado.

UMENOMON MAKADO 梅廼門真門

書初に
江戸の若水
すりいれし
赤間硯の
石のむらさき

kakizome ni
edo no wakamizu
suriireshi
akama suzuri no
ishi no murasaki

For the first calligraphy of the New Year the first water of the year in Edo, rubbed with an ink stick on the Akama inkstone, has turned the stone purple.

MURASAKI EMON 紫衣紋

花瓶のうちも
匂ひに
やハらけて
氷らぬ水を
うかす梅は

kebyō no uchi mo
nioi ni
yawaragete
kōranu mizu o
ukasu ume wa

The fragrance of plum blossoms has softened the water in the vase and keeps it floating without freezing.

御摺ものの歌まいらすべきおほせことうけ給ハりて
on surimono no uta mairasubeki ōsegoto uketamawarite

KUJAKUEN SENHIKO 孔雀園千彦, deeply honoured to present this poem for the *surimono*

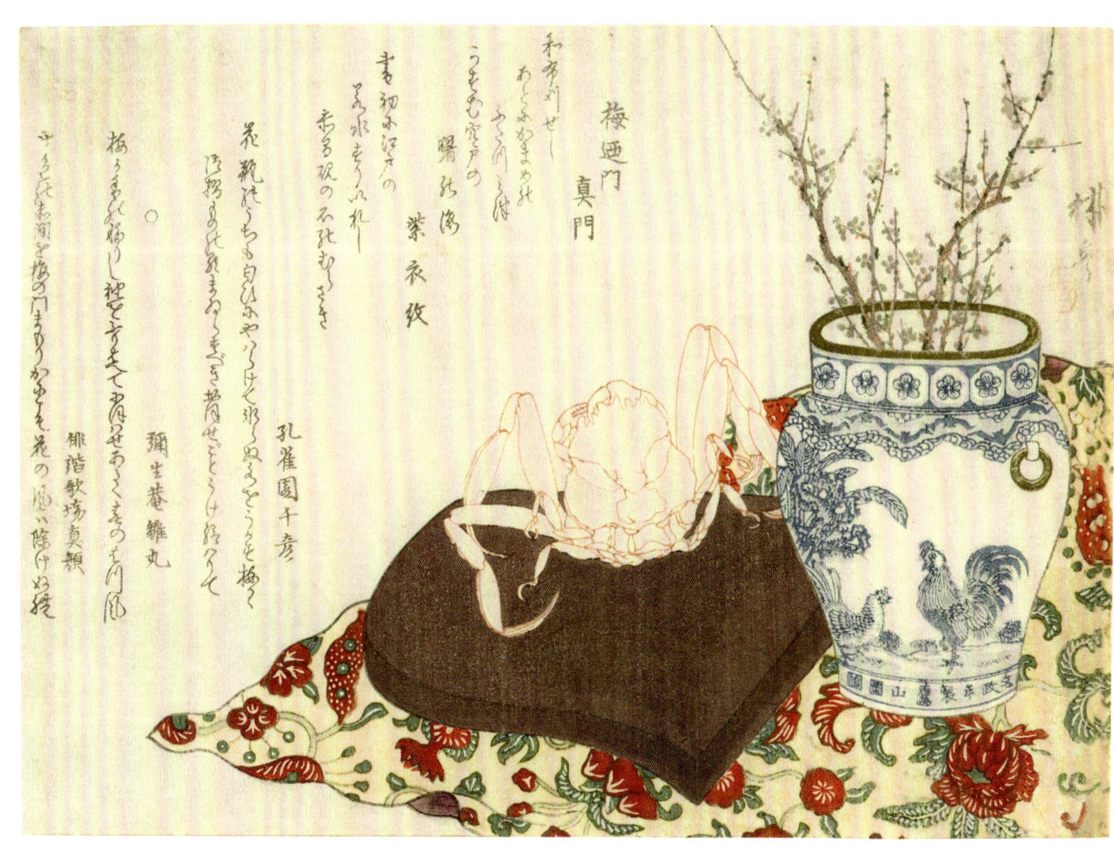

梅か香の
移りし袖を
ふりはへて
にほはせある
く春のはつ風

umegaka no
utsurishi sode o
furihaete
niowase aruku
haru no hatsukaze

She waves her sleeves deliberately as she walks, releasing the scent of plum blossoms into the first spring breezes.

YAYOIAN HINAMARU 弥生菴雛丸

其色の
赤間を梅の
門まもり
かにゝそ花の
風は除けぬれ

sono iro no
akama no ume no
kadomamori
kanini zo hana no
kaze wa yokenure

The colour of Akama is the colour of a crab that becomes a talisman to protect local plum blossoms from the wind.

HAIKAIKAJŌ MAGAO
俳諧歌場真顔

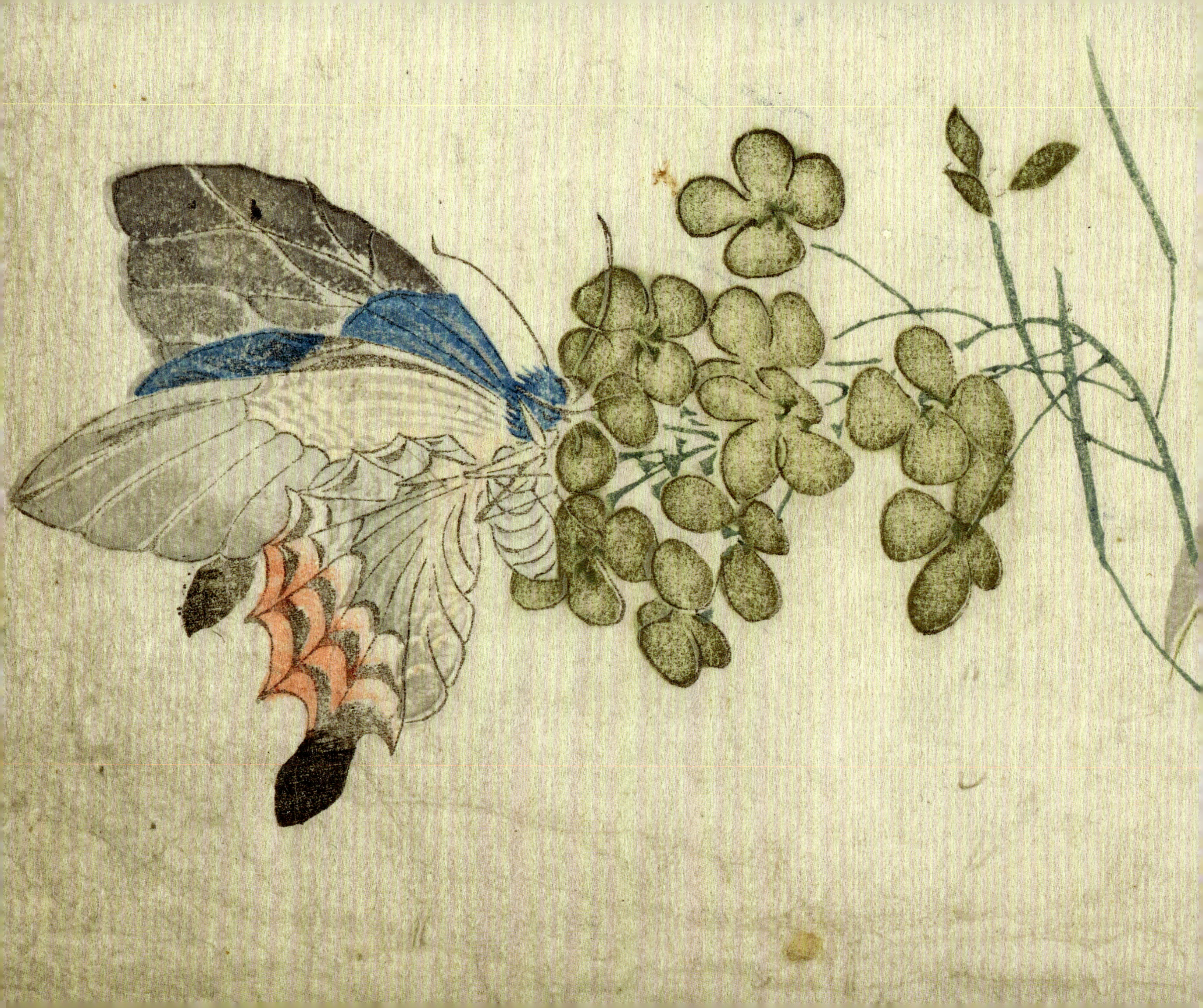

VII

The Shijō Style and *Haikai Surimono*

Most *surimono* published in the Japanese capital of Edo were illustrated in the *ukiyo-e* style seen in commercial prints. However, many of the *surimono* published by poetry clubs in the Kyoto-Osaka or Kamigata region, some 500 km to the west of Edo, were designed by artists of the Shijō school. This painting style is named after the Kyoto street on which the movement's founder, Matsumura Goshun (1752–1811), had his studio.

Shijō artists took their subjects from nature and everyday life. Rather than focusing on exact depiction, they aspired to capture the *spirit* of a subject through the use of soft colours and loose, expressive brushwork, often executed with an element of playfulness and humour. The poets who commissioned Shijō-style *surimono* were usually, though not always, *haikai* poets, who composed the 17-syllable poems better known today as *haiku*. The light, painterly Shijō images, which pared a subject down to its essence, complemented the aesthetics of *haikai* poetry. Matsumura Goshun was himself an accomplished *haikai* poet.

Although it is *kyōka surimono* made in Edo that have received the most attention from modern collectors and scholars, *surimono* based on *haikai* in fact played an important role in the history of the genre. *Haikai surimono* were published from the seventeenth century, and from the beginning of the eighteenth century were accompanied by illustrations. It was partly from this tradition that *kyōka surimono* developed in Edo in the 1780s. *Haikai surimono* continued to be produced steadily until the early twentieth century, well after the decline of *kyōka surimono* in the 1830s.

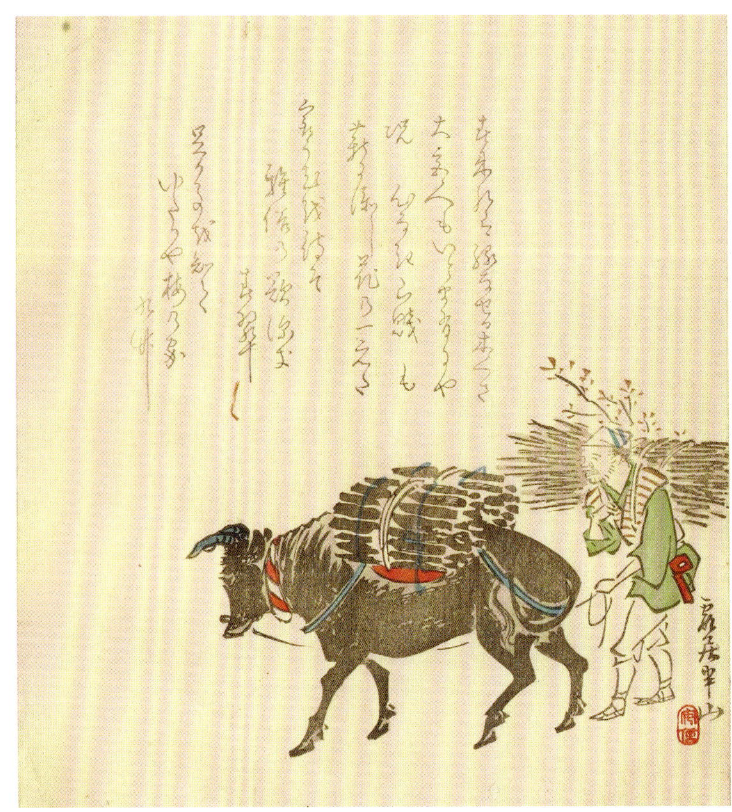

Fig.22 *Woodcutter and ox with firewood*. Matsukawa Hanzan (1818–1882). Artist's signature: Kakyo Hanzan 霞居半山. Mid-nineteenth century. Colour woodblock print, 18.7 × 16.8 cm, *shikishiban* format. Presented by Mrs E. M. Allan and Mr and Mrs H. N. Spalding from the Herbert H. Jennings Collection, EAX.4570

39

Butterflies and Japanese rapeseed blossoms

KUBO SHUNMAN (1757–1820) 窪俊満
Seal: *Shunman* 俊満
1813 (Spring, Year of the Rooster)
Colour woodblock print
19.8 × 26.8 cm, *chūban* format
Presented by Mrs E. M. Allan and Mr and Mrs H. N. Spalding from the Herbert H. Jennings Collection, EAX.4602

This elegant *surimono* has been excuted with fine, soft brush strokes and restrained hues. It depicts a carefully observed butterfly and two moths around a flowering rapeseed (*nanohana*) plant. The viewer's eye is first drawn to the magnificent swallowtail butterfly sucking the nectar from the blossoms in the lower left-hand corner. It is then led along the stalks of the plant up towards the two moths hovering over the flowers in the upper right-hand corner. The colour in this print has been applied without black outlines in the 'boneless' style typical of the Shijō school. The dark leaves of the plant with their soft, blotted gradation of colour are reminiscent of the '*nijimi*' technique used in the Kyoto Rinpa tradition, in which the ink or pigment spreads through the paper fibres beyond the original brush lines. Although the Shijō style was most commonly used to illustrate *haikai surimono*, the poems on this print are actually *kyōka*.

Kubo Shunman was one of the greatest of all *surimono* designers. He was a pupil of the *ukiyo-e* artist Kitao Shigemasa (1739–1820) and his art name was Shōsadō (the *sa* of the name meaning 'left', reflecting the fact that he was left-handed). Shunman was also an accomplished *ukiyo-e* artist, book illustrator, print-maker, author of popular stories and poet of *waka*, *haikai* and *kyōka*. He learned *kyōka* from the Rokujuen circle poet Ishikawa Masamochi (1753–1830) and used the poetry name Hitofushi no Chizue. He also used the *haikai* poetry name Shiokarabō. Shunman is said to have begun producing *egoyomi* picture calendars in the late eighteenth century and to have designed over 500 *surimono* in the following 33 years until his death.

長閑さに
色もことなる
菜の花の
きなりに遊ふ
蝶の一むれ

nodokasa ni
iro mo kotonaru
nanohana no
kinari ni asobu
chō no hitomure

In the stillness even the colour of the rapeseed flowers seems different – a flock of butterflies flits freely.

CHIKUSESSŌ NAGABUMI
竹雪窓長文

菜の花の
ちるをハいとへ
春風に
とふもみことな
はくの蝶々

na no hana no
chiru oba itoe
harukaze ni
tobu mo migotona
haku no chōchō

Not wishing to scatter the rapeseed blossoms, the gorgeous silvery butterflies fly freely in the spring breeze.

CHIKUYŌTEI UOTO 竹葉亭魚人

すう露も
あなミつ神と
覚へけり
菜種の供御に
遊ふ蝶々

suu tsuyu mo
anamitsukami to
oboekeri
natane no kugo ni
asobu chōchō

Sucking the dew, sweet as the nectar of the gods, butterflies hover around their sacred offering of rapeseed.

SASA'AN 笹庵

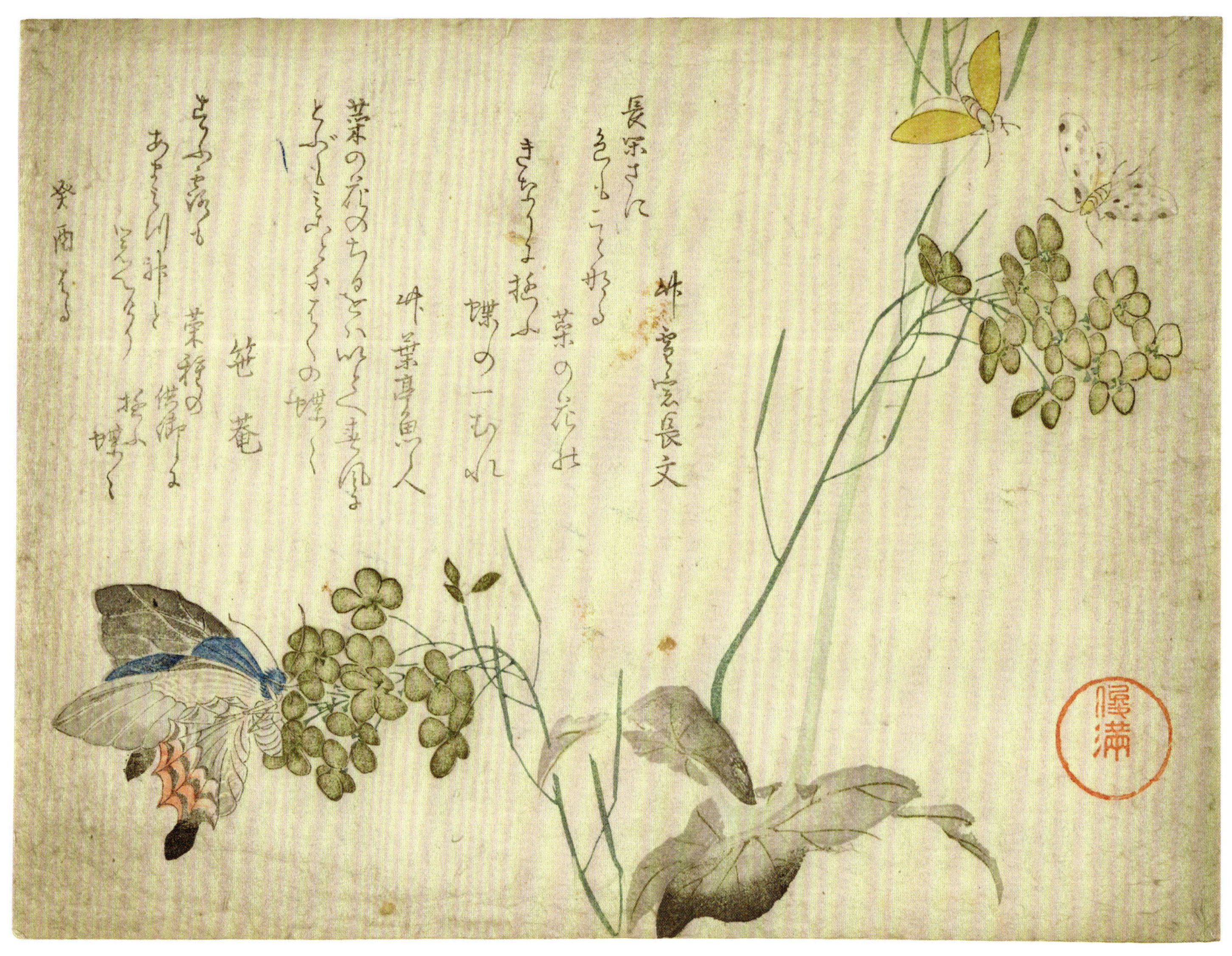

40

Two sheets of *haiku* poems with chrysanthemums

Commissioned by the poet Tomioka Rochō
Artist unknown
1851
Colour woodblock print with embossing
19.5 × 28 cm, *chūban* format
Acquired 1979, EA1979.21

The left-hand sheet of poems on this *surimono* begins with the inscription 'Tomioka Rochō celebrates his early old age (*Tomioka Rochō ga shorō o gasu*)'. This indicates that the poems were composed to celebrate Rochō's 41st birthday (40th birthday by modern age-reckoning) and we may assume that it was Rochō who commissioned the *surimono*. The poems were composed by Rochō himself and by friends wishing to share in his auspicious longevity. In Japan it was traditional to commemorate one's own longevity at significant age milestones, a custom known as '*ga no iwai*'. Traditionally the first celebration of age, known as *shorō* or 'early old age', commemorated the 41st birthday. Subsequent celebrations were held every ten years, at the age of 51, 61 and 71. In Japan today such celebrations typically begin at the age of 60, with an event known as '*kanreki*' (see also cat.11, p.56).

It seems that poets gathered from all over Japan to contribute to Rochō's milestone celebration. Their usual places of residence are listed together with their names: Kyoto, Awa Province (modern Tokushima Prefecture), Edo (modern Tokyo), Mutsu Province (modern Aomori and Iwate Prefectures) and Chiba Prefecture. The poems are packed with autumnal imagery, including references to autumn plants (chrysanthemums, bush clover, maples and rice, which is harvested in the autumn), geese (traditionally associated with melancholy autumn skies) and the plaintive sound of cloth being pounded with a mallet on the wooden *kinuta* fulling block, also long associated with autumn. The verses also include numerous poetic terms for the moon in autumn, from '*nochi no tsuki*' (the moon of the thirteenth night of the month, a waxing moon) to '*fumizuki*' (the seventh 'literary' month), '*tsukikoyoi*' (the moon of the fifteenth night of the eighth month – the mid-autumn full moon) and *meigetsu* (the harvest moon).

The image, executed in the watercolour-like Shijō style, depicts two sheets of 17-syllable *haikai* poems (also known as *haiku*) – poetry sheets within a poetry sheet. The sheets are framed by stems of red and white chrysanthemums, the white chrysanthemums delicately embossed. Chrysanthemums are also associated with autumn. The *surimono* is dated (on the right-hand sheet) to autumn 1851, with all the poems focusing on autumnal themes. Poems were often inscribed on beautifully decorated paper, and within this *trompe l'oeil surimono* the artist has depicted (on the right-hand poetry sheet) an elegant type of paper with decorative bands of stylised mist.

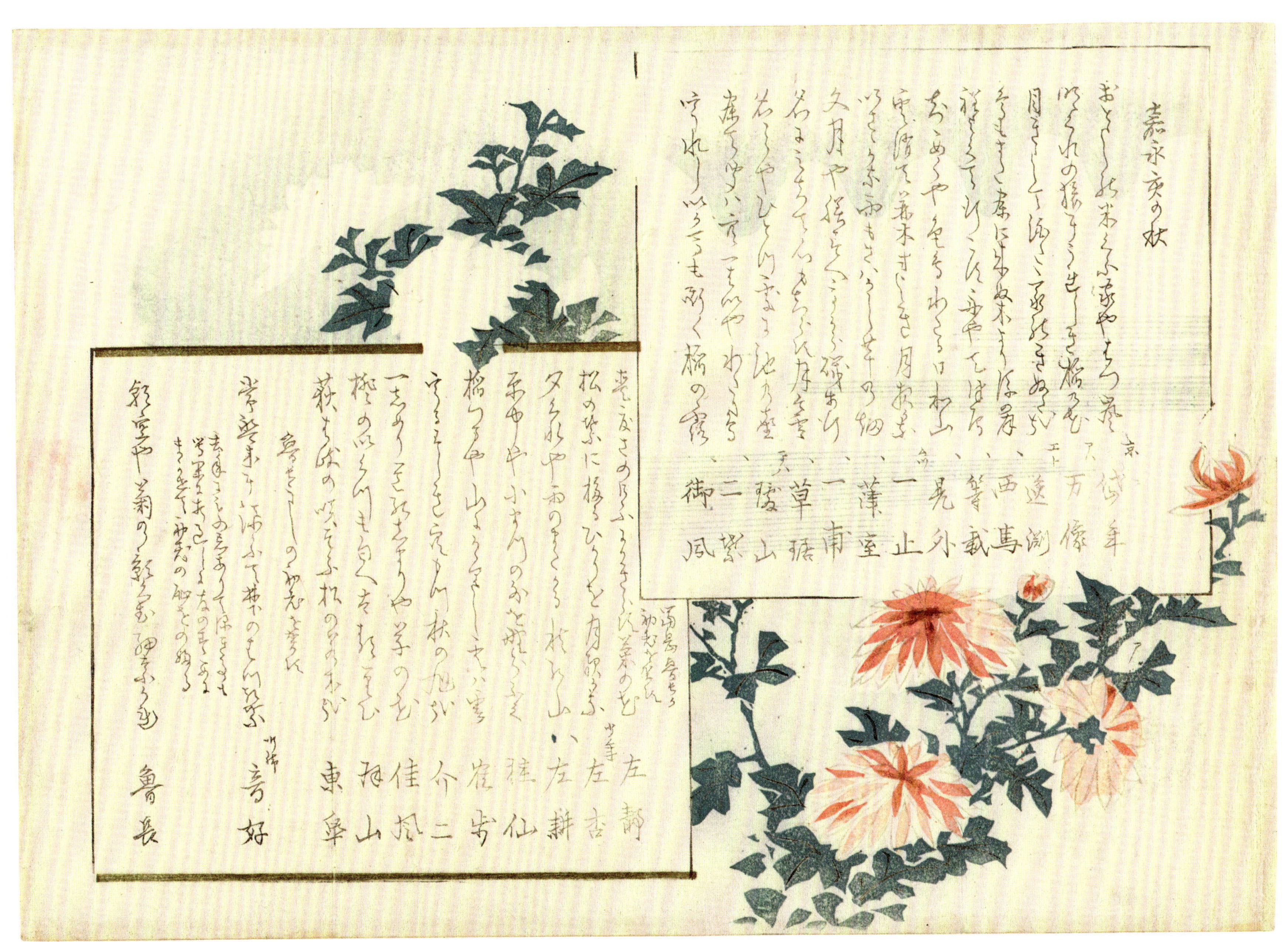

Right-hand poetry sheet, cat.40

嘉永亥の秋

kaei i no aki

Autumn 1851, Year of the Boar, Kaei era.

おとゝしの
米くふ家や
はつ嵐

otodoshi no
kome kuu ie ya
hatsuarashi

The household that eats rice from the year before last encounters the first storm of the year.

TAINEN of Kyō (modern Kyoto) 京 岱年

明くれの
旅にうれしき
稲の花

akekure no
tabi ni ureshiki
ine no hana

Travelling day and night I delight in the flowers of rice plants.

BANSHŌ of Awa Province (modern Tokushima Prefecture) アハ 万像

目きゝして
泊た家の
きぬたかな

mekiki shite
tomatta ie no
kinuta kana

At the house where I stayed after giving an appraisal, the sound of the fulling block.

ITSUEN of Edo (modern Tokyo) エト 逸渊

鳥もまた
寝に来ぬ木よ
り後の月

tori mo mata
ne ni konu ki yori
nochi no tsuki

Rather than roosting in the trees, the birds prefer the ninth-month moon.

SAIBA, also of Edo 西馬丶

程もえて
行こす舟や
天津鳫

hodomo ete
ikikosu fune ya
amatsukar

Over the boat at just the right moment, a flight of geese.

TŌSAI, also of Edo 等栽丶

ちゝめくや
色鳥わたる
日和山

chichimeku ya
irodori wataru
*hiyoriyama**

Chirping loudly colourful birds fly over Mount Hiyori.

KŌGAI, also of Edo 晃外丶

* Mount Hiyori was a small mountain with a view over Toba Bay in Shima Province (modern Mie Prefecture), where sailors came to observe and forecast the weather at sea.

雲消えて
並木すゝしき
月夜かな

kumo kiete
namiki suzushiki
tsukiyo kana

The clouds have cleared – the cool shade of roadside trees on a moonlit night.

ISSHI of Mutsu Province (part of modern-day Aomori and Iwate Prefectures) ムツ一止

いさゝかな
雨もさはかし
芋の畑

isasakana
ame mo
sawagashi
imo no hata

Even the gentle rain falls loudly in the potato fields.

RISSHITSU, also of Mutsu Province 葎室丶

文月や
膳すへてから
磯歩行

fumizuki ya
zen suete kara
isohokō

In the seventh month, after setting the dinner table, I walk on the seashore.

IPPO, also of Mutsu Province 一甫丶

名にミちて
心もしらす
月今宵

na ni michite
kokoro mo shirasu
tsukikoyoi

Worthy of its fame, the autumn full moon makes its presence known.

SŌKYO, also of Mutsu Province 草鋸丶

名月や
ひとつ処に
池の塵

meigetsu ya
hitotsu tokoro ni
ike no chiri

The harvest moon; in one part of the pool the dust gathers.

KENZAN of Chiba Province チハ钀山

寝て聞は
空一ぱいや
わたり鳥

nete kiku wa
sora ippai ya
wataridori

Lying in bed, I hear the sound of migratory birds filling the skies.

NISHI, also of Chiba Province 二紫丶

うれしいか
馬も嘶く
稲の露

ureshii ka
uma mo inanaku
ine no tsuyu

Looking joyful, even the horse gives a neigh – dew on the rice plants.

GOFŪ, also of Chiba Province 御風丶

Left-hand poetry sheet, cat.40

富岡魯長か初老を賀す

tomioka rochō ga shorō o gasu

TOMIOKA ROCHŌ celebrates his early old age.

愛度さのきょうにかきよす菊の花

medetasa no
kyō ni kakiyosu
kiku no hana

Today, an auspicious day,
I gather chrysanthemums.

SASEI 左静

松の葉に移るひかりを月夜かな

matsu no ha ni
utsuru hikari o
tsukiyo kana

On a moonlit night, the reflection of moonlight on pine needles.

the young man SAKYŌ 少年左杏

夕くれや雨のまたかる秋の山

yūgure ya
ame no matagaru
aki no yama

In the twilight, rain spreads over the autumn mountains.

the young man SAKŌ 左耕

原中やこまつの外を野分ふく

haranaka ya
komatsu no soto o
nowake fuku

In the field an autumn windstorm blows around the pine saplings.

KEISEN 桂仙

稲つまや山にかゝりし雲は雪

inazuma ya
yama ni kakarishi
kumo wa yuki

A flash of lightning reveals the clouds hanging over the mountains to be snow.

SAIHO 崔歩

うるわしき空もつ秋の旭哉

uruwashiki
sora motsu aki no
asahi kana

In the beautiful sky of autumn, the sun rises.

KAIJI 介二

一しめり道のしまりや草の花

hitoshimeri
michi no shimari ya
kusa no hana

After a spell of rain, the path dries up and the grass begins to flower.

KEIFŪ 桂風

橙のいくつも匂へはるのひ

daidai no
ikutsu mo nioe
haru no hi

Giving out their scent on a spring day, so many bitter oranges!

UZAN 羽山

萩はきの咲そふ松の若木哉

hagi wa ki no
sakisou matsu no
wakagi kana

The bush clover flourishes next to the young pine tree.

TŌKŌ 東皐

魯長主の初老を賀す

rochō aruji no shorō o gasu

Celebrating the early old age of Master Rochō.

常盤木に添ふて梺のはつ紅葉

tokiwagi ni
soute fumoto no
hatsumomiji

Beside the evergreen trees at the foot of the mountain, the first autumn maples.

The itinerant priest OTOYOSHI 行脚音好

去年にもの忘ありて深き事も等閑に打過しに友のすゝめにまかせて初老の恥をのふる

kozo ni monowasure arite fukaki koto mo naozari ni uchisugoshi ni tomo no susume ni makasete shorō no haji o noburu.

Last year I became forgetful and began to leave even the gravest problems neglected, so I took my friends' advice and gave an account of my shameful early old age.

朝空や菊の影くむ細なかれ

asazora ya
kiku no kage kumu
hosonagare

Under the morning sky
I scoop the reflection of chrysanthemums in the narrow stream.

ROCHŌ 魯長

41

Tea bowl and tea whisk

FUKUNAGA KŌBI (1872–1934) 福永公美
Artist's signature: *Kōbi* 公美
Artist's seal: *Kūzan* [*characters unidentified*] 空山□□
Spring 1914
Colour woodblock print
19 × 17.2 cm, *shikishiban* format
Presented by Mrs E. M. Allan and Mr and Mrs H. N. Spalding from the Herbert H. Jennings Collection, EA1979.20

A tea whisk rests inside a black Raku tea bowl decorated with a design of white plum blossom – the symbolic spring flower that is the first to bloom in the New Year. Low-fired, hand-built Raku earthenware bowls were first produced by the Raku family in the 1580s in Kyoto. With their subdued monochrome palette, functional simplicity and tactile forms, Raku tea bowls are closely associated with *wabicha*, the style of tea ceremony promoted by tea master Sen no Rikyū (1522–91); they are characterised by the idea of refined austerity and simplicity. Rikyū is said to have instructed the potter Raku Chōjirō (d. 1589) to produce the first Raku tea bowls according to Rikyū's principles of *wabi*.

The artist Fukunaga Kōbi seems to have adapted his design from a *surimono* of 1853 by Okamoto Tsunehiko (1816–91), an artist of the Shijō school (see British Museum no.1980,1022,0.12). Okamoto's earlier *surimono* depicts an almost identical tea bowl and whisk, but the motif on the tea bowl is Mount Fuji – another auspicious symbol of the New Year. White plum blossoms lie next to the bowl. The use of Mount Fuji as a decorative motif was common in the Raku tradition. In his design Kōbi has gently challenged this tradition, replacing the Fuji motif on the bowl with a design of two plum blossoms. In a formal tea gathering a tea whisk would be placed in a tea bowl with the handle facing up; a tea scoop would then be placed across the top of the bowl next to it. The irregular placement of the whisk shown here suggests a playfully relaxed mood.

Kōbi was a pupil of the *ukiyo-e* print designers Toyohara Kunichika (1835–1900) and Ogata Gekkō (1859–1920). Kōbi took the '*kō*' 耕 character of his art name from his master Gekkō's name, although he later changed it to a different character 公, which is also pronounced '*kō*'.

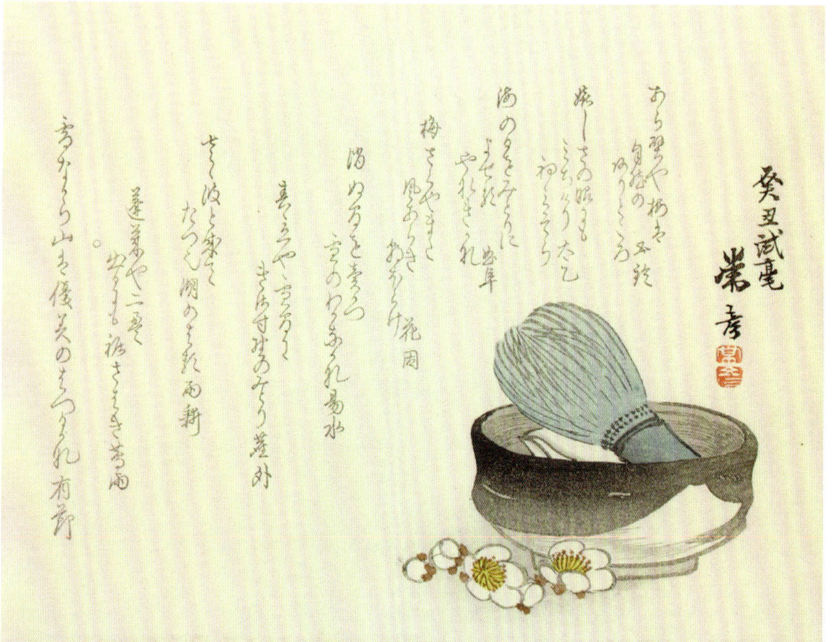

Fig.23 *Tea bowl, whisk and plum blossom*. Okamoto Tsunehiko (岡本常彦). 1853. Colour woodblock print, 19.1 × 25.2 cm. © The Trustees of the British Museum, no.1980,1022,0.12

日のうちは
覗くはかりや
嫁か君

hinouchi wa
nozoku bakari ya
*yome ga kimi**

During the daytime the mice keep on peeping in.

CHARAI 茶雷

**Yome ga kimi* is a euphemism used for a mouse seen during the first three days of the New Year.

元日や
むかしにかへる
人こゝろ

ganjitsu ya
mukashi ni kaeru
hitogokoro

On New Year's Day people's minds are drawn back to the olden days.

暮るゝ年
さなから早う
思ひけり

kururu toshi
sanagara hayō
omoi keri

The year draws to a close. How fast the passing of time feels!

手もとりの
寒さも見えす
月と梅

temodori no
samusa mo miezu
tsuki to ume

The cold has returned but the moon and the plum tree do not care at all.

Three poems by KIGŌ 騏鄕

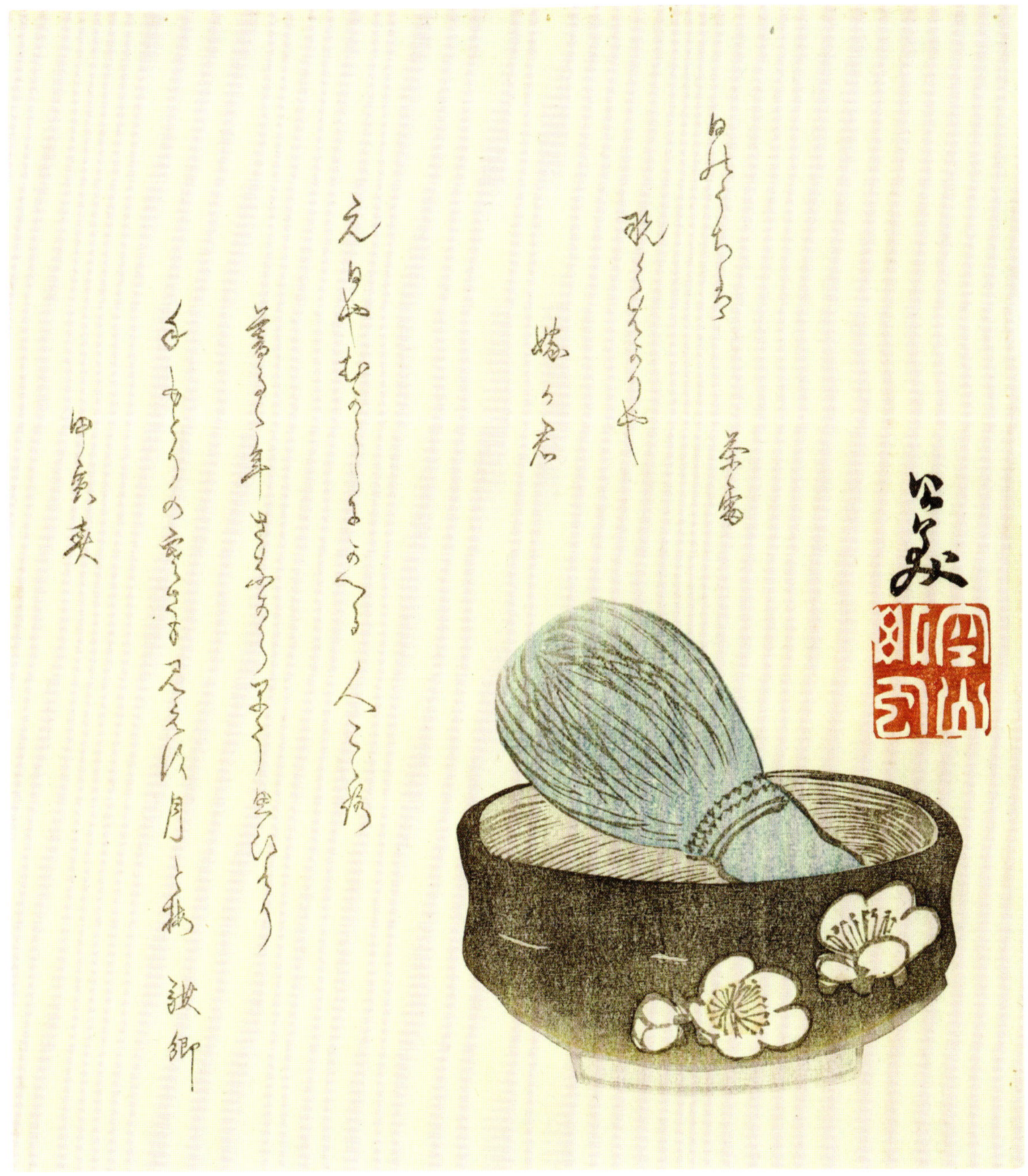

42

Autumn grasses by moonlight

Probably commissioned by the poet Yūshi
IIJIMA KŌGA (1829–1900) 飯島光峨
Artist's seal (right): *Kōga* 光峨
Poet's name (left): *Yūshi* 幽止
Poet's seal: *Shikian* 四季庵
Late 1800s
Colour woodblock print
19 × 9 cm, *koban* format
Acquired 1979, EA1979.25

This *surimono* was probably commissioned by the poet Shikian Yūshi as a change of address announcement and as an invitation to a moon-viewing party on the occasion of his house move. It was probably intended to be sent to his friends and his new neighbours.

In Japan a great emphasis is placed on seasonal customs and events. The majority of *surimono* relate to New Year's activities, but one of the most popular autumn events is moon-viewing (*o-tsukimi*). '*Tsukikoyoi*', mentioned in the *haiku* on this *surimono*, is the full moon that occurs on the fifteenth night of the eighth month of the lunar calendar. This equates to the full moon closest to the autumn equinox in the solar calendar (typically around 15 September). On this night rice dumplings, Japanese pampas grass (*susuki*) and seasonal food such as sweet potatoes are displayed as offerings to the moon.

The round bamboo lattice window depicted in the *surimono* represents the full moon. Through the window, delicate fronds of *susuki* grass appear silvery in the moonlight. The way in which the window is only partially visible emphasises the poetic effect of the image; in the *wabi* aesthetic that underlies much of Japanese art, poignant beauty is found in the imperfect and incomplete. The depiction of the moon with autumn grasses is a traditional motif in Japanese poetry and art, often featured on screens, tea bowls or lacquerware. The design was associated with the landscape of Musashi Plain located to the west of the city of Edo, and is thus known as '*Musashino*' (Musashi Plain). Viewers of this motif would immediately associate it with a mood of romantic, autumnal melancholy.

The artist Iijima Kōga studied under the Kanō school painter Oki Ichiga (1798–1855). Kōga was known for his paintings of flowers and birds in the naturalistic Shijō style, characterised by the use of soft colours and spontaneous brushwork. After the death of his master Kōga also immersed himself in the literary world.

山下街に 居を移して

yamashita-machi ni kyo o utsushite

On moving house to Yamashita town.

来る人の
顔珍らしや
月今宵

kuru hito no
kao mezurashi ya
tsukikoyoi

People arriving
brand new faces
in the night of the autumn full moon.

YŪSHI 幽 止

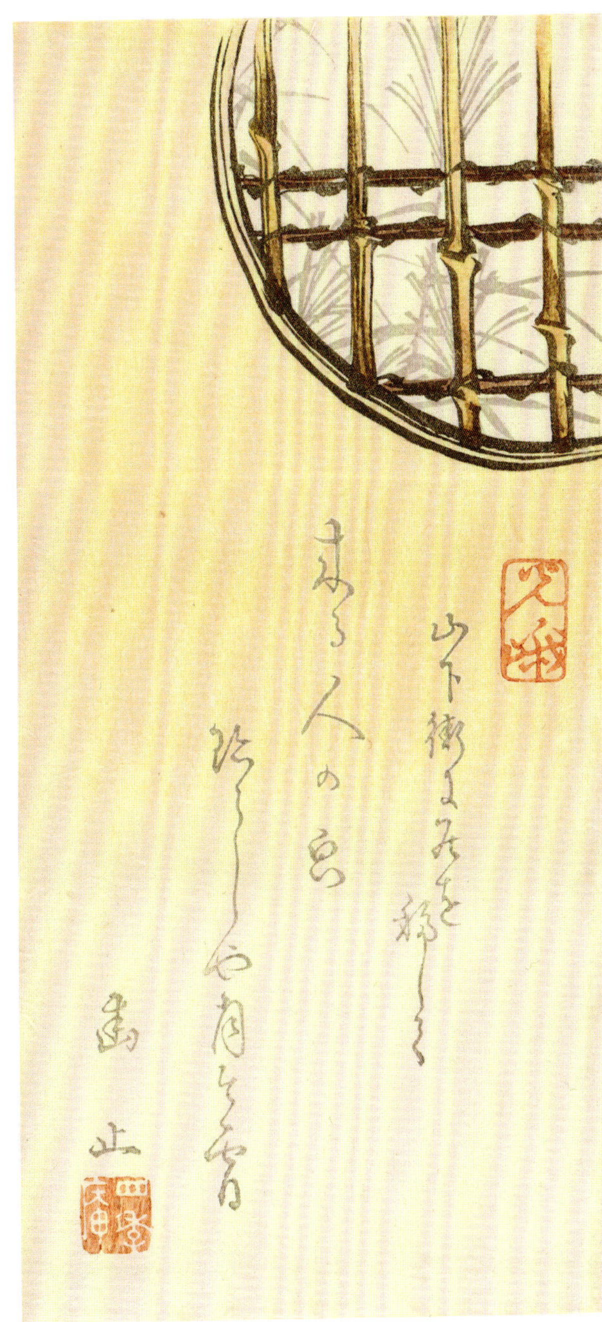

43

New Year's calligraphy

SHIBATA ZESHIN (1807–91) 柴田是眞
Artist's signature: *Zeshin* 是眞
Artist's seal: *Reisai* 令哉
1866
19 × 18.3 cm, *shikishiban*
Colour woodblock print with metallic pigment
Acquired 1979, EA1979.19

This *surimono*, illustrated by the celebrated painter and lacquer artist Shibata Zeshin, is wittily designed to look like a sheet of calligraphy. On a square sheet of paper, the top-right corner of which is folded into pleats, are two poems by Shūki. The poems are not composed in the strict 5-7-5-7-7 syllable structure of traditional *waka* verse, but are written in a freer style while still following the standard line lengths (the first poem is written in a 5-7-5-7-5-syllable format, the second 5-5-7-5). They are written in Zeshin's own calligraphy. His cursive writing is executed with characteristic fluency. Zeshin's signature and his red seal 'Reisai' can be seen on the very left of the poem sheet. On the back of the sheet is the inscription '*hinoe tora saitan shigō* 丙寅歳旦試毫', 'the first calligraphy of the Year of the Tiger'. From this we can infer that the *surimono* was produced in 1866.

Shibata Zeshin was born in Edo. He first trained as a lacquerer and later studied painting under Suzuki Nanrei (1775–1844), a renowned artist of the Shijō school. Zeshin also travelled to Kyoto, where he studied under another Shijō school artist, Okamoto Toyohiko (1773–1845). An accomplished *haikai* poet, Zeshin was highly regarded for his sophisticated and fluent brushwork and for his innovative and daring sense of design in lacquerware, paintings and prints. This *surimono* is a good example of the artist's wit and creativity.

Both poems allude to the close of the old year and the dawning of the new. The first verse, which extols the subtle beauty of the lifting of darkness before dawn over the more obvious glories of the sunrise itself, expresses the Japanese aesthetic known as *wabi*. This notion was developed by the tea master and disciple of Zen Buddhism Murata Shukō (*c*.1423–1502), who famously remarked that the moon was more pleasing when partially obscured by cloud. The second poem refers to the Japanese custom of ringing out the year with the tolling of temple bells. The bells are struck 108 times in all: 107 times on New Year's Eve, and the final bell sounded as New Year's Day arrives at midnight. The number 108 is significant in Buddhism. It represents the 108 mental defilements, or *bonnō*, that cause the suffering inherent in the repeated cycle of birth and death. These include greed, hatred, delusion, evil passions and the appetites of the flesh. The sound of the bells tolling, known as *joya no kane*, acts as a kind of purification, driving out the earthly desires with each peal.

一とせの
空を定めて
初日影
さきたらぬかけ
猶ゆかし

hitotose no
sora o sadamete
hatsuhikage
sakitaranu kage
nao yukashi

At my abode of the past year, the first sunrise of the year – how much more beautiful the light before the sun is fully risen.

月と梅
除夜のかね
心もとして
眠りけり

tsuki to ume
joya no kane
kokoro mo tojite
nemuri keri

The moon and plum tree and the temple bell ringing out the old year; I have put my mind to rest and have fallen asleep.

Both poems by SHŪKI 秀奇

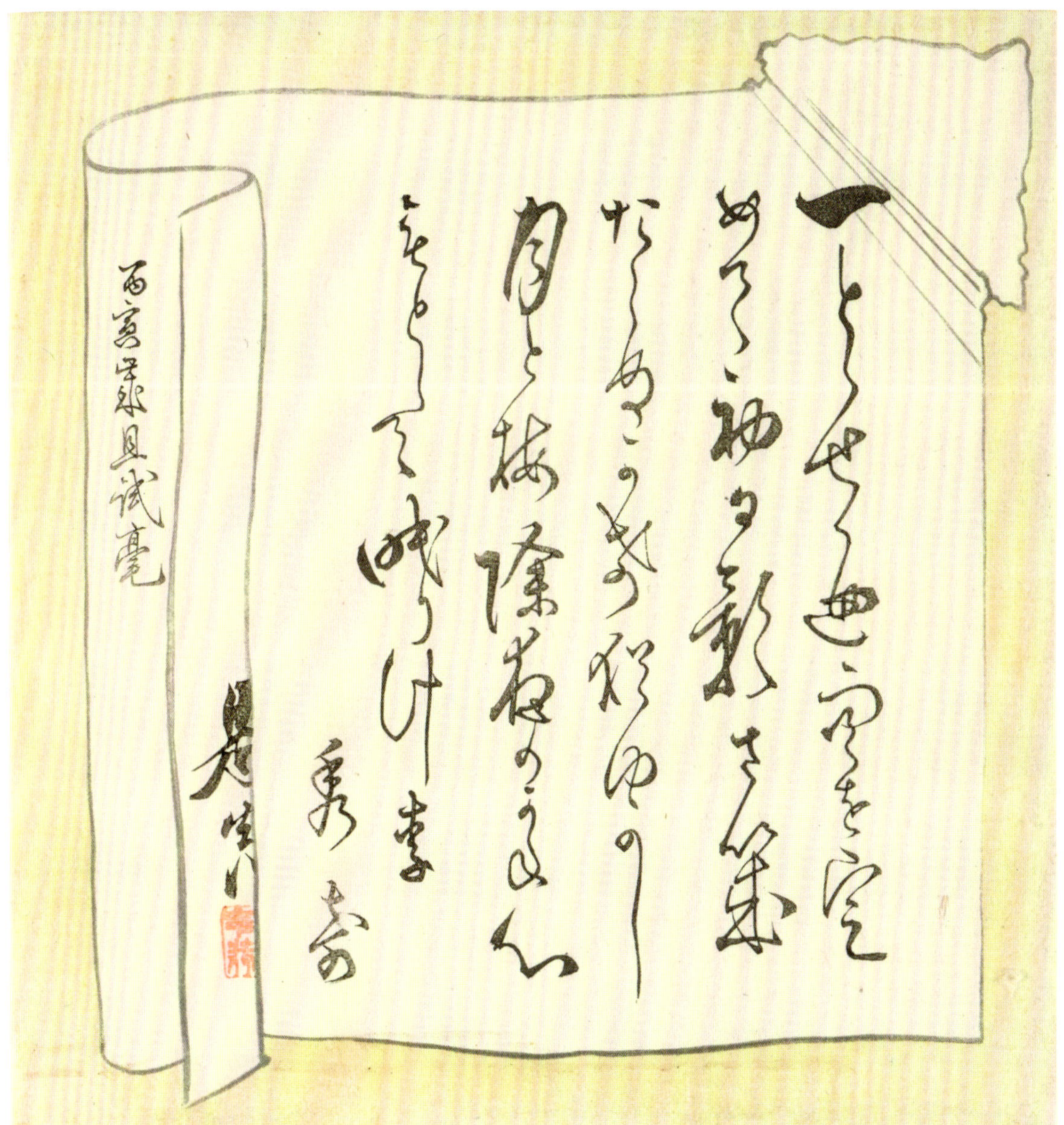

Surimono Additional Details

This list includes sources of information relating to Ashmolean *surimono* and indicates where other copies of *surimono* can be found.

cat.1

A Korean cook on horseback, smoking a pipe

Kasutani 2016, pp.2–4

Asano 2014

cat.2

A monkey carrying off a platter of sweets

Goslings 1992

Kanō 1928, p.98

Keyes 1974, p.9

Rijksmuseum Amsterdam, no.RP-P-1991-631 (see Forrer 2013, cat.174, p.101)

cat.3

Still life with hair ornaments

The Chester Beatty Library, Dublin, no.J2427 (see Keyes 1985, vol.1, cat.23, p.66)

cat.4

Daikoku with an abacus and a woman with a white rat

—

cat.5

An *arhat* with a tiger

Kokuyaku Himitsugiki Hensankyoku 1991, p.272

Tanaka and Hoshiyama 2008, cat.634, pp.629–30

Umehara 1981, cat.338, pp.299–301

cat.6

Two women on the beach at Enoshima

Schaap 1998, p.247 (see also cat.188, p.175 for a *surimono* pentaptych with a similar theme)

Suzuki 1996, p.225

Marino Lusy Collection, Museum of Design, Zurich, nos.111–1 and 111–2 (see Carpenter 2008, cat.212, p.334)

cat.7

A courtesan as the strongwoman Okane

Kanō 1928 *Kyōka Jinmei Jisho*, p.51

Harvard Art Museums / Arthur M. Sackler Museum no.1933.4.931

Rijksmuseum, Amsterdam, no.RP-P-1958: 309 (see van Rappard-Boon 1982, cat.121, p.71; Forrer 2013, cat.382, p.208)

cat.8

A Chinese warrior on a prancing horse

Brooklyn Museum, New York, no.1993.201.2

Marino Lusy Collection, Museum of Design, Zurich, no.11 (see Carpenter 2008, cat.88, p.215)

cat.9

A courtesan in front of a screen depicting sheep

Clark 2017, fig.4. p.25

Hirakawa 1797, pp.4–6

Yu 2015, p.13

cat.10

Manzai performers with a monkey on a ferry boat on the Sumida river

Manzai performers with a monkey in a *tayū* costume

The Chester Beatty Library, Dublin, no.J1428 (see Keyes 1985, vol.1, cat.237, p.268)

See Harvard Art Museums / Fogg Museum, no.1933.4.1468 for another print from the same series depicting a monkey trainer with a dog

cat.11

A mother with her two children feeding chickens

Polster & Marks, cat. no.14, p.12

Rijksmuseum, Amsterdam, no.RP-P-1991-547 (see Forrer 2013, cat.505, p.264)

cat.12

A group of travelling entertainers

—

cat.13

First bath of the New Year

—

cat.14

Rat calculations

—

cat.15

A courtesan with a *koto* and a dog

Ishizaki 1996, cat.119, pp.4–5

Lane 1989, pp.25–34

cat.16

Butterfly

Mirviss & Carpenter, 2000, cats 71–5, pp.121–2 (for the full set of five *surimono*)

Museum of Fine Art, Boston, no.11.19861

cat.17

Ono no Tōfū

Harvard Art Museums/Arthur M. Sackler Museum, no.1933.4.1971

Metropolitan Museum, New York, no.JP1035

Rijskmuseum, Amsterdam no.RP-P-1958-375 (see van Rappard–Boon 2000, no.140 and Forrer 2013, cat. no.291, p.159)

cat.18

Henjō, who has fallen

http://www.asahi-net.or.jp/~sg2h-ymst/yamatouta/sennin/kanajo.html

Inoue 1931, p.59

Kokusho Jinmei Jiten, vol.11, pp.219, 160

Rijksmuseum, Amsterdam no.RP-P-1991-653, (see Forrer 2013, cat.532, p.277)

cat.19

The Kuronushiyama festival float

Chester Beatty Library, Dublin, no.J2106 (see Keyes 1985, cat.291, p.338)

cat.20

Genzanmi Yorimasa

Museum of Fine Arts, Boston, no.11.20490

cat.21

Dancing at Furuichi for the Hisakataya circle, a pentaptych

Kanō 1928, p.85

The Chester Beatty Library, Dublin, nos.J894a, b & c, J502a & b (see Keyes 1985, vol.1, cat.48–52, pp.90–2)

Cleveland Museum of Art, nos.1921.330 to 1921.334

Harvard Art Museums / Arthur M. Sackler Museum, no.1949.146.2 (no.3 of the set)

Metropolitan Museum of Art, New York, nos.JP1964 to JP1966 (nos.1–4 of the set)

Princeton University Library, no.GA 2008.01182

Rijksmuseum no.RP-P-1958-405 and RP-P-1958-406 (see van Rappard-Boon 1982, cat.243, p.129; Forrer 2013, cat.430a & b, p.230)
Waseda University Tsubouchi Theatre Museum, Tokyo, nos. 201-5231–201.5235

cat.22
Two courtesans in front of a screen with Mount Fuji
Bibliothèque Nationale, Paris, no. od.171 (see Narazaki 1990, cat.211)

cat.23
The Immortal Rogō
Inoue 1931, p.28
Polster & Marks, cat. no.100, p.99
Yura 1979, p.208
Arthur M. Sackler Museum, Harvard Art Museums, no.1933.4.1616
Marino Lusy Collection, Museum of Design, Zurich, no.85-1 (see Carpenter 2008, cat.50, p.177)
Rijksmuseum, Amsterdam no.RP-P-1958-391 (see van Rappard-Boon 1982, cat.235, p.123; Forrer 2013, cat.415, p.222)
Schoff Collection (see Mckee 2006, cat.50, p.176)

cat.24
A courtesan as the Chinese monk Kanzan
Chiba Museum 1997, cats 83, 84
Rijksmuseum, Amsterdam, no.RP-P-2006-103 (see Forrer 2013, cat.370, p.203)
See Metropolitan Museum of Art, New York no.11.25829 for an *ukiyo-e* version by Shigenobu of the same subject

cat.25
At the Yōrō Waterfall
—

cat.26
Rochishin
Forrer 1983, pp.1–4
Mirviss and Carpenter 2000, cat.55, pp.104–5
Polster & Marks, no.221, p.193
Schoff collection (see McKee 2006, cat. no.57, p.161)
Art Institute of Chicago, no.1954.575
British Museum, no.1906,1220,0.605
Harvard Art Museums / Arthur M. Sackler Museum, no.1933.4.1855
Metropolitan Museum of Art, New York, no.JP1297
Museum of Fine Arts Boston, no.21.9283
Rijksmuseum, Amsterdam, no.RP-P-1958:320 (see van Rappard-Boon 1982, *Hokusai and his school*, cat.195a, p.105)

cat.27
The Palace of the Moon
Takemura 2006, pp.73–86
The Chester Beatty Library, Dublin, no.J2136 (see Keyes 1985, cat.138, p.170)
Museum of Fine Arts, Boston, no.11.19634 & 21.10399

cat.28
A Daoist sage with a tiger
Benten with a dragon, playing the *koto*
Harvard Art Museums / Arthur M. Sackler Museum, no.1933.4.1725 (Benten)
Metropolitan Museum of Art, New York, no.JP1433 (Benten)

cat.29
A Kabuki actor in the role of Umeōmaru
—

cat.30
Kabuki actors in the 'armour-tugging' scene
Mirviss & Carpenter 2000, cat.97, pp.142–3
Museum of Fine Arts, Boston, no.00.1941
Spencer Museum of Art, no.0000.1475 (see Keyes 1984, cat.37, p.96)

cat.31
The courtesan Komurasaki
Rijksmuseum, Amsterdam, no.RP-P-1991-542 (see Forrer 2013, cat.596, p.308)
Marino Lusy Collection, Museum of Design, Zurich (see Carpenter 2008, cat.215, p.337)

cat.32
Portrait of Ichikawa Danjūrō VII with his two sons and an *onnagata* actor
—

cat.33
A young couple on a balcony
Mostow & Ikeda, 2013

cat.34
Two folding fans decorated with emblems of longevity
Metropolitan Museum of Art, New York, no. JP2397
Minneapolis Institute of Art, no.P.75.51.28
Taliesen West Frank Lloyd Wright Collection no.FLLW FDN 3014.018 (see Mirviss & Carpenter 1995, cat. no.148, p.226)

cat.35
The Divine Horse Grass
Asano 2003, pp.61–4
Mirviss & Carpenter 2000, cat. no.9, pp.56–7
Miyashita 1974, p.197
Polster and Marks, cat.260, p.235
Satō 2010, pp.29–30
Harvard Art Museums / Arthur M. Sackler Museum, no.1933.4.1792
Schoff collection (see McKee 2006, cat. no.27, pp.94–5)

cat.36
***Yōkan* jelly from Funabashiya in Saga-chō, Fukagawa**
Asano, 1997
Tanaka October 1993, pp.3–4

cat.37
Pipe case and tobacco pouch with a *netsuke* and chain
Harada 2008

cat.38
A vase with plum twigs and a crab on a court hat
—

cat.39
Butterflies and Japanese rapeseed blossoms
Mirviss & Carpenter 2000, cat. no.82, pp.128–9
Chiba City Art Museum (see Asano 1997, cat.280, pp.138, 196)
Schoff Collection (see McKee 2006, cat. no.15, pp.66–7)
Tanaka July 1993, p.31

cat.40
Two sheets of *haiku* poems with chrysanthemums
—

cat.41
Tea bowl and tea whisk
—

cat.42
Autumn grasses by moonlight
—

cat.43
New Year's calligraphy
—

Glossary

chūban (medium-sized sheet): a *surimono* format made by cutting a full sheet of *hōsho* paper into half horizontally and then cutting that in half vertically; approximately 21 × 28 cm.

eboshi: a type of formal court hat made of black, lacquered fabric or paper. Different types of *eboshi* were worn by high-ranking court nobles, warriors or Shinto priests.

egoyomi (picture calendar): a print in which calendar markings (the long and short months of the year) were incorporated into the design. The word for a calendar was *koyomi*; when pictorial elements (*e*) were added, the calendar was known as an *egoyomi*.

engo (associative words): two or more words linked by meaning, sound or poetic convention, used in *waka* and *kyōka* poetry to evoke a particular image or concept or to provide unity of imagery within a poem or poems. For instance, terms such as 'plum' (*ume*), fragrance (*ka*), breeze (*kaze*) and sleeve (*sode*) were invariably associated with spring, and also with the elegant world of the Heian court (794–1185).

haikai: short for '*haikai no renga*', an informal version of *renga* linked verse (see *renga* below).

haiku: A 17-syllable poem that developed from the *hokku*, the opening section of a longer *renga* sequence (see *renga* below).

haimei (*haikai* or *haiku* poetry name): a *nom de plume* used in writing *haikai* poetry and other poetic forms. *Haimei* is also used for the literary name taken by Kabuki actors and artists on the occasions when they composed poetry.

homonyms: words that have the same sounds but different meanings.

honkadori (taking from an original verse): the practice of borrowing lines or distinctive phrases from a well-known classical poem and reworking them within a new composition. This may be to create humour, to borrow the associations of an ancient verse or to add an extra layer of meaning. The most common sources of inspiration were the *Kokin wakashū* and the *Hyakunin isshu*, both classical poetry anthologies.

kakekotoba (pivot word): a kind of pun used in *waka* and *kyōka*, in which a word has a double meaning depending on whether it is read with the words that precede it or the words that follow. This is one of the most commonly found devices in *kyōka*.

Kamigata: the region of Japan comprising the cities of Kyoto and Osaka. The term is most commonly used in relation to aspects of urban culture of the Edo period (1603–1868) such as *ukiyo-e* and Kabuki, and in comparison to the urban culture of the Edo (Tokyo) region.

kigo (seasonal word): a word or phrase associated with a particular season, used in traditional forms of Japanese poetry.

koban (small format): a general term for small-size print formats, up to approximately 21 × 14 cm.

kokonotsugiriban (a ninth cut): a *surimono* format made by cutting a full sheet of *hōsho* paper into nine equal parts, each approximately 14 × 19 cm. The format is often seen in *egoyomi* and early *kyōka surimono.*

kotohajime (something for the first time): On the second day of the New Year – considered an auspicious occasion – it was customary for Japanese people to practise activities such as calligraphy, sewing and playing musical instruments for the first time. In so doing they set a good pattern for the rest of the year.

kyōka (crazy poems): a 31-syllable, humorous style of poetry in *waka* form, characterised by its abundant use of puns, wordplay and allusions. *Kyōka* verses were 'crazy' or 'playful' because they broke conventions relating to the language and subject matter used in classical poetry. The style became especially popular during the late eighteenth to early nineteenth centuries.

kyōmei (*kyōka* poetry name): a *nom de plume* used by poets when writing *kyōka* poetry.

makurakotoba (pillow word): a figure of speech or conventional poetic epithet, in which particular words or phrases are used with certain other fixed words or phrases to heighten a poet's rhetorical style. In *surimono* this device was most commonly used to enhance the spring-like feeling of an image. An example is the phrase '*aoyagi no ito*' ('green willow strands'), in cat.17, p.72: here '*aoyagi*' (green willow) is the *makurakotoba*, invariably used with '*ito*' (strands, threads).

mitate (to see and compare): a form of gentle parody that juxtaposes celebrated Japanese or Chinese historical figures or events with contemporary ones, often substituting the high or aristocratic with the low or vulgar. The ironic references were enjoyed by the educated classes.

nagaban (long sideways format): a *surimono* format made by cutting a full sheet of *hōsho* paper horizontally into two equal parts, each approximately 21 by 57 cm.

shikishiban (*shikishi* poem sheet format): a roughly square *surimono* format in the form of traditional paper boards used for calligraphy or painting; they measure approximately 20 × 18 cm (also called *kakuban*). The majority of *surimono* were made in this format from around 1810 until the 1830s.

renga (linked verse): a style of verse in which two or more poets provided alternating stanzas of three lines (of 17 syllables) and two lines (of 14 syllables) respectively to make poems of varying lengths. The opening stanza of a *renga*, called the *hokku*, became the basis for the modern *haiku* form of poetry.

ukiyo-e (pictures of the floating world): prints and paintings from the sixteenth to the nineteenth centuries that were made for townspeople and mostly depicted actors, courtesans or landscapes.

utamakura (poem pillow): place names included in poetry to evoke a special meaning, mood, season or historical event particularly associated with that place.

waka (Japanese poem): originally encompassing several genres of traditional court poetry, the term is most commonly used to refer to verse composed in 31 syllables, arranged in five lines of 5-7-5-7-7 syllables each.

yarō-bōshi (man's cap): a purple silk scarf used by Kabuki actors playing female roles; also known as *murasaki-bōshi* (purple cap).

Selected Bibliography

Asano Shūgō 浅野秀剛, ed. *Suijintachi no okurimono, Edo no surimono* 粋人たちの贈り物：江戸の摺物 (Cultivated Gifts: *Surimono* of the Edo Period, 1600–1868). Chiba: Chiba City Art Museum and Yomiura Shinbunsha, 1997.

— translated by Timothy T. Clark. 'An Overview of Surimono', *Impressions* 20, 1998, pp.17–37.

— 'Surimono Art and Literary Circles: The *Genroku kasen kai awase* and *Umazukushi* series', in Gian Carlo Calza, ed. *Hokusai*. London: Phaidon, 2003, pp.58–64.

— '*Zei o tsukushita ichimai no okurimono*' 贅を尽した一枚の贈り物 (The height of luxury in single-sheet gifts), in *Hanga geijutsu* 版画芸術, no.35, 2007, pp.36–7.

— '*Makanaikata Chōsenjin-zu no keifu*' 賄方朝鮮人図の系譜 (The lineage of images of the Korean cook, *Bi no tayori* 美のたより (Newsletter of the Friends of Yamatobunka Museum), no.185, January 2014.

Bowie, Theodore, in collaboration with James T. Kenney and Fumiko Togasaki. *Art of the Surimono*. Bloomington, Indiana: Indiana University Art Museum, 1979.

Carpenter, John T., '*Kyōka* and *Ukiyo-e* Print Designers', in Amy Reigle Newland, ed., *The Hotei Encyclopaedia of Japanese Woodblock Prints*, 2 vols. Amsterdam: Hotei Publishing, 2005, pp.170–224.

— ed. *Reading Surimono: The Interplay of Text and Image in Japanese Prints, with a Catalogue of the Marino Lusy Collection*. Leiden: Hotei Publishing, 2008.

— 'Cultural Symbolism in Still-life Surimono', in Maribeth Graybill, ed., *The Artist's Touch, the Craftsman's Hand: Three Centuries of Japanese Prints from the Portland Art Museum*. Portland Art Museum, Oregon, 2011, pp.109–31.

Clark, Timothy, ed. *Hokusai: beyond the Great Wave*. London: The British Museum, Thames and Hudson, 2017.

Forrer, Matthi. *Egoyomi and Surimono: Their History and Development*. Uithoorn, The Netherlands: J. C. Gieben, 1979.

— 'Two new original *surimono* by Hokkei', *Andon* no.10, Summer 1983, pp.1–4.

— *Surimono in the Rijksmuseum Amsterdam*. The Netherlands: Brill, 2013.

Gonse, Louis. *L'Art Japonais*. Paris: A. Quantin, 1881.

Goslings, Jan H. Willem. 'Calendar Prints: *Egoyomi* and *Surimono*', *Andon* 10/4, no.40 (1992), pp.105–9.

Harada Kazutoshi 原田一敏著. *Kottō 'Rokushō' tokushū: Kiyomizu Sannenzaka Bijutsukan korekushon suina kitsuengu* 骨董「緑青」, vol.36. 特集 清水三年坂美術館コレクション 粋な喫煙具 (Collection of Kiyomizu Sannenzaka Museum: Sophisticate Smoking Paraphernalia), April 2008.

Hasegawa Tsuyoshi 長谷川 強 and Howard. S. Hibbett. '*Edo no warai*' 江戸の笑い (The laughter of Edo), in *Kokubungaku Kenkyū Shiryōkan kyōdo kenkyū hōkoku: Nihon Bungaku no tokushitsu* 国文学研究資料館共同研究報告—日本文学の特質 (National Institute of Japanese Literature joint report on characteristics of Japanese literature). Tokyo: Meiji Shoin, 1989.

Hillier, Jack. 'Still-life in Surimono', in Matthi Forrer et al., ed. *A Sheaf of Japanese Papers in Tribute to Heinz Kaempfer on his 75th Birthday*. The Hague: Society for Japanese Arts and Crafts, 1979, pp.75–84.

Hirakawa Kai 広川獬. *Nagasaki bunken roku* 長崎聞見録 (Recorded information about Nagasaki), vol.1. Osaka: Maekawabun'eidō, 1797.

Inoue Kazuo 井上和雄. *Ukiyo-eshi den* 浮世絵師傳 (History of *Ukiyo-e* Artists). Tokyo: Watanabe Hangaten, 1931.

Ishizaki Yoshio 石崎芳男. '*Yūjo-e no sagegami kō*' 遊女絵の下げ髪考 (Studies on *sagegami* in pictures of courtesans), in *Ukiyo-e Geijutsu* 浮世絵芸術 (Ukiyo-e Art, The Journal of the Japan Ukiyo-e Society), 1996, no.119, pp.4–5.

Kanō Kaian 狩野快庵, compiled. *Kyōka jinmei jisho* 狂歌人名辞書 (Dictionary of names of *kyōka* poets). Bunkōdō: Hirota Shoten, 1928.

Kasutani Masakazu 糟谷政和. '*Edo jidai Tsuchiura sairei emaki no naka no Chōsen tsūshinshi kasō gyōretsu ni tsuite*' 江戸時代土浦祭礼絵巻の中の朝鮮通信使仮装行列について (Costume parades of the Joseon missions to Japan, as seen in the Edo period Tsuchiura Festival scroll), in *Ibaragi Daigaku Jinbun Komyunikēshon kagaku ronshū* 茨城大学人文コミュニケーション学科論集 (A Collection of Essays in the Humanities Department, Ibaragi University), no.21, January 2016, pp.1–7.

Kenney, James T. 'A brief history of Kyōka and the Edo Kyōka Movement', in Bowie 1979, pp.24–43.
Keyes, Roger. 'The Van Reed Surimono Album', *The Stanford Museum*, vol.III, 1974.
— *Surimono: Privately Published Japanese Prints in the Spencer Museum of Art*. New York: Kodansha International, 1984.
— *The Art of Surimono: Privately Published Japanese Woodblock Prints and Books in the Chester Beatty Library, Dublin*. 2 vols. London: Sotheby Parke Bernet, 1985.
Kishi Fumikazu 岸文和. *Kaiga kōiron: ukiyo-e no puragumatikusu* 絵画行為論ー浮世絵のプラグマティクス (The theory of actions in images: the pragmatics of *ukiyo-e*). Kyoto: Daigo Shobō, 2008.
Kobayashi Fumiko. 'Surimono to Publicize Poetic Authority: Yomo no Magao and his Pupils', in John T. Carpenter, ed. *Reading Surimono: The Interplay of Text and Image in Japanese Prints, with a Catalogue of the Marino Lusy Collection*. Leiden: Hotei Publishing, 2008, pp.46–53.
Kokuyaku Himitsugiki Hensankyoku 国訳秘密儀軌編纂局, ed. *Shinhen butsuzō zukan* 新編仏像図鑑 (An illustrated book of Buddhist figures, revised edition). Tokyo: Kokusho Kankōkai, 1991
Kondō, Eiko 近藤英子. *Les Objets Tranquilles: Natures Mortes Japonaises VIIIe–XIXe siècles*. Paris: Galerie Janette Ostier, 1979.
Lane, Richard J. *Hokusai: Life and Work*. New York: E. P. Dutton, 1989.
Makino Satoshi 牧野聡. 'Group Portrait of the Shippō Poetry Circle: The Kyōka Master Fukunoya Uchinari and Surimono Designer Gakutei Sadaoka', in Carpenter 2008, pp.54–61.
McKee, Daniel. *Japanese Poetry Prints: Surimono from the Schoff Collection*. Ithaca, NY: Herbert F. Johnson Museum of Art, Cornell University, 2006.
— 'Leaves of Words: The Art of Surimono as a Poetic Practice.' Ph.D. dissertation, Cornell University, 2008.
Meissner, Kurt. *Woodblock Prints in Miniature: The Genre of Surimono*. Rutland, Vermont: Charles E. Tuttle, 1970.
Mirviss, Joan B., with John T. Carpenter. *The Frank Lloyd Wright Collection of Surimono*. New York: Weatherhill, Phoenix: Phoenix Art Museum, 1995.
— with John T. Carpenter. *Jewels of Japanese Printmaking; Surimono of the Bunka-Bunsei Era (1804–1830)*. Tokyo: Ōta Memorial Museum of Art and Nihon Keizai Shinbun, 2000.
Miyashita Akira 宮下章. *Kaisō* 海藻 (Seaweed). Tokyo: Hōsei Daigaku Shuppankyoku, 1974.
Joshua S. Mostow and Asato Ikeda, with the assistance of Ryoko Matsuba. *A Third Gender: Beautiful Youths in Japanese Edo-Period Prints and Paintings (1600–1868)*. Leiden: Hotei Publishing, 2016.
Nagoya City Museum 名古屋市博物館 et al., eds. *Utagawa Kuniyoshi ten seitan 200-nen kinen* 歌川国芳展: 生誕 200年記念 (Exhibition to commemorate the 200th anniversary of Utagawa Kuniyoshi's birth). Tokyo: Nihon Keizai Shinbun, Inc., 1996.
Narazaki Muneshige, ed. *Hizō ukiyo-e taikan, 8, Pari Kokuritsu Toshokan* 秘蔵浮世絵大観8パリ国立図書館 (Ukiyo-e Masterpieces in European Collections, vol.8, Bibliothèque Nationale, Paris). Tokyo: Kodansha, 1990.
Narazaki Muneshige, ed. *Hizō ukiyo-e taikan, 14, Puruverā korekushon* 秘蔵浮世絵大観14プルヴェラ–コレクション (Ukiyo-e Masterpieces in European Collections, vol.14, Pulverer collection). Tokyo: Kodansha, 1990.
Ōta Memorial Museum, ed. *Shokusanjin Ōta Nanpo: Ōedo maruchi bunkajin kōyūroku* 蜀山人大田南畝ー大江戸マルチ文化人交遊録 (Records of friendship with multiple groups of cultured people in Great-Edo). Tokyo: Ōta Memorial Museum, 2008.
Polster, Edythe and Alfred H. Marks. *Surimono: Prints by Elbow*. Washington DC: Lovejoy Press, 1980.
Rappard-Boon, Charlotte van et al. *Hokusai and his School: Japanese Prints c.1800–1840*. Catalogue of the Collection of Japanese Prints, Part III. Amsterdam: Rijksmuseum, 1982.
— and Lee Bruschke. *Surimono: Poetry and Image in Japanese Prints*. The Netherlands: Hotei Publishing, 2001.
Redfern, Mary. *The Art of Friendship: Japanese Surimono Prints*. Dublin: The Chester Beatty Library, 2017.
Satō Miho. 'Uma-zukushi' 馬尽 (All about Horses), in *Uma no Hakubutsukan kenkyū kiyō* 馬の博物館研究紀要, 17, 2010, pp.29–30.
Schaap, Robert. *Heroes and Ghosts: Japanese Prints by Kuniyoshi (1797–1861)*. Leiden: Hotei Publishing, 1998.
Schmidt, Steffi and Setsuko Kuwabara. *Surimono. Kostbare japanische Farbholzschnitte aus dem Museum für Ostasiatische Kunst, Berlin*. Berlin: Dietrich Reimer Verlag, 1990.

Suzuki Jūzō 鈴木 重三. *Ehon to ukiyo-e: Edo shuppan bunka no kōsatsu* 絵本と浮世絵 : 江戸出版文化の考察 (Printed picture books and *ukiyo-e*: reflections on Edo publishing culture). Tokyo: Bijutsu Shuppansha, 1979.

— ed. *Utagawa Kuniyoshi ten: Seitan 200-nen kinen*. Nagoya: Nihon Keizai Shinbunsha, 1996.

Takemura Noriyuki 竹村則行. '*Chōseiden yakuchū*' 長生殿』訳注 (十三) (Hong Sheng's Changshengdian, 13), in *Kyūshū Daigaku Chūgoku Bungakkai, Chūgoku bungaku ronshū* 九州大学中国文学会 中国文学論集 (Studies in Chinese Literature, The Chinese Literature Association, Kyūshū University), December 2006, pp.73–86.

Tanaka Tatsuya 田中達也. 'Kubo Shunman no kenkyū' 窪俊満の研究 (Research on Kubo Shunman), *Ukiyo-e Geijutsu* 浮世絵芸術, no.107 (January 1993), pp.3–31; no.108 (July 1993), pp.3–43; no.109 (October 1993), pp.3–28.

— 'Kubo Shunman no kenkyū' 窪俊満の研究 (Research on Kubo Shunman), *Ukiyo-e Geijutsu* 浮世絵芸術, no.108 (July 1993), pp.3–43.

— 'Kubo Shunman no kenkyū' 窪俊満の研究 (Research on Kubo Shunman), *Ukiyo-e Geijutsu* 浮世絵芸術, no.109 (October 1993), pp.3–28.

Tanaka Yoshiyasu and Hoshiyama Shin'ya. 田中義恭, 星山晋也. *Me de miru butsuzō: rakan, soshi* 目でみる仏像・羅漢 祖師 (Viewing Buddhist Sculpture: *arhats* and founders of religious sects). Tokyo: Tokyo Bijutsu, 2008, pp.629–30.

Uhlenbeck, G. C., ed. *The Poetic Image: the Fine Art of Surimono*. Leiden: Hotei Publishing, 1987.

Umehara Takeshi 梅原猛. *Butsuzō: rakan* 仏像・羅漢 (Buddhist sculpture: Rakan) 梅原猛著作集 2 (Writings of Umehara Takeshi, vol.2). Tokyo: Shūeisha, 1981.

Yu Dujie and Qu Yanchun 于笃杰,曲延纯. '*Woguo gudai "yang" de mingcheng kao*' 我国古代"羊"的名称考 (A study of the word 'sheep' in ancient China). See www.guoxue.com/?p=26544, 015-02-13.

Yura Tetsuji 由良哲次. *Sōkō Nihon ukiyo-e ruikō* 総校日本浮世絵類考 (Complete revised history of Japanese *ukiyo-e* prints). Tokyo: Gabundō, 1979.

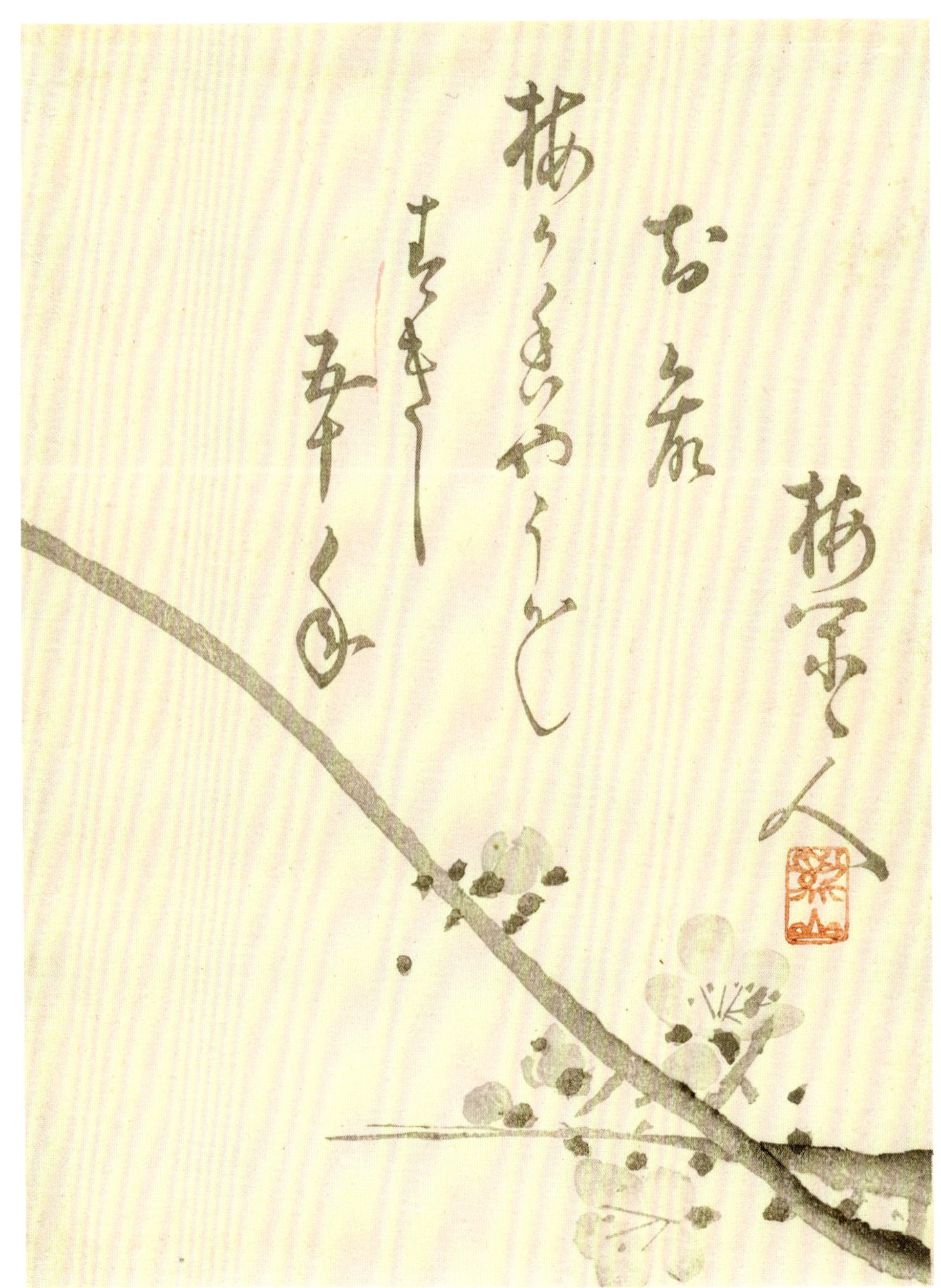

Fig.24 Spray of plum blossom. Baika Kanjin (active late nineteenth century). EA1979.23